Praise for *The Cage-Busting Teacher*

"It can be difficult to navigate the world of teacher leadership without knowing exactly what that looks like or how to get your ideas implemented. In *The Cage-Busting Teacher*, Rick Hess offers real-world advice for helping teachers go from idea to action to impact. This book is a manual for all teachers, like myself, who see changes that need to be made but aren't sure how to go about getting the job done. Not for the faint of heart—be prepared to see leadership in a whole new light."

**—Caroline Corcoran, fifth grade teacher
and Teach Plus Teaching Policy Fellow**

"*The Cage-Busting Teacher* is a giant step forward for teacher leadership. Rick Hess has penned an important book that is bracing, practical, and enormously useful. In allowing teachers to tell their stories of triumph and struggle, Hess offers a no-nonsense guide for teachers ready to transform their schools."

**—Katherine Bassett, president, National
Network State Teachers of the Year**

"I don't always agree with Rick Hess, but I always learn something valuable when he speaks. And when that speaking takes the shape of a book that is the result of many conversations with teachers and that seeks to imagine what life could and should be like for teachers, I'm especially interested in what he has to say. There is so much buzz around teacher leadership today that we run the risk that the concept will lose its meaning. *The Cage-Busting Teacher* keeps us on track, and Rick Hess has provided a worthy compass for this difficult work."

—Ronald Thorpe, president and CEO, National Board

"The message of this important new book by Rick Hess is clear: There's a lot of talent among the teachers in our schools, and it needs to be unlocked and set free. In other words, teachers need to have the professional latitude and auton-omy, as well as the support and preparation, to do their jobs. Here's hoping that the leaders who were the focus of his first book on cage-busting will work with teachers like these—or at least get out of their way—so that we can reclaim the promise of American public education for the students we serve."

**—Randi Weingarten, president,
American Federation of Teachers**

"I appreciate Rick Hess talking straight about teacher leadership and calling out the lip service and fuzzy language with which teachers are seemingly appreciated, infantilized, and muted. I cringe when I hear, "You must be so wonderful—you are a teacher!" not because I am ungrateful but because teaching is a complex, emotionally grueling, and uplifting profession. Rick helps empower teachers to see the cages that limit the deployment of our full talent, and he calls on us to recognize the power we have to bust out and take over the field."

—**Maryann Woods-Murphy, New Jersey State Teacher of the Year 2010**

"Teacher leadership is one of the most powerful and yet undervalued forces improving our schools. Rick Hess provides clear examples of what great teacher leaders can do and the impact they can have when they practice key management and advocacy skills. I highly recommend the book to any educators who want to lead their colleagues while remaining in the classroom."

—**Jonas Chartock, CEO, Leading Educators**

"No teacher is an island. They are all part of schools and systems that can amplify or muffle their effectiveness. In *The Cage-Busting Teacher,* Rick Hess provides an invaluable resource for teachers who are looking to break free from the isolation of their classrooms and to use their influence, efforts, and expertise to create powerful learning environments for students."

—**James E. Ryan, Charles William Eliot Professor of Education, dean of the Harvard Graduate School of Education**

"Imagine an education system in which we finally do what we all say is necessary but too often fail to do: rely on teachers as the experts in our field. With support from *The Cage-Busting Teacher,* we could have such a system, because it provides practical steps for how teachers can speak out, lead, and make change. *The Cage-Busting Teacher* is for veteran teachers, beginning teachers, and union leaders. It is also for the principals, district leaders, and state officials who want to support teachers in busting through cage bars—including those bars we may have inadvertently put in their way."

—**Deborah A. Gist, commissioner, Rhode Island Department of Elementary and Secondary Education**

"*The Cage-Busting Teacher* exposes an important dynamic happening within the teaching profession. All across the country, talented teachers are creating greater opportunities for their students, schools, and colleagues. Their stories deserve this spotlight and the chance to influence systematic change within public education. We hope these stories will inspire policy leaders to engage the voice of educators as a driving force in policy making."

—Sydney Morris, co-CEO, Educators 4 Excellence

"In *The Cage-Busting Teacher,* Rick Hess has found a way to say what has, up to this point, existed only in the minds of teacher leaders. This book is a must-read for anyone looking to strengthen our schools in ways that are practical and real."

—Alex Kajitani, California State Teacher of the Year 2009, and author of *The Teacher of the Year Handbook*

"In *The Cage-Busting Teacher,* Rick Hess creates a unique toolkit to help teachers strengthen their school communities so that ultimately they can better serve students. Written in a compelling and straightforward manner, with a nuanced view of the complexities surrounding education, the book offers practical tips for leveraging existing resources to create positive change. Hess's work will empower teachers to collaborate successfully with their principals, parents, colleagues, and policy makers and to continue to have an impact on their students and communities year after year."

—Elisa Villanueva Beard, co-CEO, Teach For America

"Rick Hess provides a practical resource for teachers not only to recognize the cages they are trapped in but to also earn the freedom and satisfaction of breaking free from those cages. Hess's real-life examples and practical tips help teachers move beyond the paralysis of the cage and become change agents in their schools."

—Sherri McPherson, high school English teacher and Hope Street Group Fellow

"In *The Cage-Busting Teacher,* Hess combines his usual straight-talking, irreverent voice with dozens of practical examples to show what is possible when teachers become active, relentless, purposeful problem solvers. This is a book for teachers who have ideas but don't think anyone will listen to them and for teachers who are excelling in spite of, rather than because of, the conditions in which they practice."

—Elizabeth A. City, lecturer and director of the Doctor of Education Leadership (EdLD) Program, Harvard Graduate School of Education

"*The Cage-Busting Teacher* should give every teacher in America who feels powerless the power to do what they know is right for kids. With real-life examples, Hess proves the possible."

—**Duncan Klussmann, superintendent,**
Spring Branch Independent School District, Texas

"*The Cage Busting Teacher* starts with the refreshing premise that teachers should not have to be martyrs fighting the system 'on their own time and on their own dime.' Instead, author Rick Hess offers guidance on how teachers can best use their finite supply of time and energy to impact their workplaces and profession. The book offers practical advice from a variety of perspectives, giving special attention to areas that can be weak points for teachers, such as communicating with lawmakers, speaking through the media, and working with difficult bosses."

—**Roxanna Elden, National Board Certified Teacher and**
author of *See Me After Class: Advice for Teachers by Teachers*

"Rick's book on teacher leadership adds to a growing knowledge base on how and why teachers must lead without leaving the classroom. In his must-read narrative, Rick makes it clear that teachers are 'hungry to be heard.' Now is the time to build demand among policy makers and reformers to hear what teachers have to say and to work with them as legions of classroom experts lead bold policy and pedagogical reforms."

—**Barnett Berry, CEO, Center for Teaching Quality**

"I can't wait for my teachers to read this book. 'Cage-busting' is something that my most dynamic teachers do instinctively. Plenty of teachers have fantastic ideas but just aren't sure how to push them forward. This is a book that helps them do just that. Hess shows how teachers can reach beyond classrooms to create schools where they can do their best work."

—**Kaya Henderson, chancellor, District of Columbia Public Schools**

"Rick Hess is not quite urging civil disobedience, but he comes close. He shows teachers how they can expand their role in schools and can even step outside the boss/worker cage and create schools where teachers are in charge . . . the way professionals often are in other white-collar vocations."

—**Ted Kolderie, senior associate, Education Evolving**

The Cage-Busting Teacher

THE EDUCATIONAL INNOVATIONS SERIES

The Educational Innovations series explores a wide range of current school reform efforts. Individual volumes examine entrepreneurial efforts and unorthodox approaches, highlighting reforms that have met with success and strategies that have attracted widespread attention. The series aims to disrupt the status quo and inject new ideas into contemporary education debates.

Series edited by Frederick M. Hess

Other books in this series:

The Strategic Management of Charter Schools
by Peter Frumkin, Bruno V. Manno, and Nell Edgington

Customized Schooling
Edited by Frederick M. Hess and Bruno V. Manno

Bringing School Reform to Scale
by Heather Zavadsky

What Next?
Edited by Mary Cullinane and Frederick M. Hess

Between Public and Private
Edited by Katrina E. Bulkley, Jeffrey R. Henig, and Henry M. Levin

Stretching the School Dollar
Edited by Frederick M. Hess and Eric Osberg

School Turnarounds: The Essential Role of Districts
by Heather Zavadsky

Stretching the Higher Education Dollar
Edited by Andrew P. Kelly and Kevin Carey

Cage-Busting Leadership
by Frederick M. Hess

Teacher Quality 2.0: Toward a New Era in Education Reform
Edited by Frederick M. Hess and Michael Q. McShane

Reinventing Financial Aid: Charting a New Course to College Affordability
Edited by Andrew P. Kelly and Sara Goldrick-Rab

The Cage-Busting Teacher

Frederick M. Hess

HARVARD EDUCATION PRESS
CAMBRIDGE, MASSACHUSETTS

Second Printing, 2015

Copyright © 2015 by the President and Fellows of Harvard College

Library of Congress Control Number 2014952435

Paperback ISBN 978-1-61250-776-7
Library Edition ISBN 978-1-61250-777-4

Published by Harvard Education Press,
an imprint of the Harvard Education Publishing Group

Harvard Education Press
8 Story Street
Cambridge, MA 02138

Cover Design: Wilcox Design

The typefaces used in this book are Minion Pro and Helvetica Neue.

For Joleen, who makes all things possible.
And for Grayson, in the hope that you'll know
what it is to walk into schools filled with
greatness, wonder, and joy.

Contents

PREFACE

Before We Get Started

A COUPLE YEARS BACK, I wrote a book called *Cage-Busting Leadership*. In it I argued that K–12 leaders have much more power than they think to create great schools and systems. The problem is that they are routinely trapped in "cages" of their own design. They're stymied by urban legends, timidity, a failure of imagination, or not knowing what they're already free to do.

Since the book was published, I've spent a lot of time talking about these ideas to gatherings of school, state, or system leaders. At most of those, there'd be at least a few teacher leaders in attendance. I was curious what kind of response *Cage-Busting Leadership* would get from them. After all, I was encouraging leaders to be bolder about how they might rethink staffing, spending, and schooling. Such talk can sometimes make teachers nervous, at least in my experience. The teachers who approached me, though, didn't want to quibble about any of that.

Instead, what I mostly heard was, "Rick, I basically like what you had to say. But here's the problem: all your advice is really geared to assistant principals, principals, and district leaders. Most of it doesn't really apply to teachers." As one teacher put it, with admirable frankness,

> I liked what you said. We do need to look with fresh eyes, question routines, and get smarter about using time and money. But here's the thing—your advice doesn't really help me. You talk about shifting federal funds, reexamining state laws, reading contracts closely . . . That has nothing to do with *my* cage. *My* cage is that my principal is a knucklehead, the district won't support my program, my association is off in left field, and the people writing the laws don't give a crap what I think. So, what do you have for *me*?

It was a really good question. It stumped me. I stammered a bit, thought about it, and then could only spread my arms and admit (sounding a bit like a flustered game show contestant), "I've got nothing." The more I thought about it, the more it seemed clear that teachers inhabit cages of their own, but ones quite different one from those that ensnare school or system administrators.

That was the genesis of this book. After all, I'm struck by how often even acclaimed teachers tell me that they feel muffled, stifled, ignored, under-valued, and marginalized . . . and aren't sure what to do about it. Some react with anger. Others grow bitter. Most retreat to their classroom and close the door.

So, I spent a year interviewing a couple hundred teachers, teacher advocates, union leaders, and others about how teachers can bust out of *their* cage. The more I thought about it, and the more I talked to teachers, the clearer it became that teachers lack the ready access to *organizational authority* that school and system leaders can use to bust free. They have little control over budgets and staffing.

What teachers do have, though, is the ability to tap the *authority of expertise* and to summon *moral authority*. The problem, it seems to me, is that most teachers have little understanding of this authority, how to marshal it, or how to best wield it. Indeed, those who claim to speak for teachers can undermine this authority without ever realizing it. Making matters worse, teachers mostly get bad advice on dealing with all of this.

The Cage-Busting Teacher seeks to offer practical guidance on how teachers can break free from that cage. I believe this is sorely needed for teachers' mental health—and because the success of grand plans to improve schooling will depend on whether educators are ready, able, and willing to make them work.

WHY THIS BOOK?

Education can seem a tale that's equal parts passion and frustration. Well-meaning efforts crash into ugly realities and things don't work out as intended. If teachers feel like they're taking refuge in their classrooms from out-of-touch bureaucrats, it's hard to see how they can create a sustainable culture of excellence. If teachers regard policy makers as pig-headed and anti-teacher, even the best-intentioned policy changes are in for an uphill slog. If teacher involvement is no more than a litany of empty words and symbolic initiatives, nothing will change.

Escaping this kind of standstill begins with cage-busting teachers ready to step out of their classrooms, deal with policy makers in good faith, and make teacher leadership more than an empty phrase. It requires teachers eager to champion excellence, identify important problems, offer concrete solutions, and bring those solutions to life. The more teachers do that, the more trust they'll win, the more policy makers will back off, and the more room they will have to put their expertise and passion to work. That has the promise to flip today's vicious cycle, where micromanagement leads to resistance, which leads to more micromanagement, which leads to more resistance. Cage-busters can create instead a virtuous cycle in which problem-solving educators earn the trust of lawmakers and administrators, yielding more autonomy and more opportunity to make smart decisions for kids.

Policy debates are caught up in large questions about how to measure teacher effectiveness, what to do with low-rated teachers, how to reward high-rated teachers, and so on. These are important questions, but they're focused on the crude task of managing a workforce of millions. The cage-buster's charge is less sweeping and more uplifting. The cage-buster focuses on unlocking the talent waiting to be set free in our schools. The cage-buster's question is: how does a good teacher go about creating the school and system where she can do her best work? If *Cage-Busting Leadership* was about helping thousands of assistant principals, principals, district administrators, and state officials find ways to do great things, this is a volume that seeks to help millions of teachers do the same.

WHO'S THIS BOOK FOR?

How do you know if this book is for you? Well, when it comes to cage-busting, I've found there are at least three kinds of educators. First, there are those who already have the cage-busting mind-set but are hungry for tips and practical ideas. If you're one of these teachers, my hope is that *The Cage-Busting Teacher* can serve as a handbook, a resource, and a reminder that you're not alone. For networks of teachers who already get this, I hope the book can provide a common language and a framework for talking frankly about successes and setbacks.

Second, there are those educators who've never had much opportunity to look through the cage-busting lens. They've been busy in their classroom, unsure about how one might reach out to leaders or lawmakers, or new enough that they've just not yet had much chance to think about any of this. If you're one of these teachers, I hope *The Cage-Busting Teacher* may both inspire you and make the case that embracing your inner cage-buster can help you create the school and system that you seek. I hope you'll see how cage-busting can help you teach your students better, enjoy more ownership of your school, collaborate more powerfully, and create a less taxing but more rewarding professional life.

Finally, there are the skeptics who find the stuff of cage-busting a distraction. They may not be interested in dwelling on the harsh realities discussed in the pages that follow. They may simply disagree about how principals think, the motivations of lawmakers, or the necessity of re-thinking familiar routines. And that's cool. It's a free country. If you're in this bucket, you'll likely want to pass on this book. All I'd suggest is that you give the first few pages a look to make sure you actually do disagree before presuming that this isn't for you.

Education is rife with efforts to promote teacher leadership, voice, and engagement. I hope that *The Cage-Busting Teacher* may prove a useful resource for those kinds of preparation, advocacy, and professional development (PD) efforts. On that score, let me be crystal clear: cage-busting is not a substitute for attention to classroom practice, curriculum, and instruction but, rather, a complement. I hope teacher preparation and professional developers see cage-busting not as a faddish new shortcut but as a means of equipping teachers to create the schools and systems where they can do their best work.

A WORD TO NEW TEACHERS

If you're a new teacher or preparing to be a teacher, you may wonder what to make of all this. After all, you've probably got a full plate just dealing with lesson planning, instruction, and discipline. As Teach For America co-CEO Matt Kramer puts it, "We want new teachers entirely focused on the classroom in their first two years. We tell them that they can't afford to be distracted." That's sensible advice.

Nonetheless, I think there's much of use here for new or aspiring teachers. Think about it the same way you would if you were a new hire at a law firm or a nonprofit. You're coming into an existing culture with its share of routines and frustrations. New teachers can alienate colleagues and irk their principal without even realizing it, or they can go about their business in ways that build trust and avoid unnecessary headaches. They can fall into bad habits, grumbling, complaining, and feeling shut out, or they can make sure that they're not part of the problem. *The Cage-Busting Teacher* can help you stay on the right side of those lines. Along the way, new teachers may also just find that much of what we cover will offer a sense of possibility and an understanding that things needn't be as they are.

WHY ME?

I've been involved in K–12 schooling for a quarter-century as a researcher, writer, and educator. In that time, I've been puzzled by the lack of concrete, tough-minded guidance for teachers on how to deal with the world beyond their classroom. This first struck me when I was getting my teaching credential twenty-five years ago, and it's something I've wondered about ever since. After all, teachers have been blessed with some terrifically useful books in recent years by authors like Doug Lemov, Steven Farr, Barnett Berry, Linda Darling-Hammond, Roxanna Elden, and Charlotte Danielson. Intriguingly, though, as we'll discuss in chapter 1, while some fantastic classroom guides *sound* like they should be Bibles for the cage-busting teacher—with titles like *Teach Like a Champion* and *Teaching as Leadership*—they generally provide little (if any) guidance on how teachers can bust the cage.

As Lemov, author of *Teach Like a Champion*, told me in our discussions about teacher leadership, "My unit of analysis is the classroom. I'm writing for the teacher. In a lot of schools, I can teach you to make your classroom substantially better, but it can be a pyrrhic victory if the school culture is driven exclusively by the principal. You need second- and third-tier leaders to drive the change." *The Cage-Busting Teacher* doesn't claim to offer wisdom on classroom practice. But I believe it does offer some useful thoughts on ensuring that your efforts add up to more than pyrrhic victories.

Now, some fair-minded observers might wonder what qualifies me to write this book. After all, I'm long removed from the classroom. What I am is a political scientist and policy analyst who studies and works with schools, districts, and states. I've been trained in a school of education, mentored teachers, and taught at various ed schools for more than fifteen years. But I spend the vast majority of my time outside the schoolhouse.

The funny thing is, I think that all this is what equips me to pen this volume. Most of the academics and consultants who write for teachers are teacher advocates or else offer advice drawn from their instructional experience in particular schools or systems. Naturally enough, those who spend their days absorbed in the rhythms of K–12 can come to regard its policies, practices, cultures, and routines as givens.

Much of what I do is question the verities that veteran educators may take for granted. I ask questions that more agreeable scholars might be disinclined to raise and have the opportunity to spend a lot of time talking to educators in lots of systems and lots of roles. I was able to tap the expertise of organizations including the American Association of Educators, the American Federation of Teachers, the California Teachers Empowerment Network, Elevating and Celebrating Effective Teaching and Teachers, Educators 4 Excellence, the Hope Street Group, Leading Educators, the National Board for Professional Teaching Standards, the National Education Association, the National Network of State Teachers of the Year, the Rodel Teacher Council, Teach For America, Teach Plus, the U.S. Department of Education Teaching Ambassador Fellows, and VIVA Teachers. And I owe all of these organizations my gratitude and heartfelt thanks.

ONE LAST THING

Now, I want to be clear from the get-go. If you're looking for a book to reaffirm how wonderful teachers are, this isn't it. If you're seeking a treatise that savages school accountability, charter schooling, or the Gates Foundation, you'd do better looking elsewhere. I have no patience for suggestions that would-be reformers are "corporatist swine" or that rethinking teacher benefits is an attack on the profession. At the same time, I've enormous sympathy for teachers frustrated by half-baked policies or simpleminded declarations that schools must either work miracles or be considered "failing." And I've no use for those who scapegoat teachers or shill for flavor-of-the-month reforms that treat teachers as an afterthought. Make of that what you will, but I figure it's good for you to know where I'm coming from before we get started.

So, this isn't a book that will necessarily make teachers *feel* better. That said, it just may help teachers create schools equal to their aspirations, schools where they can teach and lead to the best of their ability. I hope that feels like a decent deal.

1

The Classroom Cage

PHIL: What would you do if you were stuck in one place, and every day was exactly the same, and nothing that you did mattered?

RALPH: That about sums it up for me.

—*Groundhog Day*

Lift up your eyes upon
The day breaking for you . . .
The horizon leans forward,
Offering you space to place new steps of change.

—MAYA ANGELOU, *On the Pulse of Morning*

OVER THE YEARS, I've seen accomplished teachers take pride in doing things the hard way. They talk of working late, planning intricate trips, and writing a slew of micro grants. They're changing lives, there's no doubt about *that*. But they're doing it on their own, because so many see their schools and systems as unhelpful or even as obstacles that drain their time, passion, and energy.

Teachers have responded by taking refuge in their classrooms. They seek to excel *despite* their schools and systems. They do it on their own time and their own dime, seemingly accepting that as their lot in life. I don't think they should, and I don't think they need to. This is a book for those who agree.

Terrific teachers can grow so used to the way things are that they don't even see the problem. Dysfunction can come to seem normal, hard to change, and therefore not worth worrying about. This approach might pass muster if teachers were independent operators, like a psychiatrist with a home office. But they aren't. Their classrooms are part of a larger school, and what happens there has a profound effect—for good or ill—on what happens once their doors are closed.

There are big problems with retreating to the classroom and closing the door. It forces passionate teachers to wear themselves out. It makes it brutally difficult for mere mortals to be successful. An isolated teacher's impact is limited, absent support from the larger school. And it's just not that much fun for teachers to spend their time, passion, and energy battling "the system"—especially when great schools and systems can *amplify* their best work.

Teachers work in a world where administrators, union negotiators, and lawmakers decide how many minutes they have for instruction, how many students they teach, which instructional materials they use, when an assembly or announcement will interrupt class, what kinds of technology they get, how often they'll assess students, what kind of professional development they'll receive, and even when they can eat lunch or go to the restroom. Teachers can feel like decisions are being made by those who don't understand teaching or learning.

That's a little bit nuts. After all, the right school norms, colleagues, and culture can help turn an okay teacher into a terrific one, and the wrong setting can undermine even the most polished practitioner. This isn't unique to education. The same is true for professors, football players, and Marines. We're all made better or worse by our workplaces and colleagues. And educators have much more power than they may realize to bust out of their classroom cage and change the schools and systems in which they work.

A few readers may take issue with the notion of the "cage." One award-winning teacher told me, "I think describing the classroom as a 'cage' is so negative! I don't think it's good for any of us to start from the negative." Fair enough. However, of the hundreds of teachers I interviewed for this book, no one else took offense. Indeed, many embraced the metaphor, seeming relieved to be reassured that they're not the only one who feels this way and *that perhaps something can be done about it.*

WHAT IS THE "CAGE"?

The cage consists of the routines, rules, and habits that exhaust teachers' time, passion, and energy. The cage is why educators close their classroom doors and keep their heads down. So, what does this cage look like?

Peggy Stewart taught high school social studies in Vernon Township, New Jersey, when she was named the state's Teacher of the Year in 2005. After that stint, with the backing of a supportive superintendent, she spent five years attracting funds to develop new programs. She launched a school-wide Model United Nations program with grants funding student travel to Pakistan and China. Stewart says, "We did a graduation ceremony on the Great Wall of China because our kids didn't want to miss the program—even for graduation. My principal left me alone. He would joke, 'I don't care what you do, Stewart, just don't interfere with my golf game.'" Then the superintendent left, "and the new administration did not welcome any of this. The programs that we had started were disbanded. Teachers were relocated to other buildings." Her principal told her, "Sorry, but I can't help you. I'm taking flak." Stewart says, "We had contractual time after school on Mondays; we'd used that time to design our programs. We were told we could no longer meet at that time." After a year, Stewart left the district. Two years later, so did the superintendent. That's the cage—when everything a teacher has built can be undone by administrative churn.

Madaline Edison founded Educators 4 Excellence Minnesota because, as a first grade teacher, she saw that she could work her tail off and still know that her students "were sort of doomed to fail because the system was set up to fail them." In her third year, she started talking to some veteran colleagues and saying, "We're a small charter school. We can change things up. We need to get an evaluation system in place. We need professional development based on student achievement data. How do we do this?" She recalls, "Basically, what they told me was, 'Get used to it, kid. That's not within our purview. Stay in your lane. It's going to drive you crazy if you try to work on all of these things that are outside your classroom.' It got me thinking. These veteran teachers were amazing, they were doing great things with their kids every day in their classes, but they felt helpless to change these bigger systems—even at our small charter school." That's the cage—when even talented teachers wearily warn young colleagues to "stay in your lane."

Ashley Monteil, Houston's Teacher of the Year in 2012, thought she had a pretty good deal. She taught fourth grade in a Blue Ribbon elementary school and had a principal she liked. Still, it took her three years to summon the courage to offer suggestions to her principal. Once she did, they were consistently shot down. Ideas for tutoring, departmentalization, role changes all were dismissed. Monteil says, "The principal would keep explaining that you don't mess with a successful school." She says, "We were doing well, but we could have been doing much, much better. We had huge room for growth." Monteil finally threw in the towel; she left to become an assistant principal at a local charter school. That's the cage—when teachers find that sensible ideas are dismissed because a school is "successful enough."

Finn Laursen, a teacher and administrator for more than four decades, says, "I hear continually, 'I'm all alone in my room, and nobody is asking what I think, nobody cares, and nobody's listening.' There's this amazing feeling of isolation, in frozen forty-five-minute segments." Michelle Collay, author of *Everyday Teacher Leadership*, observes, "School cultures and physical structures—from policies that forbid teachers to leave their classrooms unsupervised to the long hallways . . . [mean that just] talking with a colleague during the day can be an accomplishment."[1] National Education Association (NEA) president Lily Eskelsen García says, "Once you leave the confines of your room and go out into your hallways, you become undocumented and the border patrol is looking for you." In *The First Days of School*, Harry Wong notes, "Teacher isolation is a reality. Many teachers become comfortable in their isolation."[2] That's the cage—professionals working in a culture of abject isolation.

Stacey Holmes taught English in the largest high school in Bridgeport, Connecticut. Holmes laments, "It felt like the school was focused on pushing kids through and making it look like things were okay." She says that several members of the English department thought things needed to change, "So one day, the four of us decided to send an e-mail to the department, saying, 'Do you guys want to stay after school one day, clean out the English office, and talk about getting the curriculum in order? If so, let's start meeting every Tuesday.' It was clearly voluntary. My colleagues asked me to send the e-mail. The next thing I know I'm in the principal's office for threatening the department leadership. And none of the teachers spoke up, because they were scared. My assistant principal called me in and said, 'Look, I really like you, so I'm just going to say something. You gotta shut up. Until you're tenured, I don't even want to know your name. Shut your door, shut your mouth, and just teach your kids.'" That's the cage—getting reprimanded for trying to do more because you haven't waited your turn long enough.

Alex Lopes was Florida's Teacher of the Year in 2013. The state's new evaluation system mandated that 50 percent of a teacher's evaluation be based on student achievement, with teachers in nontested grades scored using schoolwide achievement. As a preschool autism teacher, Lopes had no tested students; thus, he was judged using schoolwide results from his high-poverty, low-performing school. His score was predictably poor. He was labeled ineffective and rendered ineligible for teacher leadership roles. Now, no one meant for this to happen. But no one prevented it, either. That's the cage—stupid policies that have destructive effects that no one intended.[3]

When Joiselle Cunningham began teaching at a struggling school in New York City, she led a team that hustled to raise $100,000 in grants for English language learners. She later earned teaching awards and national recognition for her work. For all that, when she wanted to hold afterschool tutoring sessions for her kids, she was told, "Nope"—an administrator needed to be in the building when students were present, and that wasn't in the cards. Cunningham responded by working even longer hours and "making home visits, setting up appointments at the public library, McDonald's, wherever." Her passion was inspiring, and won her several honors, but she still found herself working harder and harder to compensate for administrators refusing to rethink their routines. That's the cage—teachers wearing themselves out to make up for obdurate administrators.

THE BARS OF THE CAGE

The cage is all those accumulated rules and routines that waste teacher time, passion, and energy. But it's useful to take a moment to consider some bars in that cage a bit more fully, because seeing the cage clearly is essential if teachers are to escape it.

An "Overflowing Bucket" of Well-Intentioned Directives

Well-intentioned lawmakers and leaders produce a hail of rules, regulations, laws, and directives that rain down on teachers. Seemingly reasonable directives can combine to breed confusion and paralysis. Sharon Gallagher-Fishbaugh, president of the Utah Education Association, sighs, "This year, the legislature proposed 148 bills that would affect schools. Eighty passed. They included a parental bill of rights, testing mandates, suicide prevention, and sexual abuse curricula. Many are good ideas, but they all require time. How much can we pack into a year? You have well-intentioned people pouring raindrops into a bucket, and the bucket is overflowing with new policies. You wind up doing a bit of everything, but none of it very well."

Utah is no anomaly. In 2013, state legislatures approved 1,105 new education bills. In 2012, they enacted 1,345.[4] I think of the Texas school leader lamenting to me in 2014, "I'm in my eighth year as a principal, and I've never had the same accountability rules for two years in a row." Even if administrators are aware of all this, no one owns the resulting mess. This is hardly a new phenomenon. Tom Loveless, a senior fellow at the Brookings Institution, recalls teaching in California in the 1980s when the special *The Day After* showed on TV. Portraying the aftereffects of a nuclear strike on Kansas City, the show was a national sensation. Shortly after, the California legislature passed a new requirement that schools "spend two hours a year teaching nuclear awareness." Each new directive can seem innocuous enough, but the result can leave teachers feeling stretched and overwhelmed.

Teachers Have Their Time Casually Wasted

Sarah DuPre taught first grade in rural Mississippi. She says, "I tried to account for every minute, including bathroom and water breaks. [But] every day, I'd be hit with last-minute disruptions, so we'd never keep to the schedule. Some days we'd make it to the 10:35 lunch on track, then I'd be called into a last-minute IEP meeting, where I'd be lectured for being late—even though I'd only just learned about the meeting and had to dash out in the middle of my math lesson. An afternoon assembly would run an hour longer than expected, so forget science. Or the extension teacher would be absent and the administration would forget to notify us; kids were sent back to class, so my planning period disappeared and everything got pushed up forty-five minutes." Asked if she brought any of this up with her principal, DuPre says, "Nope. I didn't think it would make a difference." This kind of thing can come to seem normal—but it shouldn't.

The most valuable resource that teachers possess is time with their students. More time to teach, coach, mentor, and encourage doesn't mean students *will* learn, but a lack of time pretty much ensures that they won't. Across the nation, most teachers have perhaps six hours of instructional time a day, 180 days a year. That's 1,080 hours. Then start knocking out hours and days for testing, assemblies, early release days, and absences. In fact, researchers have found that only about 65–70 percent of school time is devoted to academic instruction, and even that time is disrupted by attendance taking, announcements, paper passing, pullouts, and the rest.[5] Indeed, the typical elementary student loses more than forty-three days of math instruction a year to all of this.[6] The consequences touch teachers of every stripe. For instance, districts scramble to find speech-language pathologists, yet practitioners spend an average of 450 hours a year on paperwork and in meetings.[7] Administrators encourage teachers to spend more time filing comprehensive lesson plans, displaying student work, and posting "big goals" in their classroom. But the result can easily turn into busywork, endless punch lists, and inane demands. This makes it hard for teachers to "just close the door and teach."

No Upside for Excellence

Too often in schools the reward for good work is more work. Think of the terrific third grade teacher whose reward is his principal strolling up to him in the spring and genially saying, "We've got three second graders who are a real handful. You're the only one I trust to handle them, so I'm going to give you all three next year, okay?" Now, it would be one thing if these requests came with recognition, compensation, or opportunities. But they usually come with nothing more than personal pleas, intimations of guilt, and assertions that it's the right thing to do. The result takes excellence for granted while encouraging all but the foolhardy to duck and keep their heads down. Roxanna Elden, a National Board certified teacher and author of *See Me After Class,* wryly notes, "Teacher leadership can mean a lot of things, but it almost always means unpaid time you're going to be putting in."

Not only is excellence not rewarded, but seniority-driven systems can make performance an afterthought. A 2014 analysis of policies in 114 large school districts found that more than 60 percent used seniority as the primary factor when deciding which teachers to let go during staff cuts, and just 10 percent made performance the primary consideration.[8] When job security is that unrelated to performance, it says something. Forty-nine percent of teachers say that their school and district officials "do not reward outstanding teachers." Meanwhile, 80 percent of teachers favor additional pay for teachers who work in low-income neighborhoods, 64 percent for those accredited by the National Board for Professional Teaching Standards, and 58 percent for those who consistently receive outstanding evaluations.[9] How excellence should be defined or rewarded is a question about which thoughtful people will differ, but teachers agree that today's stifling norms aren't good enough.

Blindsided by Accountability

Teachers can feel bludgeoned by pointless tests, simple-minded accountability systems, and ludicrous expectations. As one deputy superintendent marveled to me, "We held a meeting where we just realized we have twenty-eight different tests. Nobody had ever realized it. We finally started writing them all down. Most aren't mandated, and we realized that nobody keeps track of them all. It was just one thing tossed atop another." In Florida, a 2013 review of testing calendars found that the typical district required ninety-eight local tests in addition to the state's mandated assessments. Meanwhile, plenty of teachers report that accountability systems have meant boiling the school day down to reading and math. As one teacher put it, "By January, we've dropped science, art, social studies, and everything else. It's reading for the first half of the day and math for the second half. It's all about trying to make our numbers."

Observers recall a teacher telling the then-superintendent of Philadelphia's schools that the district bureaucracy was making it harder for her to teach well, and the superintendent replying, "What we need are teachers who don't make excuses. I don't want to hear about bureaucracy . . . We are looking for young people who say, 'I can teach a rock to read.'" Since No Child Left Behind (NCLB), these kinds of ridiculous expectations have made accountability sometimes feel like a "gotcha'" exercise. As Chester Finn Jr. and I observed many years ago, NCLB's "grand ambition [of 100 percent proficiency] provided a shaky basis for policymaking, rather as if Congress had simply announced that America would suddenly no longer have any crime, pollution, or poverty."[10] Even when targets are practical, teachers can worry about the consequences of placing too much weight on testing. As American Federation of Teachers (AFT) director of field programs Rob Weil says, "Right now, the single measure of test scores is so important that people feel locked in. Persistence, the stuff that makes kids successful, gets lost . . . We're so caught up in the measures that the learning gets lost." These concerns are aggravated when, as is the case today, just 25 percent of teachers think that standardized tests accurately reflect student learning and just 45 percent think that students take the tests seriously.[11]

THE SHAPE OF THE CAGE

A remarkable number of teachers say that they have come to accept feeling alienated, disempowered, and frustrated as just another part of the job, like glitchy technology or aimless staff meetings. These feelings are so deep-seated that the results of teacher surveys can seem nonsensical unless one recognizes that teachers take the cage for granted. For instance, 81 percent of teachers believe that unions are needed to protect teachers from school politics and abusive administrators. In another survey, teachers ranked dead last—behind coal miners and truck drivers—when asked whether their work environment is "trusting and open" and if they are "treated with respect."[12] Yet, *at the same time*, 85 percent of teachers report that their principal is doing an "excellent or a pretty good job."[13] This only makes sense if teachers think that administrators will be abusive and that schools will be lacking in trust and respect *even when schools are led by "good" principals.*

Eighty-six percent of teachers say they have to do "too much paperwork and documentation," and 71 percent say they have very little control of what happens in school.[14] Less than one-third report that they're professionally engaged.[15] And 69 percent don't think their voices are adequately heard in education debates.[16] Public Agenda's Jean Johnson has summarized the state of affairs, writing, "70 percent of teachers believe that they are left out of the loop in the district decision making process [and] 80 percent feel that they are rarely consulted about what happens in their schools."[17] Yet, *at the same time*, Gallup reports that teachers rate their quality of life more highly than do members of any other occupation, save physicians. Teachers are more satisfied than are professionals, managers and executives, or business owners. Gallup similarly finds that teachers have the second highest Emotional Health Index score of all occupations, again trailing only physicians.[18] This only makes sense if teachers *expect* to be disengaged and ignored as a matter of course.

While teachers feel unappreciated and undervalued, survey researchers report that the United States ranks slightly above average when comparing respect for teachers around the globe. The United States ranked ninth of 21 countries on this count in 2013, outpacing Germany, Switzerland, Japan, and the United Kingdom.[19] American teachers might feel like they're dealing with a hostile public, but the data suggests they actually enjoy more respect than do their Japanese or German counterparts.

Teachers fear abusive leaders and report that their work environments are lacking in trust and openness, yet they give their principals extraordinarily high marks. Teachers feel disempowered, ignored, and forced to spend much time on trivial tasks, yet they report high levels of personal and professional satisfaction. Teachers feel disrespected, yet American educators fare better than average in terms of public esteem. The easiest way to reconcile these contradictions is to recognize that teachers have grown accustomed to their cage. Teachers accept dysfunction as routine, so they don't blame principals for stifling cultures. They accept administrivia as normal, so they settle for grumbling quietly about it. They feel powerless, so they figure that's the way it goes. They believe themselves to be disrespected and without support, so they respond accordingly. The cage is so familiar that it's practically invisible. Cage-busting starts by illuminating, with flares and floodlights, the bars of that cage.

WHO'S TO BLAME?

In writing this book, I talked to hundreds of teacher leaders who lamented the dysfunction they experience each day, even as they exhibited a remarkable willingness to accept it as the norm. Few voiced a clear sense of what they might do to change things. Instead, there was a lot of resignation, wry humor, and talk of classroom sanctuaries. The cage ensnares teachers, sucks their energy, consumes their time, and can leave them thinking that the smartest move is to mind their own business within their classroom's four walls.

Who is to blame for this? Everyone and no one. There are rules, regulations, and routines that have stacked up over the decades. The cage is the product of staffing norms, accounting practices, and collective bargaining agreements that have created a world where administrators won't think twice about having a talented educator waste an hour watching children board buses or eat lunch. This isn't anybody's *fault*, per se. Leaders have historically felt little urgency or obligation to address all this. Teacher preparation and professional development offer little guidance on how teachers can influence principals, system leaders, or policy makers. Most resources for teachers eschew such topics, focusing instead upon pedagogy, curricula, and how teachers can "survive" in their classrooms.

All of this is reinforced by bad habits and mental blocks that can trap teachers and keep them from acknowledging the cage or trying to do something about it. There are at least four familiar traps.

The MacGyver Trap. Readers of a certain age may remember the 1980s TV show *MacGyver*. Each week MacGyver found himself in impossible situations, only to escape by devising some ingenious contraption. Trapped in a Bolivian jail with a belt buckle and a bedspring, he'd design a flamethrower, break out, and save the world. You'll see a lot of Mac-Gyver in many of today's great teachers. They work ridiculous hours raising funds and scoring favors from old friends in central administration. Their tales of ingenuity and remarkable accomplishment are inspiring. But MacGyverism creates an ironic trap. When non-MacGyvers point out the problems posed by the cage, they get told they're "making excuses," that they should "just look at how well MacGyver is doing." Meanwhile, the truth is that MacGyver is getting worn out.

The "Take Refuge in the Classroom" Trap. Good teachers frequently describe their classroom as a refuge from outside distractions and annoyances, so they're tempted to just close the door and teach. The result, however, can undermine their best efforts. Elisa Villanueva Beard, co-CEO of Teach For America (TFA), recalls her early years as a second grade bilingual teacher. Her students were doing well, she says, but "when I looked around, I realized that the third and fourth grade teachers couldn't keep it going—one of them hardly spoke English. I realized that I could do everything in my power to teach my kids, but if our school couldn't sustain that progress, so much would be lost." A teacher content to spin her magic within her room may never even notice all her good work being undone by the school and system around her.

The "Think Locally, Act Globally" Trap. You've seen the bumper sticker that reads "Think Globally, Act Locally." The idea is simple: be mindful of important, universal questions, but concentrate on the specific things that you can change. A problem is that too many teachers stand this logic on its head; they let concrete frustrations with policies, pay, tests, bureaucracy, or what-have-you provoke them into vitriol that's so broad ("testing, charter schooling, and Teach For America are evil!") that it's more the diatribe of a café anarchist than an actionable call for change. They wind up thinking locally and acting globally. The irony is that this turns their passion into a recipe for inaction.

The "This Too Shall Pass" Trap. Teachers have seen lots of reforms come and go. In my first book, back in the 1990s, I found that the typical urban school districts launched a major new reform every few months.[20] The most sensible response for teachers faced with this sort of insanity is to keep their heads down, close their door, and know that "this too shall pass." As one teacher put it, "Teachers don't engage because they've seen reforms come and go over the years and don't believe this one is here to stay either." You know what? It's hard to quibble with that skepticism. But keeping heads down and doors closed means that teachers stay stuck in the cage, victims of the decisions made by a parade of system leaders.

A sense of helplessness can serve to reinforce or supersize the bars of the cage. As Suzy Brooks, a third grade teacher in Falmouth, Massachusetts, puts it, "I am in a professional and personal cage because I allow myself to be there. I censor my responses, suppress my opinion, let others speak up because my fear gets in the way."[21] Much of the cage is built out of fear, uncertainty, and lack of know-how. Busting through that requires more than great teaching or "teacher leadership." It requires understanding the shape of the cage.

WHAT *IS* CAGE-BUSTING?

Cage-busting is concrete, precise, and practical. It asks what the problem is, seeks workable solutions, and figures out how to put those into practice. It asks precisely why schools are doing this and tallies the number of minutes wasted annually by demanding that. Cage-busting teachers are less interested in what policy makers or district leaders *ought* to do than in how teachers can *make those things happen.*

Cage-busting teachers don't necessarily grab attention. What they do can often seem like nothing more than the commonsense behavior of a savvy professional. Guess what? That *is* cage-busting. Cage-busting is not about garnering headlines or picking fights; it's about creating great communities of teaching and learning, one step at a time.

Most teachers have limited experience leading adults, thinking about systems, or talking policy. Thus, even when problems are obvious and sensible solutions easy to imagine, teachers can stumble. It needn't be this hard. Teachers frequently try to lead by squeezing through the bars of the cage—to move steel through sheer force of will. Cage-busting is about going at things differently so that life is less exhausting, opportunities more plentiful, and efforts more rewarding.

Michelle Shearer, a high school chemistry teacher in Frederick, Maryland, and the 2011 National Teacher of the Year, observes, "Many teachers have internalized the belief that the classroom is a cage and that you can't get anything done outside your walls. Often, when I'm talking to teachers, including those who've been named Teachers of the Year, they'll say, 'If I had my dream, I would do this, but it'll never happen.' I always stop them and ask, 'Why do you say that? Have you made a proposal? Have you worked it through the appropriate channels?' Far too often, the answer is, 'No.' So, the truth is, they don't really know what they can do."

Cage-busters know more is possible than teachers may imagine. As Bill Raabe, a veteran educator and the NEA's longtime authority on collective bargaining, says, "The truth is, teachers can usually do a lot more than they think. Teachers often start from a deficit model. They assume, 'There's nothing we can do—because of the contract or because of policy.' They should be asking, 'What do we want to do?' and then figuring out how to make that happen."

Jacob Pactor, a high school English teacher at Speedway High School in Indianapolis, was charged with improving support for failing students. His plan involved having teachers report student data monthly rather than waiting for quarterly intervals, in order to help them catch problems early. Teachers were on board, but, after a while, says Pactor, "The principal didn't like seeing all of the Fs. And he wasn't willing to let us follow through on any of our proposed consequences—stuff like afterschool detention where students would have to do their homework. So he cut the practice off." Pactor explored his options. He asked the school secretary if there was a way to update the online grade book in real time. She said that would be easy, requiring only a simple change—meaning teachers could now get updates every day instead of every nine weeks. Pactor went to the principal with the idea, and the principal told him, "Sure." Pactor reflects, "Without having to institute a formal policy, teachers now knew how students were doing in each other's classes. They could plan interventions accordingly."

Brent Maddin, provost at the Relay Graduate School of Education, recalls teaching in Franklin, Louisiana:

> Our school had this policy that students had to be in the top of the class to take the ACT. The guidance counselor would not give other kids an ACT packet. The philosophy was: if other kids took the test, their scores would make the school look bad. I called ACT and got some packets myself. I started dealing them from my back porch, like I was trafficking in something illegal, not ACT materials. The guidance counselor was furious. She said, "I work with the ACT." Ultimately, though, the principal said, "If you're going to hand out packets, then you need to do prep." So we began running afterschool and Saturday prep. By the end of the year, once they thought about it, the administration was on board. After all, that's why we were all there. But, if we were doing it, they wanted the school to look good. Two years later, we'd added an official ACT prep course.

Sometimes, cage-busting is just getting school or system leaders to pursue policies more sensibly. Casie Jones teaches English at Martin Luther King Jr. Student Transition Academy in Memphis, Tennessee, a district that piloted the Gates Foundation's massive Measures of Effective Teaching (MET) project. The project featured a commitment to incorporating student feedback in teacher evaluation using the Tripod survey. Memphis's Teacher Effectiveness Measure included student achievement, student growth, observations, and the Tripod score. While Tripod accounted for just 5 percent of a teacher's score, Jones says, "The scores were a freak-out moment for a lot of teachers because we were going to eventually be paid on these scales, and we didn't think they were fair or accurate. The motivation was good, but I'm an alternative teacher. My students struggle in reading, and the survey was 75 questions long. They'd get bored and stop answering." She says a lot of teachers just complained, but she made a point of focusing on what changes she wanted to see. She says, "I conceded that students are biased and shouldn't have the greatest voice but that if anyone knows how teachers are doing, it's students. When I'd meet with the district's teacher ambassadors, I'd advocate for Tripod but explain why they needed to shorten the survey." She helped shape the concerns into a memo "with a positive spin—here's a question and an idea of what should be done." She relates that the district agreed to cut the survey to forty questions. It's easy for teachers to grumble, "Nobody cares what I think." That's especially true when dealing with a major, multi-million dollar district initiative. But Jones didn't grumble. She identified a problem and got it solved.

Jeffrey Charbonneau, a science teacher at Zillah High School in Washington State and the 2013 National Teacher of the Year, wanted students at his small, rural high school to receive dual enrollment credit for his chemistry, physics, and engineering courses. Charbonneau says, "I knew my courses were demanding enough." After more than a decade in the classroom, Charbonneau was confident that receiving college credit would make students much more likely to matriculate—especially his predominantly Hispanic students, many of whom would be the first in their family to attend college. He reached out to Eastern Washington University and asked, "What do I need to do to for my chemistry course to count for college credit?" They said, "Sorry, we don't do that."

> I talked to the chair of the department and got a "no." It was a problem that I didn't have at least a master's in chemistry. I spoke to the dean. I continued up the chain and just kept asking. I had three different meetings at the university. They'd ask, "How do you know you're teaching to a high enough standard?" I'd show them work examples. They asked how they'd know that my lectures were okay. I said, "Let me come guest lecture on campus and show you. Don't even tell me what class it is until the night before." What I was asking was, "Set the bar as high as you want, but give me an opportunity to meet that bar." After that, the faculty voted to allow it on a one-year trial basis . . . You need to understand their perspective. They have accreditation issues. Their accreditor is looking at the degrees that faculty have. I didn't realize that, but it helped me see why they were saying no. I went out and got National Board certification to help demonstrate that I'm teaching to a high level.

Meanwhile, Charbonneau took care to think about what was in it for the colleges. He says, "They get to influence exactly what kind of physics and chemistry is being taught. It helps them with recruitment. And dual enrollment generates financial benefit for them."

Of Zillah's 100 eleventh graders, sixty took chemistry for college credit in 2013. The partnership now includes not just Eastern Washington but also Central Washington University and Yakima Valley Community College. And other teachers followed suit. Zillah students can now accumulate sixty-nine college credits during high school—nearly a year and a half of college credit. Charbonneau says, "At the start, I must've got twelve 'no's' in a row. But I kept coming back with reasons why they should and how they could." Oh, and Charbonneau's efforts caught the eye of the governor and got him appointed to Washington's Student Achievement Council—a state board that focuses on higher education. This is such a nice example of cage-busting because, once Charbonneau figured it out, it kept paying dividends. Colleagues could piggyback on the precedent. And he had relationships that he could tap in the future.

WHAT CAGE-BUSTERS BELIEVE

Cage-busters believe that actions change culture, and that talk does not. They heed the advice of Larry Bossidy, veteran CEO and coauthor of *Execution: The Discipline of Getting Things Done,* who argues, "We don't think ourselves into a new way of acting, we act ourselves into a new way of thinking."[22] They know that "culture change" can otherwise be short-lived.

Cage-busters believe that teachers can have enormous influence but need to earn it and harness it. Cage-busters recognize that earning influence and professional respect requires reshaping a profession that has accepted uninspired management and ineffectual routines for too long.

Cage-busters believe that *management*, not teachers, ought to be blamed if management fails to address mediocrity anywhere in a school system but that *teachers* ought to insist that management do its duty. If teachers don't do that, cage-busters believe that they'll have trouble convincing observers of their professionalism and commitment to excellence.

Cage-busters believe that "teacher leadership" is a cheery, amorphous term that's only meaningful when it gets concrete. Cage-busters are less interested in debating "Who's *really* for the kids?" than asking, "What's the problem we need to solve and how do we solve it?"

They believe in the value of precision and clarity. They believe it's better to say "an extra forty-five minutes a day of instruction" than "extended learning time" and "an extra thirty minutes of computer-assisted tutoring" than "blended learning."

Cage-busters believe that a focus on problem solving, precision, and responsibility can help teachers to create the schools and systems where they can do their best work. They don't cage-bust *instead* of tending to curriculum and instruction. Rather, they cage-bust because they believe it will help forge schools and systems where their time, passion, and energy make the biggest difference for kids.

Cage-busters believe that the lucky get luckier. While I was writing this book, educators would sometimes ask me about it. After I'd share a story or two, most would half-sigh and say, "That's interesting—but these are the exceptions." They'd explain that these educators were teachers of the year or National Board certified or part of some privileged network or blessed with a great principal. In other words, they were the lucky few. What's easy to miss is how often these teachers make their own luck. Candice Willie-Lawes, a special education teacher in New York City, says, "I intentionally built a good relationship with my [assistant principal], who is now my principal. Currently, she's assigned me a teaching schedule with an alternate population of fifteen students and five wonderful paraprofessionals/teaching assistants. I can do my thing because I have that trust. I built it up over the past eight years. No one is going to respect you unless you've earned it. But once I earned it, it freed me to bust out of the cage." Cage-busters identify problems, offer solutions, find strength in numbers, manage up, and—gosh—they keep getting lucky.

Finally, cage-busters don't just believe—they *know*—that this stuff is hard and there will be plenty of missteps. But because each win dismantles another piece of the cage, they also know that time is on the cage-buster's side. This is a great place to introduce Maddie Fennell, whom we'll hear from several times in the chapters ahead. An elementary school teacher in Nebraska, Maddie has enjoyed enormous success and chaired the NEA's Commission on Effective Teachers and Teaching.[23] She's also had her share of setbacks. One was the time she was deposed as union president. She recalls, "In 2007, after being named Nebraska Teacher of the Year, I was elected president of my local union." She says, "I was flying high. I'd been doing that for a year and a half and we had the highest membership in fifteen years. Then I went away for a week and a half." When she returned, the union board demanded her resignation. It turned out the board had been swayed by an ambitious vice president who wanted to be president and who thought Maddie was driving the members too hard. Maddie agreed to step down. She says, "I cried for two weeks. I didn't want to get out of bed. Then I knew I had to get back into the classroom. I was back in my element. And, you know what? I was stronger for it." Cagebusters believe that stumbles and setbacks are part of the journey, not the end of the road.

TEACHERS POSSESS TWO KINDS OF AUTHORITY

Teachers are often unsure how they might bust the cage. After all, teachers don't have a lot of formal authority in schools. This means it's especially important that they be clear and strategic about tapping the authority they do have. After all, while teachers do lack *positional authority*, they have two powerful sources of authority at their disposal: the *authority of expertise* and a potentially powerful *moral authority*. Teachers rarely employ these to their full extent. Many aren't even aware of the power they possess.

The *authority of expertise* comes from the fact that teachers know more than anyone else about how policies and practices actually affect students and classrooms. Teachers know what's working, what's not, and what's really going on. They know how evaluation systems play out and how new technology gets used. They know which colleagues aren't pulling their weight and where well-intentioned reforms are falling flat. If teachers share this knowledge clearly and constructively, they can profoundly influence policy and practice. In all walks of life, there's a deep-seated desire to trust the expertise of professionals. People want to lean on the advice of their dentist, plumber, or mechanic, just because life is so complicated that people want someone with know-how to tell them what they need to do about a tooth, a faucet, or a car. The same holds true for schooling.

Moral authority is a different animal: it comes when professionals are seen as the guardians of the public interest. Now, there are a *lot* of efforts to sloganeer the way to moral authority—by saying things like "we're for the kids." Those slogans *do not* produce moral authority. Moral authority doesn't come from *saying* that one is fighting for students. It comes with a track record of clear, consistent action to promote professional excellence. It derives from a record of doing things to help teachers get better, get systems to stop wasting time or money, and ensure that mediocre employees (whether they work in the central office or in classrooms) are dealt with appropriately. Moral authority is *earned*. It's the product of teachers convincing parents, voters, and policy makers, "We've got this."

The authority of expertise is only effective when professionals are deemed trustworthy. If people grant the expertise of auto mechanics, but believe that too many are ripping people off, it undermines the moral authority of all mechanics. The result is a public that second-guesses mechanics and asks elected officials to do something to pluck out the bad apples. The authority of expertise is bolstered by moral authority, and moral authority isn't a question of what people think of this or that mechanic—but what people think of mechanics in general. For teachers, moral authority is not what people think of *you*, but what they think of the teachers at your *school,* or in your *system*, or throughout the *profession*. Moral authority is a team sport. That's why retreating to the classroom is so debilitating.

PUTTING THAT AUTHORITY TO WORK

Powerful examples of teacher authority are scarce because schools aren't in the habit of encouraging it, and because few teachers know how to gather it or to apply it. For one thing, the cage is mostly ignored in teacher preparation and professional development.

When teachers do pursue change beyond the classroom, they often go about it in ways that seem calculated to disappoint. They'll raise reasonable concerns, but in vitriolic language that marginalizes their points and alienates potential allies. Too few teachers are really versed in the political or policy realities that permeate schooling. Few know who is making a decision or have thought much about how they might win over lawmakers and leaders.

Teachers have also been hindered by a reluctance to police their profession. Teachers have long stood silent as principals give high marks to mediocre colleagues or as unions protect those who shouldn't be in classrooms. They've rarely challenged superintendents to do something about lousy professional development or ineffectual spending. The profession has suffered for this geniality.

Administrators dismiss sensible concerns as "complaints" and tune out useful suggestions. Teachers can conclude that no one is listening or cares what they think. And this is how things will remain, until teachers learn to put their expertise and moral authority to work. (See "Cage-Busters Make Things Happen.")

CAGE-BUSTING MOSTLY GETS IGNORED

It's not like teachers are hurting for advice. After all, a search of Amazon for the word *teacher* turns up more than three hundred thousand book titles. There's a lot of smart guidance out there for teachers seeking advice on instruction, pedagogy, curriculum, and culture. What's missing, though, is guidance on how teachers can deal with the cage. Indeed, because most of this advice emphasizes instruction and collegiality, it can have blind spots regarding policy, the policing of the profession, or the nitty-gritty of teacher leadership. David Imig, former president of the American Association of Colleges for Teacher Education, says, "Teachers may take a course here and there on teacher leadership, but what's striking is how overwhelmed even exceptional teachers are by their principal, environment, department chair, and everything else." Teachers are mostly left to their own devices when it comes to addressing dysfunction, knucklehead principals, or problematic policies.

A Passive Profession?

Even smart, thoughtful resources seem to start from a presumption that teachers just don't have that much power to change things. Advice often

Cage-Busters Make Things Happen

"Any new teacher will feel trapped within their four walls," reflects Jeff Austin a high school economics and government teacher at Social Justice Humanitas Academy, "and that's okay to start. You have to develop that part first." Over time, though, Austin and his colleagues have learned to escape those walls in order to do their best work.

Austin started teaching in the suburbs. When he moved to Los Angeles, he says, he got "a quick slap in the face." No matter how well he taught his students for one hour a day, he realized he could do his very best and still not make a real difference for too many kids. A few years before Austin arrived to teach twelfth grade, a couple of tenth grade teachers had started to coordinate their curriculum, modeling their efforts on the "small learning communities concept." A few eleventh grade teachers liked what they saw and wanted in.

In 2005 Austin and his colleagues approached the principal armed with improved student achievement and discipline data and asked if they could rework classroom placement to ensure continuity for students in the program. Austin says, "We said, 'How about we just give you our matrix and all you have to do is plug it in? We're not asking you to create it—we'll create it.' The more we brought solutions, the more people just said, 'Okay.' Why would that principal stop us? We were literally taking work out of her hands. We were improving graduation rates and test scores without her having to do anything."

By the third year, they had a school-within-a-school for grades 10–12 in social studies, art, and English. Seeking to expand further and incorporate all subjects, they asked the principal for the authority to hire math and science teachers to teach within their collaborative. The principal said it was okay with her, so they went to the superintendent. Leading with their achievement, graduation, and college acceptance data, they asked for clearance to work directly with human resources. The superintendent agreed.

Within a few years, they had a full, self-contained high school, covering all subjects for grades 9–12. At that point, Los Angeles launched a new "pilot school" initiative that offered autonomy to approved schools. Austin and his colleagues thought about applying, discussed it with the superintendent, and then, says Austin, "kind of let him think that he convinced us not to do it." In return, they got laptop carts, a copy machine, science equipment, and new space.

The next year they decided to apply for pilot status. Austin says, "We were teaching and staying after school until 8:00 p.m. to work on the proposal. It was tiring but energizing, too. The LA Education Partnership gave us some office space. We were there Thanksgiving week, just writing and editing." Because the process involved a vote of community members, parents, and students, they held dozens of community meetings. There were four spots for eleven applicants. Austin's Social Justice Humanitas Academy snagged one.

Since the launch, Austin says, the challenge has been exercising the promised autonomy. "They let us believe we'd run the principal interview process," he says, and then the district gave them a list of candidates. Austin says a district HR official told them, "'I'll need to be at the interview and I need to ask these questions.' We told him, 'This is a teacher-led school. You're welcome to attend, but this is our interview.' The HR director totally, completely backed down. It was crazy."

After year one, smiles Austin, "We got our state test results back, and we were the highest-scoring public high school in Los Angeles." Three years on, in 2014, Social Justice Humanitas Academy was graduating 97 percent of its students and boasting the highest student attendance rates in the district. Austin and his colleagues remade the world in which they worked. The payoff for their hard work wasn't a plaque or more work; it was a school where they could be the teachers they always wanted to be.

emphasizes "survival," as in popular resources like *The First-Year Teacher's Survival Guide,* Scholastic's monthly "New Teacher Survival Guides," and offerings like *The Classroom Teacher's Technology Survival Guide* and *The English Teacher's Survival Guide.* Survival is fine, but it's not usually the measure of professional success.

Well-meaning advice for teachers routinely begins, "If you have a supportive principal . . ." The 2013 book *Everyone at the Table* offers smart guidance on how teachers can help shape teacher evaluation. But, when the authors note that teachers may be in places "where leadership does not support such an effort," they kind of shrug and tell teachers to be prepared "if and when the current leadership becomes more supportive."[24] That can make for a long, frustrating wait. Cage-busters don't wait to work with leadership that gets it. They help leaders who don't get it *to* get it.

In *The First-Year Teacher's Survival Guide*, Julia Thompson advises, "Because it is almost impossible to cheer up people who are determined to be negative, associate with upbeat people who are focused on learning to be outstanding teachers instead."[25] It's not that this advice is wrong so much as it's docile. Cage-busters refuse to accept negativity and obstruction as givens; they're unwilling to settle for just trying to steer around them.

This passivity is especially striking when coupled with otherwise valuable advice. In *Teacher Leadership That Strengthens Professional Practice*, Charlotte Danielson, an icon who has provided the profession with vital tools and insights, explains, "The culture to promote teacher leadership must be established and maintained first of all by district and site administrators."[26] She writes, "The culture of inquiry is established first by the administration. In a school with a well-developed culture of inquiry, administrators ensure that every teacher is aware of an expectation for ongoing professional engagement."[27] Danielson is right that good leaders should do these things. But sometimes they don't. And she doesn't have much to say about what teachers can do when their principal isn't making this happen.

Inattention to the cage is the rule, not the exception. Consider what's addressed in some of the most widely recommended volumes for teachers. A search of the top 30 lists on Google's "Recommended Books for Teachers," combined with the top 20 books on the Goodreads "Teaching" shelf, produced 29 widely recommended books for practitioners. An in-text search of these 29 books found that some topics were repeatedly discussed, and others were not.[28] Familiar classroom topics having to do with instruction, collaboration, and "social justice" were easy to find. *Technique* showed up 466 times, *discipline* 402, *culture* 159, *poverty* 131, *multicultural* 125, and *communication* 98. Teachers who want more advice on discipline or culture have plenty of places to turn. Yet, there's much less attention paid to the practical frustrations that can trip teachers up. If teachers are struggling with leaders, technology, wasted time, bureaucracy, or professional development, the most widely recommended texts have little to say. *Grant writing* showed up 26 times. *Work rules* and *bureaucracy* showed up a dozen times each. And, altogether, practical frustrations like *wasted time, bad technology, bad professional development, bad principal, bad meetings, bad teacher, interference, district administrator, Title I, collective bargaining,* and *central office* showed up just a couple dozen times. The bottom line is that there are important, practical topics that just don't usually get addressed.[29]

Cage-Busting and Great Classroom Practice Are Complements

When teachers ask me about resources for cage-busting, the books I get asked about most often are Doug Lemov's terrific *Teach Like a Champion* and Steven Farr's stellar *Teaching as Leadership* (see "*Teaching as Leadership*").[30] Both authors provide teachers with techniques that can help them take their instruction to the next level. Indeed, Farr's vision of leadership purposefully focuses on leadership *inside* the classroom, not outside it. He says, "When we were working on *Teaching as Leadership*, the question was, 'What are teachers doing in those classrooms to get these great results?'"

Cage-busting, though, deals with something different—how teachers can alter their larger schools and systems. Doing so can make it more possible for teachers to truly, as Lemov puts it, "practice perfect." Cage-busting helps teachers create the conditions where they can better use the advice proffered by the likes of Farr, Lemov, and Danielson. Classroom practice and cage-busting are not substitutes and they're not in competition. They're complements. Cage-busting can help teachers create schools where they can more effectively deliver instruction, mentor students, provide peer feedback, and promote collaboration.

In *Building a Better Teacher: How Teaching Works (and How to Teach It to Everyone)*, journalist Elizabeth Green tells the story of Spartan Village, a professional development school that partnered with the education school at Michigan State University to serve as a lab for teaching strategies, including how to use high-quality observations to transform teacher education. The principal, Jessie Fry, energetically sought to alter the school calendar, adopt a new floor plan, and add staff time. Despite promising results, though, Green writes, "strains began to appear. Each time a new superintendent arrived . . . [Fry] had to defend the Spartan Village exceptions.

Every time budgets grew tight, the school board always seemed to turn to Spartan Village." Whether or not the school was on the right track turned out to be irrelevant, as the effort "proved unsustainable." The lesson: promising instructional ideas will only deliver when coupled with the cage-busting needed to see them through.[31]

HOW DID WE GET HERE?

Teachers feeling isolated, frustrated, undervalued, and under attack is nothing new. In fact, that's kind of how our K–12 system was designed. Dan Lortie, the University of Chicago's famed chronicler of teaching, observed nearly four decades ago in *Schoolteacher* that practitioners historically haven't had a lot of say about schooling: "Teachers never did gain control of any area of practice where they were clearly in charge and most expert; day to day operations, pedagogical theory, and substantive expertise have been dominated by persons in other roles."[32]

How did we get here? In 1800 teaching was a predominantly male profession. It was feminized by nineteenth century Common School reformers as they sought a large pool of inexpensive educators. The Common School expansion was fueled not by a grand strategy to boost student achievement but by the fear that a flood of Catholic immigration presented a threat to American values. School expansion was intended to make sure that lots of Catholic children would be reading the King James Bible under the tutelage of Protestant educators. This plan required cheap, available labor—and the solution was to turn teaching into women's work. By 1900, most teachers were women.[33]

In the early 1900s Progressive reformers decided that disorganized, decentralized schools could be improved through the insights of "scientific management." These reformers, including business leaders and education professors, championed top-down management structures, salary schedules, professionalized school administration, and standardized record keeping. They eagerly imported the best practices of the industrial era, giving managers tight control over what the workers did and where and when they did it. Reformers trusted that smart, well-trained administrators (mostly

Teaching as Leadership

Cage-busting is a *complement* to great classroom practice. There is no conflict between tending to instructional practice and learning how to bust the cage. In fact, it's easiest to improve instruction when teachers are no longer trapped by the cage.

Steven Farr, the soft-spoken author of the influential 2010 book *Teaching as Leadership*, says, "The question we set out to answer was, 'What are teachers doing that's producing these insane results?' It was an action-focused approach. But over the past three or four years," he says, "we have seen that that we can go into two classrooms where they're using the same powerful techniques but getting completely different results." Many times, their differences can be chalked up to what's going on in the teacher's school.

Great teachers can work in troubled schools or alongside colleagues who aren't getting it done while feeling powerless to do anything about those larger challenges. Farr says that teachers need to address that, and, if they don't, "those cages are their own."

Teachers can find themselves yielding to pressure even when they think it's wrong for kids. Farr explains, "Teachers have a number of competing priorities. Teachers may know what they should do, but it's a big deal when the principal says, 'We're using a scripted curriculum and I expect to see you on this page, this day.' Teachers think, 'I don't want to get fired, and telling me to do anything other than what my principal says is unfair.' Your principal is your boss and can hire and fire you, but if you're that intent on pleasing your principal . . . you wind up making compromises."

Farr muses, "We need to talk not just about classroom practice but about purpose, relationships, and the broader set of things that affect the work." The instructional insights that Farr offers in *Teaching as Leadership* can be undermined by caged cultures and timid teachers. Cage-busting is not an alternative to the instructional expertise offered by Farr and others but a way to help ensure that teachers can put it to the fullest use.

men) could improve schooling by using factory-style management techniques to better control the teachers (most of whom were women).[34]

There resulted all manner of capricious leadership, with teachers fired for being pregnant, allegedly harboring socialist sympathies, or failing to conform to height and weight charts. Teachers responded by fighting for protections like tenure, work rules, and salary schedules, which reflected the collective bargaining model used by workers in industries to take on powerful management. Their victories were real and important. These wins came at a price, however. Success meant school staffing practices were modeled on those of factory workers rather than those of the emerging professions. Those norms got embedded in schooling's regulations, contracts, and bureaucracies. Victories intended to tame fickle management came with a high cost, binding teachers ever more tightly into a latticework of steps, lanes, contract minutes, evaluation protocols, and more.

This back-and-forth has constructed the cage, bar by bar. It was built by reformers trying to dictate teachers' work and also by teacher advocates intent on adding new safety bars around teachers. The result is a profession with an astonishing lack of autonomy, opportunity for growth, or room for creative problem solving.

Despite one reform wave after another, the teaching job has remained remarkably static over the past century. This is true, observes Dana Goldstein in *The Teacher Wars*, even as "Americans have debated who should teach public schools; what should get taught; and how teachers should be educated, trained, hired, paid, evaluated, and fired."[35]

While other knowledge-based industries saw the emergence of more flexible and adaptable staffing models, schooling did not. Staffing systems and salary schedules continue to treat teachers as basically interchangeable, with responsibilities and pay largely divorced from a teacher's expertise, effort, or accomplishments.

Today's educators are caged by policies and practices that may have once made sense but that seem poorly suited to attract, retain, and make the best use of talented professionals in the twenty-first century. Cage-busters begin by unshackling themselves from old assumptions and asking whether there is a better way to order the teacher's role, structure time, spend funds, or organize schooling.

NOBODY IS ALTOGETHER ON MY SIDE

In recent years the education debate has featured two warring camps. On one side are those who embrace test-based accountability, differentiated teacher pay, and school choice. On the other are those who broadly reject such measures while demanding more support for teachers and kids, more professional autonomy, and more emphasis on peer assistance and portfolios.

Teachers can feel pressed to be in one camp or the other. They attend conferences where state and district officials invite them to play leadership roles by championing this reform. They get e-mails from colleagues or union officials urging them to oppose that reform. Through it all, there's a sense they're supposed to pick sides—to be for or against school accountability, the Common Core, or charter schooling. Cage-busters don't accept that premise. Cage-busters are intent on creating schools where they can do their best work, and don't have time to get swept up in someone else's grand crusade. Cage-busters work to appreciate the logic of each proposal, understand its practical frailties, embrace the good, and reject or address the bad.

In all of this, teachers can take inspiration from an unlikely source: Treebeard, the wizened, ancient Ent who befriends a couple of lost young hobbits in J. R. R. Tolkien's *Lord of the Rings*. On meeting Treebeard, in the midst of a savage war, the wide-eyed young hobbit Pippen asks him, "And whose side are you on?" Treebeard ponders the question and then laconically replies, "Side? I am not altogether on anybody's side, because nobody is altogether on my side."[36]

A cage-buster is happy with neither camp in the current debates. He knows that some teachers work harder and are better at their jobs than others and that professionals *should* be accountable. But he also knows that many proposals for strengthening accountability are half-baked and that there's reason to fear overreliance on test scores or unreliable metrics. The cage-buster believes that reformers are right, that many policies need to change if more schools are to thrive. But he also believes that school improvement is ultimately about practice and not policy. In short, it's easy for a cage-buster to look at today's scorched-earth education debates and conclude that no one is altogether on his side. The funny thing is, by saying just that clearly, firmly, and respectfully, he can make it more likely that he'll get a hearing from serious people on both sides.

CAGES AREN'T BUSTED BY CHEAP TALK AND LIP SERVICE

Teachers get lots of lip service and misty-eyed declarations of admiration. These cloying tributes are ritually offered to more than three million teachers without qualifiers or challenges. U.S. Secretary of Education Arne Duncan has insisted, "I believe that [teachers] are absolutely the unsung heroes of our society."[37] Actor Matt Damon told a Save Our Schools rally, "I flew overnight . . . and came down here because I really had to tell you all in person that I think you all are awesome."[38] Or, as Michelle Collay put it in *Everyday Teacher Leadership*, "Teaching is not just another job. Choosing to work with children and youth on a daily basis is something elevated to superhuman status."[39]

This isn't how we talk to professionals. These platitudes are the fluff of political speeches and celebrity profiles. You don't lard buckets of mushy sentiment on people you really respect. This is how we talk to Cub Scouts or t-ball players. This is the sweet, syrupy tone we reserve for little kids because they're cute and too fragile for tougher stuff. The truth is that such talk *infantilizes teachers and crowds out respect*. Real respect is earned. It's not given away freely or casually. It's a conversation between equals, and we usually don't feel obliged to shower banal praise on our equals.

All this happy talk is insincere. We know this because *nobody* honestly believes all of America's three-million-plus teachers are awesome or heroic. As one decorated teacher told me, "I am so sick of all this teacher heroism crap already. I'm a professional, not a hero." I mean, nobody thinks that every doctor, lawyer, professor, or cop is good or noble. Even Matt Damon doesn't think that every actor or screenwriter in Hollywood is "awesome." (How do I know? Well, a few years ago, Damon slammed screenwriter Tony Gilroy, saying of Gilroy's *Bourne Ultimatum* script, "This is a career-ender. I mean, I could put this thing up on eBay and it would be game over for that dude. It's terrible."[40]) Real respect starts by saying plainly, to their face, that some teachers are great . . . and some aren't and that it's the terrific teachers who deserve acclaim.

When teachers hear the empty blah-blah, they need to know that everything that follows is probably unserious—and that the real decisions are going to get made after the lights are turned out and teachers are ordered off to bed.

Cage-busting teachers don't just accept this insincere blather; they do something about it. Like what? Start by taking a page from U.S. Army captain Benjamin Summers, who took to the pages of the *Washington Post* in 2014 to flatly declare, "I have worn an Army uniform for the past eight years and deployed twice to Afghanistan. This doesn't make me a hero. Many veterans deserve high praise for their heroism, but others of us do not . . . Not every service member is a hero."[41]

The next time teachers hear someone launch into starry-eyed, infantilizing dreck, they should calmly them, "No thanks. You can keep the empty words." It's nice that Duncan, Damon, or whoever wants to pat teachers on the head. But professionals should calmly ask these allies to instead talk to them *as* professionals.

CAGE-BUSTING OFFERS A WAY FORWARD

A lot of advice presumes that if teachers are positive, passionate, and committed to their craft . . . well, things will work out. Yet, teachers can do remarkable work in their classroom only to wear themselves out as they slam again and again into the bars of the cage. Even teachers who've mastered some lock-picking tricks can find it tough to articulate or to share them.

I think of the teacher who held a PhD, had been named a "master teacher" by a national organization, and had worked eight years in the district office before returning to the classroom because her administrative job had her musing, "I could be teaching *Antigone* right now." Yet, when asked what advice she had for colleagues on dealing with school or system issues, this impressive woman could say only, "I tell them to just keep a positive attitude! I tell them to focus on teaching and learning, keep a smile on their face, trust that the administrators know what they're doing and that everything else will fall into place." Her faith was impressive, but would leave teachers stuck when administrators don't know what they're doing or things aren't falling into place.

Teachers can feel powerless. They're not. Superintendents, school leaders, and policy makers are looking for problem solvers, and teachers are better positioned to help solve those problems than anyone else. People care what teachers think. Teachers have a lot to work with, even if they don't know it.

Advocates and lawmakers have little ability to affect what really happens in classrooms. Thus, they see little recourse but to push policy and hope that helps. Unfortunately, when it comes to things like teacher evaluation or school turnarounds, experience has taught that new policies frequently disappoint. When policies fail, reformers are inclined to think, "It *would* have worked if educators had bought into it and made it work." So, reformers push for more ambitious, detailed policies. Today we are in this destructive cycle where reforms garner more pushback, prompting calls for more aggressive and intrusive policy and yielding even more pushback.

Is there a way out of this vicious cycle? Yep. It starts with cage-busting teachers. It starts with teachers earning, employing, and leveraging the authority that will make them masters of their fate. It's about a new deal, where teachers embrace responsibility for what schools do and how students fare. Enough teachers doing this successfully can reassure policy makers and the public, building the trust that makes possible a new day and a new deal.

Ted Kolderie, senior associate at Education Evolving, captures what that deal might look like. "The old deal with teachers was, 'We don't give you professional authority and in return you don't give us accountability.' Now the 'reform' deal is supposed to be, 'You *will* give us accountability even though we still don't give you autonomy.' The good deal, the new deal," he argues, "should be, 'We will give you professional authority and in return you give us accountability.'"

Cage-busters are working to make *that* deal a reality. It starts with teachers tackling the things they can readily influence. It's not about pleasing sentiments or talk; it's about action. It's action that shows seriousness, impresses observers, and changes culture.

Here's how things unfold from here. The next chapter looks more closely at key elements of cage-busting. Chapter 3 examines how to put cage-busting insights to work when dealing with school and system leadership. Chapter 4 explains why policy can be so frustrating and how teachers can make it less so. Chapter 5 shows how a cage-busting mind-set can help address the practical challenges of teacher leadership. Chapter 6 considers how cage-busters think about the teachers unions. Chapter 7 explores how cage-busters can think more broadly about what it means to be a teacher and the role that teachers play. And Chapter 8 brings it all together and seeks to offer some additional real-world advice.

With that, let's get started.

2

Choose to Be
a Problem Solver

LUKE SKYWALKER: *[finding that his ship is about to sink into the bog]* Oh, no! We'll never get it out now!

YODA: So certain, are you? Always with you, it cannot be done. Hear you nothing that I say?

LUKE: Master, moving stones around is one thing, but this is . . . totally different!

YODA: No! *No* different! Only different in your mind. You must *unlearn* what you have learned.

LUKE: All right, I'll give it a try.

YODA: No! Try not. Do . . . or do not. There is no try.

—*The Empire Strikes Back*

LLOYD: If you guys know so much about women, how come you're here at, like, the Gas-n-Sip alone on a Saturday night, completely alone, drinking beers, no women anywhere?

JOE: *[after a long moment of silence]* By choice, man. It's a conscious choice.

GUY 2: Yeah, we're choosing to be here.

—*Say Anything*

MUCH OF CAGE-BUSTING comes down to a simple choice—whether or not to accept the cage. For many teachers, choosing to seek a way out can seem nerve-racking or unrealistic. Doing so requires teachers to unlearn the habits that keep them trapped. It requires teachers to look at their world anew and refuse to accept the way things have always been. This is hard, but it is doable. And it is worth doing.

Today, even terrific teachers wind up sounding exhausted, rather than exhilarated, simply because schools make choosing excellence such a chore. I recall the State Teacher of the Year who told me,

> When I pitched my digital media proposal to the district, they said, "Sure." They would give me the room to run with it, but they didn't have the bandwidth to actively guide or support it, and they weren't going to just give me a bunch of computers. So I went to local stores, found old computers, and wrote a grant to Microsoft for the operating system. I got a classroom, but it didn't have the necessary setup and they wouldn't buy extension cords. So I bought the cabling myself, and the classroom had basically been the janitor's room before, so it wasn't ideal. But there were no air ducts, so I was moved to the library where they draped part of the room off. But we just got a fantastic new librarian who was trying to grow her own program, so neither of us had the space we wanted for what we wanted to do. Then the district said, "We're not going to support these computers. You've got to support them yourself." So I'm trying to teach and cobble together fifty-three computers that are absolute trash.
>
> I'm teaching storytelling with my right hand and trying to install software with my left. [With] my right foot, you know, I'm trying to replace a hard drive. I'm there until nine or ten o'clock, trying to get things done. I'm there and my wife's there helping me. It goes on for years this way. It's not like the district necessarily stops teachers from pursuing new programs and initiatives, but it's not the culture. And when teachers want to do it, they find they're doing it by themselves, and they often burn out.

For all of his passion and remarkable effort, his classroom is, well, a cage—one his wife even shares! Sure, there are superheroes out there, able to succeed in spite of everything. But when success requires incredible individuals working incredible hours against incredible odds, success is going to be the exception. This chapter aims to help teachers see the cage more clearly, grasp the strategies that can help unlock or dismantle it, and leverage their moral authority and expertise.

THE CAGE IS LESS CONFINING THAN ADVERTISED

The thing is, the cage is less confining than teachers often think. Each of those four bars we discussed in the last chapter is less solid than it might first appear.

That overflowing bucket of directives? Administrators and policy makers don't always know when they're causing problems. A word from you may help them avoid problems that they never intended. Maddie Fennell recalls a district decree that all principals should pop in to at least ten classrooms a week, even if just briefly. These instructional rounds were intended to be formative, and principals were instructed to find something positive to say. But, Maddie says, "this was never really explained. Teachers didn't know what the visits meant. They'd wonder, 'Why did I get a dozen visits when the teacher next door got two? Why did the principal walk out so quickly?' It was a good idea, but it wound up giving teachers more stress than support." She was as confused as anyone until she happened to see a central office presentation on the idea. She told them, "This is great, but do you realize that none of us teachers understands this, and that we're all confused and alarmed?" Of course the leadership had no idea. Maddie says, "Administrators don't know if the teachers don't reflect it back to them. These folks just honestly didn't know that they had been saying the complete opposite things because they hadn't talked to each other, and no one before me had told them."

All that wasted time and inattention to excellence? There are schools and systems that have shown it's possible to do a whole lot better. In Washington, DC, high-performing teachers can now earn more than $100,000 after less than a decade in the classroom. American Federation of Teachers president Randi Weingarten points to contracts in places like New Haven and Baltimore as models for recognizing and rewarding terrific teachers.[1] Kerrie Dallman, president of the Colorado Education Association, notes that Jefferson County, Colorado, is in the midst of a performance pay system that is delivering substantial pay bumps to high performers and counseling dozens of low performers out of the profession. Dallman says, "There are those who struggle to believe we're sincere when we talk about excellence because of preconceived notions about unions. But I'll publicly say that ineffective teachers have three victims: students in that classroom, that teacher's colleagues, and that teacher himself." That kind of frank talk makes it a lot easier for teachers to win a hearing. Meanwhile, charter schools like YES Prep, KIPP, Rocketship, and Achievement First are among those that have found ways to make more efficient and imaginative use of teacher and student time, as have districts through initiatives like Charlotte-Mecklenburg's LIFT program.

That sense of being blindsided by simple-minded accountability and teacher evaluation systems? There's nothing inevitable there, either. Teachers might not realize that even those championing the use of value-added measures agree that tests capture only a piece of what's important. Harvard University professor Tom Kane, who led the Gates Foundation's influential Measures of Effective Teaching (MET) project, readily concedes that "state tests do not measure every outcome parents and taxpayers (and students) expect from schools."[2] Indeed, Columbia University professor Jonah Rockoff, who coauthored a landmark study linking value-added scores to future earnings, notes, "We all know test scores are limited not just in their power and accuracy, but in the scope of what we want teachers and schools to be teaching our kids."[3] Teachers concerned about unrealistic goals or overreliance on tests might find more allies than they'd expect.

Charter Schools Have Their Own Cages

Some of you teach in charter schools and may be thinking, "Well, what does any of this have to do with me?" And other readers may be thinking, "Heck, I'll just avoid all this by moving to a charter school!" After all, popular accounts can give the impression that charter school teachers don't have to worry about the cage. That's a mistake. There are six thousand charter schools across the land. Some have done a phenomenal job of disassembling the cage. But many others have not. You only need to spend a little time talking to charter school teachers to realize that plenty share the same concerns and frustrations as their district school counterparts. What do I have in mind?

Madaline Edison of Educators 4 Excellence Minnesota, whom we met in chapter 1, says, "My charter school was brand new. There was turnover in our leadership and our school board was pretty hands off. And the teachers were coming from a lot of different places, some from district schools where they had worked for a decade. That mindset can get sort of entrenched if someone has been in a system that, for so long, has kept them in a cage. That becomes your operating principle. It became clear that not all of the people in my building were there because of the mission or the student population. I had naïvely thought that a charter would just have things more together than district schools do. That wasn't the case." Educators who've spent their entire career in traditional districts can all too easily bring old assumptions and norms along with them.

Cohesive schools with strong cultures can create cages of their own. Grant Shreiner, UniServ director for the Louisiana Association of Educators, says, "Some charters do not have procedures in place for things like teacher absences, teacher personal days . . . When issues arise around something that hasn't been addressed in an employee handbook or school policy manual, teachers are often afraid to say anything. That's because if you do speak up, you may not be viewed as a team player."

Charter schools can sometimes be constricting. One much-admired big-city superintendent told me that, in the previous year, he'd lost five principals to an acclaimed charter network. He said, "You know what? Within five months, all five wanted to come back. They were told, 'Come here and you'll have tremendous flexibility and won't be bogged down with people telling you what to do. But they have strict structures. It's a good model that gets results, but, like McDonald's, it's pretty much the same, wherever you go—with fixed ways they buy beef or fry the fries.'"

When we think about cages, it's natural to focus on rules and regulations that have been around for a long time. Charters are less prone to that, and plenty of charters have done much to dismantle the cage, but charters are not a cure-all.

The truth is that policy makers rarely know the ins and outs of how these systems work, and they're very willing to hear better ideas.

The cage is not as intimidating or impermeable as it may first appear.

SEEING WITH FRESH EYES

The bars of the cage are frequently further apart and frailer than they appear, though this can be surprisingly hard to see. In joining a new school or system, it's only natural to watch our p's and q's. It can be easy for that initial deference to settle into genial acceptance of the way things are. Problems and obstacles turn into immutable examples of "how things are done." That's when the cage starts to seem all-encompassing and inevitable.

The cage-buster starts by cultivating what Zen Buddhists term *shoshin*, or "beginner's mind." Cage-busters approach subjects with curiosity and an open mind, even when they think they already know the answers. In *Zen Mind, Beginner's Mind*, Shunryu Suzuki puts it aptly: "In the beginner's mind there are many possibilities, in the expert's mind there are few."[4]

Beginner's mind starts by looking clearly at what's going on, why it's happening, and asking why time, passion, and energy are being wasted. Zak Champagne was teaching elementary math in Jacksonville, Florida, but "no matter how we were teaching math, the parents didn't know what we were talking about. It was as if we were speaking a different language." Trying to do something about that, Champagne and a colleague hosted a math night, but no one came. They tried again, this time providing food; still no one showed. They tried adding daycare, and then transportation. Still no luck. Finally, instead of exhausting themselves trying to get parents to come to school, they held a "math night" at the community center. They stopped wearing suits and opted for a more casual Saturday look. Parents showed up. Then they started to hold meetings at the local church on Sundays after service. Champagne says, "We got a dramatic increase in parent support and student performance." The key? He says, "We needed to ask why our math nights weren't working."

Seeing with fresh eyes can be easier than it sounds. In fact, it can amount to nothing more than unleashing your inner kindergartener. Peter Skillman, architect of the first handheld computer, has presented a TED talk on what he calls "The Spaghetti Problem." Skillman's topic was how to help teams think creatively and devise better, smarter solutions. In exploring this question, Skillman assembled a variety of different groups—ranging from MBA students to Taiwanese telecom engineers—and broke them into small teams. He then gave each team twenty pieces of spaghetti, a meter of tape, a marshmallow, and a piece of string and told them they had eighteen minutes to create the tallest structure that would support the marshmallow. The engineers did well. The MBAs did poorly. But the winners were a team of kindergarteners. Skillman explains that the kindergarteners didn't assume the amount of spaghetti was fixed. They asked for more pieces and got them.

What's the lesson? It's not "ask for more spaghetti"—any cage-buster knows that resources are limited and you don't usually get very far by just asking for "more." The lesson is to make sure that you're not assuming limits that don't exist or supersizing the limits that do. And the best way to do this is by looking at the situation afresh, with no assumptions. Try to stand back and ask yourself, "How would a kindergartner think about this?" Sometimes that's what it takes to notice that no one said, "You only get twenty pieces of spaghetti."

WHAT PROBLEM ARE YOU SOLVING?

In schools, it's easy to get caught up in petty frustrations, grand ambitions, or the sheer number of things that need doing. Amidst all this, the cage-buster's clarifying mantra is, "What problem are you solving?" Cage-busters work to relentlessly focus on addressing one problem at a time. This helps keep things manageable. Jay Hoffman, a technology education teacher at Frederick H. Tuttle Middle School in Burlington, Vermont, was a small business owner before becoming an educator. In business, he says, "If you want to be rich, it's not about focusing on getting rich. It's about finding a need and filling it. I've applied that to everything I've done. Doing that, by default, seems to make you a leader."

Is reading performance far below where it should be? Okay. Passion is nice and moral urgency is swell, but what might be done besides car-ing more or working harder? Focus on solving the problem. What are the challenges? Is it the curriculum? Amount of time on task? Caliber of instruction? Lack of student engagement? Lack of parental support? Some of these? All of these?

Define, as concretely as possible, the problem you're trying to solve. Excuses love ambiguity. Once you focus on *this* problem, as it exists *here and now*, it's a lot easier to identify possible solutions. Take professional learning communities. Pretty much every school claims to be a PLC or aspires to be one. Of course, this requires time for teams to meet and plan, good data on learning, appropriate training, and so on. The frustration for teachers is how rarely these things actually happen. A problem-solving approach asks what's needed for a PLC to actually deliver, and how to get what's needed.

Ultimately, a problem-solving mind-set helps cage-busters focus on six key questions that can light their path:

- Is X *important*?
- If so, how well *should* we be doing when it comes to X?
- How well *are* we doing with X?
- If we're not doing as well as we should, how can we *improve* X?
- What's *stopping* us from improving X?
- How do we *remove, blast through, or tunnel under the bars* stopping us from improving X?

If you're in a hurry, you can boil pretty much all of cage-busting down to these six questions. If you're in an even bigger hurry, you can tighten it down even further—to just four. What problem are you solving? What's your solution? What's in the way of your solution? And how do you get that obstacle out of the way?

THE FIVE WHY'S

If you're having trouble getting a good grip on how to ask or answer these questions, just look around and ask why things are the way that they are. A terrific tool for flagging easy-to-overlook dysfunction is the Five Why's approach. The idea is simple: to push yourself to challenge things that are so familiar you no longer think about why they're problematic. The key is asking "why?" enough times that you start to tap into that inner kinder-gartener. Here's how it works:

> *Question 1:* Why do our students only get forty-five minutes a week of mu-sic instruction?
> *Answer:* That's all the time, funding, and staff we have for music.

> *Question 2:* Why don't we have more time, funding, and staff for music?
> *Answer:* The district has other academic priorities.

> *Question 3:* Why can't we organize music to support academic priorities and then find the resources to triple the amount of music instruction?
> *Answer:* We haven't had a chance to look into doing that.

> *Question 4:* Why haven't we looked for music programs that engage kids and have a track record of promoting academic achievement?
> *Answer:* We've been so focused on finding time and resources to support math and reading instruction that we just haven't had time.

> *Question 5:* Why don't we find the time and put forward a strategy that we could consider piloting next year?
> *Answer:* Uh, I suppose we could discuss that.

What does it look like to do this for real? Here's a simple example. A couple years ago I was working with a district that wanted to get seri-ous about stepping up its career and technical education—but they had a problem. The district didn't have an internship program. Why? (That's one.) The head of student services said the leadership team had concluded they couldn't afford one. Why? (That's two.) The problem, student services said, was state policy that required a full-time staff member on premises at any internship site. Why? (That's three.) No one could think of a good reason, and we all agreed that sounded nuts, but the language was copied there in the district's policy handbook. Why did the state require this? (That's four.) A staffer from student services called the state and asked. It turned out that the state *didn't have any such restriction*; it only required that a full-time employee regularly visit the internship site. That clarifica-tion was enough to make internships practical and affordable. The district was off to the races. And we didn't even need the fifth question.

THE VALUE OF PRECISION

Okay, so beginner's mind sounds nice in theory. But how do you know where to look or what to focus on? Actually, that part is simple. Ask yourself, "What is *my* vision of a terrific school?" Don't just ask how to run a good class. Rather, ask, "What kind of school would enable me and my students to thrive?" Don't just ask how your school is doing on reading and math metrics, but ask how many students are excelling in ways that you care about. How many kids are mastering a second language? What percentage of parents hear from their child's teacher in a given week? How many students are getting a 3 or higher on at least one Advanced Placement (AP) science or math exam? Then gauge the distance between where you are and where you want your school or classroom to be. That can help you resist the tendency to settle.

An ancient Chinese proverb advises, "The beginning of wisdom is to call things by their right names." That's why talking unabashedly about "problems," and doing so with precise measurements, is so useful. It helps pierce the fog of routine. Clarity exposes the dark corners of the cage where excuses and missed opportunities can hide. The more precision, the more readily excuses melt away—and the more possibilities start to appear.

If you'd like to tackle wasted time, get precise. How many minutes a week are wasted on administrative noisemaking? How many minutes should be? For instance, say you decide that announcements, assemblies, and other administrative disruptions should take up no more than forty minutes a week. If they're taking twice that, that's a problem. If you don't know how much time is being taken up that way because you don't track that data, that's a big problem. It's a problem even if the numbers suggest that your school is doing relatively well. Why? Because you just said so! When you identify objectives you deem important and then determine that you want your school to do better, you've identified problems. And that's great! It generates clear, concrete goals. It flags opportunities to improve. And it helps identify obstacles that may be in the way.

The value of identifying all of these possibilities is not because you'll address them all right away. It's because it helps you focus on doing better at those things *you* have flagged as important.

The best way to start is often by considering how your school uses two critical resources: time and money. If anything wears teachers down, it's wasting time or scrambling for the dollars to procure crucial supplies. Getting precise about dollars and minutes is a great way to get in the habit of asking hard questions about familiar routines.

Paul Ramirez, an English teacher in Wilmington, Delaware, says that when he started teaching in 2010, he spent a lot of time assessing students and grading quizzes. Because there was no automated scoring system, teachers would grade multiple choice quizzes by hand. He says, "I'd give weekly vocabulary quizzes. At a minute a quiz, I'd spend an hour a week marking those up for seventy students. That alone was thirty-six hours a year. There were also tons of reading assessments, SAT prep, and prep for state tests." It seemed there had to be a better way. Ramirez "looked around for a technological solution and found this online system called TRIAND.com. You just print the quizzes on printer paper and run them through the copy machine. Other teachers saw this and word got around. Four years later the district is using this in every school." As a result, Ramirez makes better use of his time and gets better data. He says he's saving more than a hundred hours a year, which means lots more time for lesson planning, mentoring, or instruction. The bonus, he says, is that making use of these easy-to-grade quizzes means "now I have more time for essays and short answers."

ACTIONS CHANGE CULTURE

Schooling is rife with talk of culture change. Michael Fullan, professor emeritus at the University of Toronto, puts it well, observing, "Transforming the culture—changing the way we do things around here—is the main point."[5] He's right. But what can get lost in translation is that culture isn't changed by good intentions, impassioned words, or policy directives; it's changed by action.

Tammy Laughner, a second grade teacher in Arlington Woods Elementary in Indianapolis, Indiana, illustrates how small actions can start to change the culture in a school and, eventually, a system. Laughner had reached the end of her rope. "I'd have success on my own little island, inside my four walls," she reflects, "but the school was a shambles. I didn't feel physically safe." Her school had an F rating. When another teacher, Dan Kriech, transferred in, they started to brainstorm. She says, "We'd write our ideas down on legal pads, let them sit there for a week, and then revisit them. We worked like that, writing our ideas down and stepping back to get a fresh perspective." Laughner and Kriech knew they needed the support of their principal, who, says Laughner, was "fatigued, feeling defeated, and eager to entertain any new idea that might help." Laughner and Kriech created Project RESTORE, featuring tests every Thursday, higher expectations, and a more demanding academic environment. Teachers would gear their instruction toward those weekly tests. Students would compete with each other and with other classes to post the best score. Weekly tracking would provide teachers with continuously updated data, while a reward system would reward student buy-in. And a newly created discipline team would handle classroom problems.

Their principal connected Laughner and Kriech with an assistant superintendent, who told them they were good to go if the faculty signed on. Laughner and Kriech explained to faculty that the changes would include more work but would have a big pay-off. After the presentation, in a secret ballot, thirty-three of the thirty-five teachers voted to go forward. There were some initial tears as teachers struggled with stress and bruised feelings, especially when dismal test results were posted. But after about two months, morale started to lift as the culture adjusted to the new routines. Laughner says, "That first year, we went from an F school to an A on the Indiana rating system."

A year later a new principal arrived, who wasn't keen on Laughner's program. By October Laughner felt like she had no choice but to send out an e-mail to about thirty people, "including the superintendent, and the state superintendent," saying that she couldn't continue as things stood. She got a meeting with central office staff within two days. Asked what she needed, Laughner told them that she needed a new principal and a new school where she could expand the program. Armed with impressive outcomes, she got both. Laughner and Kriech then helped launch Project RESTORE at a neighboring elementary. Within two weeks of the initial meeting, the problem principal was removed from Arlington Woods.

Laughner continued to teach fifth grade, while rotating teachers from the second school through her classroom to teach the practices of Project RE-STORE. At the end of that year, the second school had also leaped from an F to an A.[6]

When pondering culture change, think of a broken bone that hasn't healed quite right. Nobody wants to have to re-break and reset the bone. That's a painful, unpleasant process. So there's a natural desire to prescribe therapy and hope things will work out. But therapy rarely solves the root problem. Instead, it's a constant battle to keep things from going out of kilter. Meanwhile, re-breaking and resetting *is* painful, but then it's over. And eight weeks later the bone has healed and the soft tissue has healed around it. That's a recipe for lasting change. In schools, once new norms have been in place for six months, they start to seem routine. And the culture will change accordingly. Two years on, no one will even remember that things used to be otherwise. (See *"See Me After Class."*)

EMBRACING YOUR MORAL AUTHORITY

Brian Crosby is an accomplished teacher, author of two books, and columnist for his local newspaper. Yet, when he sits on teacher committees at his school, he often feels like he's just there for show. "The problem," he says, "is that Americans don't view teaching as a profession. They just don't think that we're hard-working professionals the same way that, say, doctors are." Earning the professional status that Crosby desires requires more than just hard work and commitment; it requires like-minded teachers to change the tenor of their profession.

When a teacher sits down with a principal or a lawmaker, they're viewed not just as an individual but also as a member of a profession. The person across the table needs to decide whether they can trust your judgment, sincerity, and professionalism even though they may hardly know you. Their view of teachers writ large will color their thinking. That's both because it's human nature and because what they do for you will inevitably apply to other teachers.

This means that your fate is in the hands of the other teachers in your school, system, state, and nation. The more teachers are trusted, the more

See Me After Class

In chapter 1, I noted that too few books offer practical advice that helps with cage-busting. One happy exception is Roxanna Elden's *See Me After Class*.[7] If you're looking for ideas on how to act in ways that will productively change school culture, Elden's got some advice to share. She explains, "This book is not *Chicken Soup for the Teacher's Soul*. It's more like *Hard Liquor for the Teacher's Soul*."

Elden offers useful advice on dealing with colleagues. Of grouchy peers, she writes, "Sometimes their complaints feel refreshingly honest. Too much time in the company of the complainers, however, can leave you feeling hopeless." She advises, "Think twice before jumping in with your own stories. You don't want this person using them as examples next time they complain." Elden also advises, "Don't let the actions of a few outspoken, ignorant people keep you from getting to know your other coworkers. The more allies you have, the less one person's attitude matters."

When it comes to your principal, Elden reminds readers, "running a school is hard, and principals face their own challenges in the school system's chain of command . . . It is unfair to assume all problems begin and end with your front office." She offers plenty of other useful tips for the savvy cage-buster. These include:

Pick one issue at a time. "Your principal is more likely to listen to your request to replace broken desks if it's not combined with an unrelated complaint about the lunch schedule. Focus on your highest priority and leave other topics for another day."

Offer a solution. "Administrators have the same problem with overwhelming to-do lists as teachers do. Your principal will be more receptive if you approach with a plan of action you'd like her to sign off on rather than a problem you hope she will figure out how to solve."

Offer to do most of the work. "When someone is trying to sell you a car or a gym membership, they handle the paperwork themselves. All you have to do is say yes and sign. Keep this model in mind when you want your principal to approve field trip requests. If you want to get the answer you want, expect to make phone calls, fill out paperwork, and collect permission slips on your own."

Elden also offers some sharp thoughts on what "your principal really wants from you." She says, "What most principals want from teachers is simple and matches what any boss wants from employees: Do your job, do your job well, do your job independently and with as little drama as possible, [and] make yourself, your students, the school, and yes, your principal look as good as possible."

Elden's is the kind of advice that teachers need but too rarely get.

weight their moral authority carries, the readier leaders and lawmakers will be to stand back and follow the profession's lead. Absent that moral authority, teachers can do great work, change lives, and still find themselves without the professional respect they seek.

The Teaching Profession Suffers for Its Reputation

Peter Greene, a veteran English teacher and former union president, notes that the profession has historically been so reluctant to discuss bad teachers "that reasonable people might conclude we refuse to acknowledge their existence." He writes, "While I think it's wrong to think teachers don't believe in bad teachers, and counter-intuitive to think so, we have refused to address the issue for so long that critics could be forgiven for concluding that we had joined the Flat Earth Society." He continues, "Teachers know full well that bad teachers exist, probably better than anyone; after all, your kid was in Mr. McNumbnutt's class for a year, but I've been working next door to him for ten . . . Some teachers, having had their chance to shape up, need to get out."[8] But lawmakers and the public rarely hear educators say any of this out loud. And that compromises the profession's moral authority.

Frances Davis, associate superintendent for human resources and talent management in Gwinnett County, Georgia, has seen a shift in the profession to where "a third grade teacher wants that second grade teacher to be accountable" for student learning. Yet, Davis laments that "in case after case, when it comes down to removing an ineffective teacher from the classroom, rarely can we depend on another teacher to weigh in. We have to depend on the evaluations done by the principal or AP [assistant principal]." This means that everything hinges on the administrators—and they're often reluctant to act. She says, "You can go in any school, and teachers know who the ineffective people are. But teachers don't want to speak up. The issue is not identifying the weak links; it's having the emotional fortitude to speak up."

No matter how impassioned or hardworking, teachers suffer from the profession's jaded stature. This isn't about blame, and it isn't personal. But the profession has paid for a lack of quality control. In 2013, 30 percent of teachers reported that having to work with less effective colleagues was one of the top three factors impeding their teaching.[9] More disconcerting, a 2014 study of 234,000 teacher records found that one out of six teachers were absent at least eighteen days a year (even after excluding teachers who had missed eleven or more days in a row, presumably due to extraordinary circumstances).[10] Yet, at the same time, administrators consistently rate 99 percent of their teachers as effective.[11] And 98 percent of principals report that their teachers are "doing an excellent or pretty good job."[12] These issues are not new. In Illinois, between 1995 and 2005 only one of every 930 evaluations yielded an "unsatisfactory" rating for a tenured teacher.[13] None of this is the *fault* of teachers per se (if anything, it's the fault of principals and district administrators), but it is teachers who pay the price in terms of credibility and reputation.

If doctors stand by silently when colleagues commit malpractice, we question their judgment and their professionalism. If police excuse reckless or irresponsible colleagues, we question their reliability. When trust in public servants falters, their professional autonomy and authority suffer. So long as mediocre teaching gets a pass—even if the blame is the fault of administrators and not teachers—it undermines efforts to empower teachers.

It's Not About Picking Fights

Teachers don't win moral authority by picking fights, insulting colleagues, or proclaiming that lots of teachers are awful. It involves something much more practical and precise. Most of all, it requires finding a way to address the handful of teachers who really are a problem. After all, even teachers think 5 percent of their colleagues aren't getting it done. Teachers report that 5 percent of those teaching in their local schools deserve an F grade (and that another 8 percent deserve a D).[14] Experts think that sounds about right. Perhaps the most influential work on teacher evaluation has been done by the Gates Foundation's MET project. MET chief Steve Cantrell noted in 2014 that Gates researchers believe that "the real number of truly ineffective teachers hovers around 5 percent," or "the single lowest performer among every twenty teachers."[15]

Cage-busters know that enhancing the profession's credibility starts with insisting that schools improve or remove the handful of teachers who aren't getting the job done. As one national authority on teaching puts it, "School culture is often driven by the three or four really negative people who say, 'Screw you, pal, you're not going to make me do this. I'll wait you out.'" All by themselves, that handful of teachers can stunt a school's culture, alienate the administration, poison the well with policy makers, and undermine the profession.

Now, some self-proclaimed teacher advocates loudly insist that any talk of mediocrity or any criticism of teachers is part of a nefarious attack on public education. (To them, all I can say is, "Sorry, I've got nothing for you." You don't get to teach the public's children, in public schools paid for with public funds, and tell the public, "Buzz off.") But, happily, most teachers are all for a stronger culture of self-policing. In 2012 Education Sector reported that 75 percent said they wanted their union to make it simpler to remove ineffective teachers and that 68 percent of teachers want the union to guide ineffective teachers out of the profession.[16] Another survey found that 89 percent thought tenure should reflect teacher effectiveness, and 92 percent said that tenure should not protect ineffective teachers.[17]

How to judge effectiveness is a big, complicated question. Cage-busters don't feel obliged to adopt any particular view with regard to value-added, classroom observations, student surveys, or evaluation systems. Reasonable people can and will disagree. What cage-busters insist is that discussion be grounded in the conviction that good teachers should be recognized and bad teachers should be dealt with appropriately. They reject those who would denounce all talk of accountability as an assault on teaching, just as they reject ill-conceived accountability systems. The problem is that policy makers, principals, and the public don't hear often or loudly enough from those with practical solutions. Instead, they hear the vitriol of the few, which leaves them distrustful, the Brian Crosbys isolated, and teachers without the moral authority they crave.

The Weakest Link

Joseph Manko is principal of Liberty Elementary in Baltimore, Maryland, a school that is consistently recognized as one of the highest performing high-poverty schools in the state (while also managing to run the most expansive field trip program in the city). Manko credits Liberty's success to its talented faculty and autonomous culture. "My philosophy on hiring is that I hire really good people and then get out of their way. I don't know why that seems so novel and unique, but that's it. Failure is allowed; it's just part of the learning process. We ask teachers to try new things and then learn from their mistakes."

Why can't all schools do this? To that point, Manko observes, "I can tell any parent coming to the school, in whatever classroom, that they're going to have a strong teacher. There are no lemons here. My rookie teacher is in her fourth year. Of our twenty-four teachers, fourteen are considered model teachers by the district. We have one of the city's highest percentages of National Board teachers." He explains, "It helps a lot to have no weak links," because it lets him delegate with confidence. That has allowed Liberty Elementary to slash its administration. Manko is the only administrator in the building.

He says, "There are no APs, deans, or coaches. All the dollars that would go for that are pushed into classrooms. That means that teachers have to take a lot of responsibility. They run the PD [professional development]. They are expected to deal with kids that are having behavioral issues in the classroom." All this is possible, says Manko, "Because our weakest link is not that weak. That helps us out a lot. Our teachers feel special that they're here. They've been vetted. And they hold each other accountable. They make each other better. And that allows me to give them more autonomy."

Teachers determine their own working day and decide how to use their ten professional days, and every formal observation is posted to a sharing site so that teachers can watch one another's videos. Manko says, "Teachers can comment and discuss, noting a missed opportunity or asking whether this question would result in a different response. Then we'll sit down during team meetings and watch the videos together. In a lot of schools that would be off the table because there's not enough trust." A lot of teachers would like to work in a school like that, and for a principal like Manko. But Manko can only lead as he does because of the faculty he has—and because he trusts that there "are no weak links." When teachers retreat to their classrooms and tune out the knucklehead down the hall, they're choosing to leave those weak links alone and ensuring that next year they'll once again be grumbling, "Why can't my principal be more like that Manko guy?"

Giving Excellence Its Due

Would-be reformers talk a lot about getting bad teachers out of the classroom. That's well and good. Cage-busters think that kind of policing is essential. But cage-busters are far more interested in building schools and systems that celebrate excellence and give good teachers the chance to shine. Cage-busters sympathize with the precocious lament from young Dash in Pixar's *The Incredibles*. When his mom insists, "Everyone's special," Dash knows to mutter, "Which is another way of saying no one is." Addressing mediocrity and celebrating excellence are two sides of the same coin. By fighting to change a culture where "everyone's special," cage-busters work to make it possible to recognize extraordinary effort and performance.

Tim Daly, president of TNTP, puts it starkly:

> The biggest mistake that we ever made with the teaching profession was rejecting the idea of distinction based on performance. If you take a sport, you see that some athletes get the star treatment. This is a good thing, for two reasons. First, they gain broad recognition and help elevate the sport. Second, they still bargain within the collective. More than inspiring division or envy, they raise the status of their peers and the sport. But in teaching, we suppress the distinction. Without that elevated status, so long as the public is as suspicious of public schools as it is, teachers aren't going to get that freedom and flexibility. But if we recognize teachers, give them distinctions and responsibilities, that can dispose the public to recognize

teachers as every bit the professionals that pro athletes are and improve the day-to-day environment of their school.

Leslie Ross has taught in Greensboro, North Carolina, for nearly two decades. In recent years, she's worked long hours planning lessons, mentoring students, and writing small grant proposals while teaching high school biology. This all unfolded with no acknowledgment and little support from her district, even as her biology students outscored their peers on districtwide assessments by more than twenty-five percentage points. Ross says, "My school said, 'It's up to you to secure those funds. It's up to you to write the proposals.' There's a lot of lip service, but that's it." Ross would spend thousands of dollars a year, out of pocket, procuring supplies and working away in isolation. She says, "When I'm in my classroom I concentrate on those four walls. That's what you're focused on and what I was passionate about. You don't think about extending your reach."

After earning TNTP's Fishman Prize in 2012, Ross says,

> I don't think my school system realized the magnitude of what I'd won. My principal went to a meeting and heard about me from the TNTP director. He called me and said, "You won't believe what's going on." They recognized me at a school board meeting and our district's annual State of Our Schools program. I got invited to have lunch with President Obama and Secretary of Education Arne Duncan to discuss equity in schools. It was an amazing experience. People started looking at me and asking, "How are you accomplishing things that no one else is?" I hadn't seen myself in that light. It changed the trajectory of my career. It made me realize that what I'm doing needs to be shared with other people. I hadn't really considered that. Until I won the Fishman Prize, I hadn't realized that I'd never received that kind of recognition. Once I got it, it felt really good to have someone say, "You've done a remarkable thing and we'd like to share it. I want those 'attaboys'" . . . and I try to do that for the teachers I work with. When you don't receive something you don't necessarily miss it, but now that I've had it, I wouldn't want it any other way.

POLICING THE PROFESSION

It's one thing to talk about policing the profession and another thing to do it. Given their lack of positional authority, teachers don't have much formal ability to deal with weak links. So what can they really do? Think of that public safety poster—"See something, say something." Actions change culture. As James Liou, a teacher-on-assignment involved in peer assistance in Boston, says, "It can be a hard thing to do and say, but we as teachers have to set the bar. We as a profession know that. No teacher wants to teach in the room next door to a teacher who is ineffective or doesn't work hard or doesn't really care about kids. It starts with setting school culture."

Maddie Fennell points out that teachers love the notion of peer assistance . . . but usually aren't eager to wade into the "review" part of "peer assistance and review." The problem, she says, is that "if teachers won't police their profession, then it's not a profession." After all, cage-busters know that autonomy will ultimately equal responsibility. Richard Ingersoll observes in his book *Who Controls Teachers' Work?* that "accountability and power must go hand in hand; increases in one must be accompanied by the other."[18] Self-policing requires more than pleasant talk. As Doug Lemov puts it, "Teachers often find peer-to-peer accountability very powerful. Especially in organizations where teachers get limited support from administration, your fellow teachers are at least as powerful and important to you as your principal."

When it comes to policing the profession, there are some pointers worth keeping in mind. The bottom line is that an individual teacher cannot police her school, much less the profession. What a teacher can do is be part of a team that works to set and enforce norms. It's easier to make the case for doing this when you recall the upshot of "no weak links"—that self-policing is the ticket to autonomy and empowerment. The model here is really nothing more than good classroom practice: set norms, enforce them, and be consistent.

Clarify the Norms. Work with your colleagues and the administration to establish clear norms for teachers. What's expected in terms of timeliness and deportment at meetings? How many missed days are too many? What's expected in terms of collaboration and planning? When you establish these things at the start of the year and talk about them as universal expectations, it's easier to get people to agree in principle. Then, when individuals come up short, you've made it easier for administrators, grade-level leads, mentors, or peers to remind them that they're failing to live up to their own commitments.

Find Strength in Numbers. It's really, really hard for an individual in any organization to address a colleague who's not getting the job done. It can feel personal or like you're picking on them. That gets unpleasant fast. Don't try to be a lone ranger. Instead, focus on establishing norms and then ensuring that most colleagues embrace them and maintain them. Find others who share your values and work together to model expectations.

Make Your Principal a Partner. Principals possess the positional authority that's critical when formalizing expectations or dealing with teachers who serially violate shared norms. "They'd added a half hour each day in our contract for collaboration to improve instruction," says Steve Aupperle, an instructional coach at Truesdale Education Campus in Washington, DC. "My principal and I both wanted to see that time maximized, but she had too much on her plate to make it happen. As a result, that time wasn't being used very often. So I handled the planning, and she made sure that everyone showed up on time. There are opportunities to work with principals if you're willing." The problem for principals is often a lack of time and information. Teachers can help by setting and enforcing norms so that it's clear when a peer is falling short. They can quietly keep the principal up to speed on potential problems. They can help brainstorm solutions. They can go to the principal in numbers and let her know that the teachers have her back but also that they expect her to act.

Put Peer Pressure to Work. It can be easy to let frustrated colleagues set the tone. Don't let that happen. Be sure that the tone is set by colleagues who are focused on the right things. One teacher quietly confided to me, "A teacher on our grade-level team just kept complaining. She was low-skill and her room was chaotic. Helping her improve her practice was one thing. But, as a team, we decided to actively ignore her carping. When she said something negative, we'd freeze her out. We wouldn't respond.

It worked well enough. She stopped complaining. She stopped being disruptive. And, by the end of the year, she was looking for another job." Maybe, in a perfect world, her peers could have figured out how to turn her around. But, in the meantime, they solved the problem.

Talk to Them Like Adults. Sometimes any of us can find ourselves in a place that's more destructive than we ever intended. We can feel hurt or marginalized and not even realize what we're doing. One veteran muses,

> We had this teacher who'd been successful before but was insecure in the building. She would complain and pick fights. It was awful. My approach was to be very direct, because she's a skilled teacher who had the kids' best interest at heart. She started crying. She said she felt like she had been put on trial for the last couple of years. If you came to work and felt like you weren't valued and were being daily accused of not being there for the kids, you'd have your back against the wall too. She knew her actions were counterproductive, but it was a gut-level thing. Once we talked, she acknowledged her actions weren't productive. Hitting her between the eyes with the information gave her no wiggle room.

If you can talk firmly and respectfully to a colleague about shared norms, sometimes that makes all the difference.

CHOOSING TO BREAK FREE OF THE CAGE

Doug Lemov has found that teachers seeking to deliver the kind of powerful instruction he preaches are hampered by the cage. He says, "I don't think people are really aware of the bureaucratic challenges around organizing time. They just don't know. We've found that we have to spend more and more time at workshops on this. It turns out to be really, really necessary. If we don't do that, they don't succeed in making change." It can seem that the routines that sap teachers' time, energy, and passion are facts of school life. Cage-busters, though, look with fresh eyes and see possibilities instead of maddening inevitabilities.

Avoid vague, sweeping declarations. Those are a recipe for inaction. Insisting, "I want school leaders to listen to teachers, to respect and draw on teacher expertise" will get a lot of nods—and not much else. It's too broad. It's not clear what it means or what "listening" would entail. In fact, rightly or wrongly, state and system leaders already think they're listening to teachers. They'll tell me that they're trying to address the very concerns teachers raise . . . and that teachers often don't realize it or don't respond to *their* efforts! Teachers who want to make change need to be clear about what should change and how to make that happen.

The coming chapters will explore how cage-busters can put these intuitions to work. But it all starts with tapping expertise, solving concrete problems, and being willing to police the profession. As AFT assistant to the president for educational issues, Marla Ucelli-Kashyap wryly says, "Accountability can't be something teachers leave to 'those darn administrators.' Almost everything negative in the policy world today can be traced to a lack of trust in teacher expertise, knowledge, and even integrity. Rebuilding that trust is the key to building a cage-free environment." The more teachers earn that trust, the more they'll be able to forge schools and systems that mirror their ambitions.

3

Managing Up

All things are difficult before they are easy.

—Thomas Fuller

A smart man can identify any obstacle
A wise one removes the non-factors 'til it's solvable.

—Dom McLennon, "Dom Speaks"

TEACHER MYTHOLOGY is littered with go-it-alone heroes. You've seen the movies. Richard Dadier in *The Blackboard Jungle*. Jaime Escalante in *Stand and Deliver*. John Keating in *Dead Poet's Society*. Glenn Holland in *Mr. Holland's Opus*. Erin Gruwell in *Freedom Writers*. Ken Carter in *Coach Carter*. You know the drill. They fight to change lives despite the obstacles thrown up by idiot administrators, blithering bureaucrats, inertia, and low expectations. These movies are stories of teachers battling the System. The heroes deliver some terrific results, but their handiwork is the product of singular gifts, charisma, or ferocious will. Their approach is exhausting. And when their flame finally burns low, the cage remains. As one teacher wryly observes, "You can only be a martyr for so long."

Cage-busting asks for more than martyrdom. In return, it offers more. Cage-busting helps teachers start to *dismantle* the cage and to morph that naysaying principal into a supportive one. This means seeing where the cage is real and where it's illusory. It requires understanding where administrators are coming from and offering them viable solutions. And it requires marshaling allies to help put moral authority to work. As Jonas

Chartock, CEO of Leading Educators, says, "If you don't know how to manage up to your principal or manage laterally to your colleagues, it's like you're alone in that cage." It may not be as cinematic, but this kind of action is much more likely to create schools where greatness is more than an extraordinary, movie-worthy phenomenon.

For all the talk one hears about teacher collaboration, the tendency to celebrate a do-it-yourself ethos is a real problem for the profession. Ben Owens teaches high school science and math in rural North Carolina. He came to teaching after eighteen years as an engineer in the private sector. He says, "In industry, for every assignment—whether a $20 million project or simply keeping a pump from failing—I was expected to tap into a network of fellow engineers. I never had to reinvent the wheel. In fact, it was taboo to work in isolation when the answer was probably already out there." But in teaching, says Owens, "it seems the prevailing mentality is to keep your cards close to your chest and to do it yourself. That's the most striking difference between the private sector and teaching." Teachers treat their classroom as a refuge, a go-it-alone tendency that has real costs. Big, sustainable changes take time, resources, coordination, and moral authority that a single teacher cannot muster but that teachers working in concert can.

Evan Stone, former New York City sixth grade teacher and cofounder of Educators 4 Excellence, saw the strength in numbers while advocating for one student. He tells of Saul, who entered his class having never passed the state math exam: "But he was eager to learn. He came to afterschool programs and even Saturday school. Eventually, I realized he understood the concepts but struggled with computation—he had to count on his fingers." Stone got Saul a 504 individual education plan and extra testing time. That year, after a lot of hard work, for the first time Saul passed the state math exam. Stone recalls, "His mom made me empanadas for weeks!" Stone says, "The next year he and his mom came back and he was in tears. He was in a new school, had just taken his first diagnostic test; his teacher hadn't given him extra time, and he had failed. I assumed that the fireproof box that had his file, which I'd sent to central, had gotten lost. So, I thought, 'No problem. I'll go talk to the principal.' I walked over a copy of his 504 form. The principal looked at me and said, 'There's nothing we can do. Giving one student more time is too difficult to do here." Stone recalls, "I went back to my classroom and stayed in the room with my head on my desk. One of my colleagues asked what was wrong. She said, 'So let's go back next week.' I said, 'There's no reason to go back, that woman's a tyrant.'" But she suggested they organize Saul's former teachers and go back as a group. "The next week, twelve of us walked over to meet the principal. And the principal was an entirely different person. She was welcoming and said she just didn't understand last week, and of course they could accommodate Saul. She said his form must have just gotten lost." He reflects, "We organized around one clear initiative that benefited one kid. You could do this at scale, more often, for a lot more kids."

PAY NO ATTENTION TO THAT MAN BEHIND THE CURTAIN

Late in *The Wizard of Oz*, Dorothy and the gang have killed the Wicked Witch and returned to the Emerald City for their triumphant audience with the Wizard—only to have Oz blow them off. Just as the gallant little gang is about to give up, dejected, Dorothy's dog Toto tugs at a curtain to reveal a man feverishly operating a booth to produce the Wizard's voice and visage. Oz famously intones, "Pay no attention to that man behind the curtain." But Dorothy peels back the curtain, revealing the man in full, and asks, "Who are you?" He stutters, "Well, I—I—I am the Great and Powerful—Wizard of Oz." She insists, "I don't believe you!" Abashed, he mumbles, "No, I'm afraid it's true. There's no other wizard except me."[1]

The same is true of so much that stifles teachers. As noted in chapter 1, there are real bars in teachers' ways. But those are fewer and frailer than is often imagined. Teachers have gotten used to hearing "you can't do this" or "you have to do that." When they ask why, they're told it's a rule, policy, or what-have-you—which is often nothing more than an order not to peer behind that curtain. Supposed prohibitions are often no more real than was the Wizard of Oz.

Lori Nazareno, a veteran teacher of twenty-five years, helped start Denver's teacher-led Mathematics and Science Leadership Academy (MSLA).

She says, "My attitude has always been 'proceed until apprehended.' If I want to pursue an idea and someone tells me I can't, I ask, 'Can you show me in contract, policy, or statute where it says that I can't?' I've found that people think policy or the contract says certain things and it doesn't. It was just the way it was done at a school where they worked." Nazareno says that when designing MSLA, it was all too easy to focus on what people were used to doing rather than on what they wanted to do for kids. "People assume that school has to be Monday through Friday, same hours every day. But that's not true. Even in the contract and district policies, start times, ending times, and hours per day are open. In Colorado they mandate annual hours of instruction but don't define the day or week."

Nazareno says, "I had numerous calls where someone would say we had to do something a certain way. I'd ask, 'Is this what we're supposed to do?' They'd say, 'I think so.' I'd say, 'Where is the board policy that says that?' They couldn't identify it. So I'd go and look for it, and, more often than not, they were making up that it was a policy. Teachers are a trusting lot, and we take people at their word. Nobody is necessarily lying, but many urban legends have been around so long that people think they're true."

Many teachers pine for the freedom to rethink curricula, schedules, staffing, and teacher evaluation. Yet, there already exist more opportunities to do this than teachers may imagine—and many go untapped. MSLA got launched when Denver's superintendent invited proposals for new charter or innovative schools and the local union president stepped up. Nazareno notes, "Teachers often see turnarounds or charter schooling as opportunities for someone else. They don't realize that the same door is there for them to walk through with a teacher-led school or their own idea."

In Delaware, the Rodel Teacher Council had raised questions about the state's new teacher evaluation system, asking whether administrators overwhelmed by mandated observations and removed from the classroom would provide the most informed or useful feedback. Several council members had asked school or system leaders about the idea of teachers doing some of the observations. They were told that the state only allowed administrators to do observations or that it would be an onerous process to get a teacher certified as an observer.

Then the teachers had a chance to sit down with Christopher Rusz-kowski, head of the Teacher and Leader Effectiveness Unit at the Delaware Department of Education. Ruszkowski recalls visiting with them: "When they started saying, 'I wish, I wish, I wish,' I jumped up and said 'You can!' We'd heard feedback that teachers wanted peer observers. They wanted some of their observations done by people who knew their content and classrooms better than the administrators did." Seeing this as a good idea, the state board of education approved a pathway to allow for credentialed observers who are not administrators.

Ruszkowski says, "All you need to do is have the district submit your name and then complete six one-hour online modules to become famil-iar with the system. You can do them in an afternoon with a book open in your lap. Then the teacher does a training workshop on the teacher evaluation and—voilà!—you'd be good to go. And this is for the formal state observations. For informal observations, they don't need anything at all." The council's coordinator recalls that the reaction among the teach-ers was, "Whoa, we didn't know that!" Ruszkowski reflects, "To me, this shows two things. One is how reliant teachers are on school leaders to give them information. The other is that the teachers said they'd never taken the fifteen minutes to read the four pages of teacher evaluation regulations on the Web. That would've showed them what's possible. And this Rodel Teacher Council was a group of real cage-busters! . . . That provision has been up for more than a year now. We assumed when we put it on the books that people would come out of the woodwork. But, so far, we haven't credentialed anyone who's not an administrator."

All along, these Delaware teachers had the power they sought. They just didn't know it. That's why you need to look around for that curtain and then give it a good, hard tug. What you decide to do after that is up to you.

INFLUENCING UP

In *Influence Without Authority*, Allan Cohen, a professor of global leader-ship at Babson College, and David Bradford, dean of Stanford University's executive program on leadership, explain that an employee is influential to the extent that he's making his boss successful.

In their subsequent volume, *Influencing Up*, Cohen and Bradford warn against falling into the "traps that large power gaps often set."[2] Bradford explains, "In the book, we say that 'high power makes you deaf and low power gives you laryngitis' . . . If you perceive you have very little power, you tend to shut down instead of offering alternate points of view."[3] The trick, Cohen and Bradford argue, is to think of yourself as a "junior partner." You don't need a perfect boss to be a good junior partner.

Make it easier for your boss to work with you by offering solutions. As Bradford explains, "Let's say your boss puts off decisions. You could say, 'Hey, Boss, my sense is you like to get as much information as possible before making a decision, but we get criticized when decisions are delayed. Is it okay if I am more active in pushing for decisions?'"[4] Keep in mind that disagreements don't have to be a bad thing. They provide a chance to air questions and speak honestly. If you speak up respectfully and with an eye on solving a problem, disagreements can spur creative thinking and stronger relationships. Says Bradford, "I know one CEO who said, 'You're allowed four Nos, and each one has to bring in new information. I will listen to your disagreements, but after the fourth time, if I still disagree, this is the way it's going to be.'"[5]

In fact, Bradford says, "In most cases when people say they have an impossible boss, on examination we find that they may be difficult but really aren't impossible. There is the tendency to give up too early . . . For example, we raise a question about an action our manager is considering and the response of, 'I think you are wrong; what's your evidence?' causes us to back down." Bradford says, "The mistake is seeing bosses as impossible when they really aren't."[6]

Speaking up can be enough to solve a problem. Michael Dunlea, a second grade teacher at Ocean Acres Elementary in Manahawkin, New Jersey, says, "I used to think you should just stay in your room, but I kept feeling pressure from local policies that didn't make sense. The district mandated giving all our students the Developmental Reading Assessment three times a year. Now, the DRA is a really valuable one-on-one assessment, but it takes 30 to 45 minutes per kid each time. Let's say you have twenty kids—that's 10 or 15 hours of instructional time gone each time you administer it. We've got a 90-minute ELA [English language arts] block, so I told the administrators, 'That's basically seven weeks that I'm not teaching. How will that improve outcomes?'" Dunlea told them he didn't need the assessment for kids who were on-level because he had other ways to track their progress. He says, "It was just a blanket policy, and no one had bothered to calculate how much time it would take. When I said all this, they said, 'Okay'" and made adjustments. "Sometimes it's as simple as having the numbers in hand and a ready answer."

Plenty of leaders *want* to hear constructive criticism. Louisiana state superintendent John White says,

> A huge percentage of our strategy was due to a teacher pointing out a flaw. I spend a lot of time on the road and talking to teachers. Our plan to convert our entire state test to Common Core this year was prompted by two math teachers who said we were making things harder by phasing it in. We'd thought it would be helpful; they convinced me we were wrong. There's no area where I've benefited more from teacher perspectives than on tests, standards, and alignment. Teachers are so close to this. They can show us the problems and how easy it would be to change . . . A state commissioner doesn't know everything that goes on in his department. During my first year, I recall talking with one teacher at a Starbucks after she e-mailed and asked if we could meet. If you're offering to solve problems, I'll always find time for that meeting. She said, "I know you were an English teacher. I want fifteen minutes to show you what your curriculum people are putting out. You're claiming there's a transitional Common Core curriculum. But that's not what this is. It's the same materials we've had, just more of them." She said we ought to focus on providing frameworks and guidance—not curricula . . . She was right.

(For some more practical advice on working with managers and colleagues, see "*How to Win Friends and Influence People.*")

THINK LIKE A LEADER

Cage-busters need to be able to think like leaders. When a teacher sits down with his principal, it's natural to focus on what that teacher thinks he needs for his students. But it's easy to forget that the principal thinks

How to Win Friends and Influence People

There's a reason that Dale Carnegie's *How to Win Friends and Influence People* has sold more than fifteen million copies.[7] It makes important truths accessible and concrete. Any cage-buster will benefit from Carnegie's 12 Principles for "How to Win People to Your Way of Thinking." Here they are, as explained by Carnegie:

Principle 1: *The only way to get the best of an argument is to avoid it.* "Nine times out of ten, an argument ends with each of the contestants more firmly convinced than ever before that he is absolutely right."

Principle 2: *Show respect for the other person's opinions. Never say, "You're wrong."* "You can tell people they are wrong by a look or an intonation or a gesture just as eloquently as you can in words—and if you tell them they are wrong, do you make them want to agree with you? Never!"

Principle 3: *If you are wrong, admit it quickly and emphatically.* "Any fool can try to defend his or her mistakes—and most fools do—but it raises one above the herd and gives one a feeling of noble exultation to admit one's mistakes."

Principle 4: *Begin in a friendly way.* "Kindliness, the friendly approach and appreciation can make people change their minds more readily than all the bluster and storming in the world."

Principle 5: *Get the other person saying "Yes, yes" immediately.* "In talking with people, don't begin by discussing the things on which you differ. Begin by emphasizing—and keep on emphasizing—the things on which you agree."

Principle 6: *Let the other person do a great deal of the talking.* "Most people trying to win others to their way of thinking do too much talking themselves. Let the other people talk themselves out. They know more about their business and problems than you do . . . They won't pay attention to you while they still have lots of ideas of their own crying for expression. So listen patiently and with an open mind."

Principle 7: *Let the other person feel that the idea is his or hers.* "Don't you have much more faith in ideas that you discover for yourself than in ideas that are handed to you on a silver platter? If so . . . isn't it wiser to make suggestions—and let the other person think out the conclusion?"

Principle 8: *Try honestly to see things from the other person's point of view.* "Other people may be totally wrong. But they don't think so. Don't condemn them. Any fool can do that. Try to understand them."

Principle 9: *Be sympathetic with the other person's ideas and desires.* "Wouldn't you like to have a magic phrase that would stop arguments, eliminate ill feeling, create good will, and make the other person listen attentively? Yes? Alright. Here it is: 'I don't blame you one iota for feeling as you do. If I were you I would undoubtedly feel just as you do.'"

Principle 10: *Appeal to the nobler motives.* "A person usually has two reasons for doing a thing: one that sounds good and a real one . . . All of us, being idealists at heart, like to think of motives that sound good. So, in order to change people, appeal to the nobler motives."

Principle 11: *Dramatize your ideas.* "Merely stating a truth isn't enough. The truth has to be made vivid, interesting."

Principle 12: *Throw down a challenge.* "Every successful person loves . . . the chance to prove his or her worth, to excel, to win."

Carnegie's volume has been successful decade after decade for a reason. It's because this stuff works.

these are *her* students too, and that things can look quite different from her side of the table. Before sitting down, make it a point to put yourself in your principal's shoes.

Think about it this way. Say students come to you with a project that they're excited about. For it to work, they explain, they need you to not test them on the current unit and to let them come and go as they please. You might be open to some or all of this, but you probably want to hear a compelling rationale and how you'll know it's working. Otherwise, your first instinct might just be to say, "No." (And your students would say, "Geez, all we ever hear is, 'No.' Our teacher is *so* close-minded." Meanwhile, you're probably thinking, "Hey, I'm open to ideas, but only if they're good ones.") Leaders are generally doing the best they can—given limited time, information, and expertise.

I remember one accomplished elementary teacher fuming that her principal was making her do reading remediation she found unhelpful. When asked how she responded, she said, "I told him how stupid this was." Asked how that had worked out for her, she admitted, "Not so well." Could she think of any justification for the principal's decision? On reflection, she said, "Our scores definitely needed to be better, and some of my colleagues needed something more structured. So maybe it made sense for some of them." Did she say this? "Nope, I really didn't. I could've, but I was so mad." Stepping back now, could she imagine how she might've acknowledged her principal's concerns? Could they have figured out how to require the approach for some, but not all, teachers? She said, "Well, sure. My kids' scores were off the charts. If the principal made it optional for teachers whose kids were doing well, that would've done it." Thinking like a leader helps you see problems more fully and can help surface solutions.

It helps to remember that school and system leaders have it rough too. Terry Kaldhusdal, who teaches sixth grade at a middle school in Kettle Moraine, Wisconsin, says, "I've been a teacher for twenty-three years. People tell me that I should go into administration. But, to me, working with kids is a dream, and sitting in an office, pushing paper, and dealing with kids in trouble doesn't sound like fun at all. I feel for the guys who are doing this. Too many times as teachers we don't even try to empathize with what it feels like to be in their shoes. Those folks have pressures on them that I'll never understand." As the AFT's Rob Weil says, "Being a school principal right now has got to be one of the hardest jobs in America. Those people get no breaks at all."

"But My Boss Is a Jerk"

Longtime AFT executive Joan Baratz Snowden recalls then–AFT president Al Shanker sitting down with a number of union leaders in the early 1990s. "Al was trying to get them to do something, and one after another they'd stand up and say, 'That's fine if you've got a good superintendent, but my superintendent is a jerk.' After three or four of these guys, Al Fondy, president of Pittsburgh Federation of Teachers for thirty-eight years, stood up and said, 'I'm sure your superintendent is a jerk, but he's the only one you've got, so you have to find a way to work with him. Figure it out.'"

Before concluding that things are hopeless because your boss is a jerk, ask yourself if you've done all you can to make things work. Teachers who feel powerless can mistake complaining for problem solving. Worse, they can delude themselves into thinking they've tried to offer solutions when they haven't. One teacher told me what an idiot her principal was for running useless PLC meetings. I asked what she'd suggested. She said, "I told him he should let us leave early on Mondays." She seemed bitter that he wasn't sold on the idea. Now, even if he was a jerk, he might have responded pretty differently if she'd offered a more constructive suggestion and done so with a bit more attention to his needs.

"You have to get a little bit psychological with your administrators," says one National Teacher of the Year. "You have to make the first step. They might not reach out, but I find they always reach back. E-mail them or stop by. You sort of have to be the principal of the principal. Theirs is a pretty lonely job. Not a lot of people reach out and ask how the principal's doing. Now, I'm not saying to suck up. I'm saying that I'm surprised more teachers don't understand it's a two-way street that can work really nicely for you and the school. It's tricky, though. A lot of people are fearful. They think, 'That's my boss; he can fire me. I don't think I can talk to him.'"

Be conscious of whether you're going to your principal with problems or with solutions. Michelle Wheatfill, a fifth grade teacher at Walter Bracken STEAM Academy in Clark County, Nevada, says, "In our school, when we go to our principal's office, we better have thought up some kind of solution and not just be going in to complain. I'll never go to my principal unless I have some idea of what we want fixed and a solution. She may give me a different solution, but at least I'm presenting an idea and not just complaining." And, sure enough, Wheatfill thinks her principal is great.

How can you be sure you're focused on problems and solutions and that you're not just complaining? Three tips. One, imagine yourself on the other side of a conversation. If a student comes to you and explains this project is problematic because of X and then offers a suggested solution, that can be really helpful. If he just tells you that all of your projects are awful, not so much. Make sure you're offering solutions. Two, make sure your solution is one that *you* might say yes to. If someone came to you with your idea, would you think it was a good one? (Be honest now.) Three, don't offer solutions that just make it someone else's problem. If your solution is that your principal needs to buy more iPads or do a better job mentoring new teachers, then you're solving your problem by creating one for him. That's not so likely to fly.

Treat Your Principal Like a Student

Jeffrey Charbonneau, who in chapter 1 was finding a way to get his students dual-enrollment credit, says about the key to cage-busting:

> It is about helping your principal see the value in what you're doing. Many times as educators, we'll work tirelessly in our classrooms to help students get it. If they don't get it the first time or the second time, we rework the lessons. That's what we need to do for administrators, too. We need to teach them. If I suggest something and they say no the first time, that's just another opportunity for me to try to teach it better. My biggest piece of advice for cage-busting teachers is to look at administrators and policy makers like they look at students. Just like with your students, the better you know your principal, the better you'll be able to teach him. The administrators say "no" to me a lot! But I treat that as a learning experience. I listen and respond to their concerns.

When a student is having trouble picking up a new idea, good teachers probe to determine where the student is getting stuck. Similarly, Charbonneau counsels, "Don't think that if someone tells you 'no' that it's entirely because of you or your idea. Try to understand the constraints *they* face." When working to get colleges to agree to grant credit for his high school courses, he says, "I couldn't understand at first why they were saying no. Once I understood their credentialing process, though, I got that it was something larger. If faculty lack the proper credentials, it can put the institution's accreditation at risk. The more you understand why someone is saying no, the more adept you are at seeing possible solutions. Had I not taken time to listen, I would've just thought they weren't seeing the vision." By listening carefully, you can pick up the knowledge needed to turn 'no' into 'yes.'

It's simple, really. Just treat your boss with the same understanding you show your students.

Solve One Problem at a Time

Don't worry about "fixing" your school. Giant problems are overwhelming. But you can transform overwhelming challenges into manageable ones by breaking them down and tackling them one piece at a time. Take one step, and then another, and then another . . . and you eventually cover a lot of ground. "The big mistake I made at first was bringing a million things to my administration," recalls Jessica Waters, a science teacher in Woonsocket, Rhode Island. "I'd show up and say, 'These are all the things that you're doing that are awful.' And I would just go down the list, saying, 'We need to change this and that and this' . . . And when there's so many, they couldn't even listen to me."

John Solet illustrates how teachers can accomplish big things by taking small actions to solve specific problems. Growing up in Terrebonne Parish, Louisiana, Solet recalls being frequently pulled from class to be checked for lice. Why? Because, he was told, Indians were dirty. Afterward he'd be given a bar of soap and told he needed to bathe because his skin was "too brown." As an adult, Solet returned to the parish to teach. In a community with 1,500 Native American students, only five to ten graduated a year. He knew that the community's racial history was a big part of the story but that there was much more to it. So he focused on tackling those challenges one at a time.

Solet noticed that the system was having difficulty getting Native American parents to school for parent meetings. So he started doing home visits, saying, "Since you can't come to us, we'll come to you. I'll bring the paperwork." Once word got around, parents who had been suspicious of the school system began coming in to school to see him. Another problem was that students didn't see much point in graduating since they thought their only career options were "working offshore or being a roughneck or a shrimp boat captain." To prod them to consider other options, he started taking juniors to Mr. Charlie's Rig Museum, a working rig used to train oil rig workers, to "show them what it actually feels like to work on an oil rig" (short answer: not easy). Next, he sought to expose students to new professional opportunities. He launched a summer program. He says, "I was the former Terrebonne Parish quarterback and homecoming king, so we did a lot of tree-shaking. I had some contacts and raised what we needed at first." The program introduced students to local politicians, council members, law enforcement officers, and so on. They would tell students, "These doors are open for you to come, ask questions, and voice your concerns." He says, "I think that we in the Native community always felt we weren't welcome in those places. Our kids had gotten the sense that these jobs, as a police officer or council member, were unobtainable."

Administrators started seeing results, and parents started pressing them to support the program. The school started providing financial support and devoting Title VII funds to it. Six years in, one hundred Native American students were graduating each year. Solet combated injustice not by wringing his hands or through grand gestures but by solving one problem at a time. Actions change culture, which, in turn, changes expectations and behavior.

Ask "How Can We Do This?"

Stymied by a caged culture, some teachers adopt the philosophy, "Ask forgiveness, not permission." Cage-busters aren't especially enamored of that advice, mostly because the forgiveness strategy rarely changes norms or routines. There's only so much a teacher can do alone, sneaking around the cage.

Cage-busters prefer an approach that can win support, expand the realm of the possible, and create new possibilities for *everyone*. The critical step is to stop asking "*Can I* do this?" and to start asking "*How can we* do this?" This shift is simple but profoundly important. Why?

It does three things. First, it changes your mind-set. You're no longer asking permission to freelance, for reasons that may not be clear to your principal. In asking "How can *we* do this?" you force yourself to explain the benefits clearly enough that others will want to make it happen. Second, it changes this from a solo endeavor to a team enterprise while inviting others onto that team. You're no longer asking them to sign off on your big idea (for which they'll catch grief if it goes south); you're seeking input and suggestions. Third, you're signaling that you're flexible. A lot of times school and system leaders say no not because they hate the idea but because they fear it's being offered in an unrealistic or naïve fashion.

Starting small makes it easier for leaders to give the go-ahead. Jon McIntosh attended college on a debate scholarship and taught debate to college and high school students before starting to teach at a KIPP middle school in Brooklyn. In 2008 he wanted to start a speech and debate club. Pitching the idea to his principal, McIntosh says, "I told him I wasn't going to ask for his attention, for any money, or for any connections, that I just wanted to use a bit of our KIPP special planning period to get this off the ground." That kind of ask makes it easy for principals to give an initial "yes."

By the second year, McIntosh's principal provided some funds and offered meals for NYU students that McIntosh had recruited to help coach the team. Other local teachers signed on as assistant coaches. By 2013 McIntosh wanted to take his students to the national middle school debate championships in Birmingham, Alabama. By that point the principal was invested in what he was doing, and it was easy to get the trip approved. McIntosh's first-time entrants claimed fourth place nationally. McIntosh didn't sidestep his principal or try to do it all himself. He made measured asks and built his program one step at a time.

LET LEADERS KNOW HOW TO HELP

I get to talk to a lot of leaders and a lot of teachers. Often, I find they're talking past each other. Teachers will say that no one wants to hear from them, even as plenty of principals and superintendents tell me that they're eager for input.

Leaders are generally willing to help, but teachers, in turn, need to make it easy for them and to let them know what's needed. Laura Strait, an elementary teacher at Aspire ERES Academy in Oakland, California, recalls that when she was starting out in Massachusetts, she wasn't getting enough support.

> It's easy to complain and vent. But you need the mind-set, "I'm going to identify my weaknesses and challenges and discuss them with administrators."

I was only getting observed once a year. That wasn't nearly enough for me to become a highly effective teacher. So, I went to my principal. I said, "I know you're busy, but is there any way you can take one day a month to observe me?" The principal didn't have time in his schedule, but it was a giant school, and he put me in touch with someone who could give me more observations, conferences, and check-ins. Still, I needed more. I asked what books I should read and what I could do. I tried to make clear it wasn't all on them. A lot of people shut down if anybody says no. Don't get discouraged. Someone can almost always help if you keep looking.

Cage-busters treat administrators with respect, but they don't fold up at the first sign of "no." Michelle Shearer, the former National Teacher of the Year we met in chapter 1, says, "Let's say I take my idea to the assistant principal and he's not open to it. I don't stop there. I would go to a different assistant principal. I would go to the principal and just say, 'I've talked to the AP on this and here are her concerns, but I'd love to get your perspective.' Some teachers feel that there are these hierarchical layers, each layer is a wall, and that if you can't get past one wall, you're doomed. Now, I'm a believer in chain of command and protocol. But I don't think any one person can be that dead-end wall. I don't think it's violating protocol to bounce your ideas off of every wall. I'll take it to the superintendent if I have to. If I've worked it through the layers, I have every right."

When you're seeking a go-ahead, "The higher up you go, the more open administrators can be," says Rebecca Snyder, a language arts teacher at Greater Latrobe Senior High School in Latrobe, Pennsylvania. "We had a supportive, knowledgeable superintendent who was willing to empower teachers. But as that trickled down to the building level, administrators weren't always willing to allow that kind of control." As you climb up any organization, you encounter more senior officials who may feel more able to shift priorities, make big changes, or sign off on unconventional ideas. So, sometimes when you're pushing a bold or unusual idea, and you're getting a reflexive "no" from your principal, you may need to go to the higher reaches of the system to find someone who feels able to give you a "yes." You need to do this respectfully and with patience, but it's a strong argument for not letting that first "no" mark the end of the road.

MAKE IT EASY FOR LEADERS TO SAY YES

Cage-busting teachers explain that there are four steps to getting a "yes" from your school or system leaders. First, you need to give them something they *can* say yes to. You need to give them a concrete, precise problem and solution. Second, you need to give them something they'll *want* to say yes to. You need to explain why your idea is going to help solve a problem that *they* care about. Third, you need to help them understand how they'll *justify* their "yes" to parents, school board members, or their supervisors. Let them know what they can say to those who might be skeptical of the decision. Fourth, reassure them that they *won't regret* saying yes. Explain how you'll stop your request from becoming a headache or hassle for them.

Mike Stryer, a longtime high school teacher in Los Angeles and now a vice president with Teach Plus, offers a nice illustration of how to do all this.

> My school only had about 5 or 10 students in tenth grade AP History. I went to my school administration and said, "Let me teach two classes of AP World History. You can put 40 or 45 kids in each class, I don't care. I'll take anyone who has even minimum qualifications." The administration was concerned our pass rate would plummet. I didn't argue with them about that. But we had lousy API [Academic Performance Index] scores, and their butts were on the line. I knew they were feeling pressure on that. I said, "If you have 80 students exposed to rigorous AP curricula, our ELA and history scores are going to go up." They thought about it and said, "Okay." Our scores shot up, and they looked good. Some teachers were skeptical. But the administration saw the need to raise those API scores, so they backed me up.

The AP passing rate—students getting 3 or higher—was strong: 75 percent. But, says Stryer, "the main thing for the administration was that the API scores really increased. That was the key for them." This is all just common sense, but it's amazing how easy it can be for teachers to ignore common sense when dealing with administrators. The result: teachers hear "no" where a cage-buster might expect to hear "yes."

You know who can be a great source of advice on how to win over principals? Principals. Adrian Manuel, head of the SEED School in Washington, DC, talks about what teachers can do to earn a principal's support.

Some teachers walk into schools where there are real obstacles and ask, "How do you find opportunities?" That's something I've seen in the teachers that I've respected the most. When everyone else was cynical, they said, "We can do this." That's how teachers break out of the cage when everyone else complains about what they can't do. But you also have to know what you're talking about, do your research, back up how your idea would work . . . Many teachers have great ideas but haven't thought through how it would be implemented. When I have teachers come to me with a plan for how it would be implemented, most of the time I'm open to that plan. Even if it's going to fail, we can learn from it. You've got to do the legwork, but that's what gets people to give your idea a careful look. You have to be your own best advocate. If you have a plan and it addresses a major challenge for the school, your principal is going to welcome you. Because it just doesn't happen that much. Administrators feel like we're the ones who are always supposed to have a plan. I almost feel like part of what teachers need to do is analyze their school a bit. Teachers have to figure out what their principals are struggling with right now and how they can help with that. Who's willing and able to help?

If you listen to Manuel and follow those simple steps, you may just find your principal's door swinging wide open.

WHAT WILL YOU DO IF THEY SAY YES?

What happens if you talk to your principal or a district official . . . and they say "yes"? What happens if they say, "Okay, I'm listening. So, what should we do?" Amazingly, a lot of teachers get stuck *here!* They get stuck because they're asking for things that leaders can't provide or don't control or because they've gotten so used to the idea they'll hear "no" that they don't have a solution to propose.

Lynn Gaddis tells an instructive tale, recounting, "When I was [Illinois] Teacher of the Year, at the beginning I was pretty naïve about how to make things happen." She says, "I got a group of Illinois Teachers of the Year together. We said, 'We want to have a voice. We want to talk to the state superintendent and the governor.' We got the meeting. I introduced myself and the superintendent asked, 'What can I do for you?' We kind of looked at each other. That was an eye opener, because we weren't prepared to answer that question. After that experience, I learned to come into any meeting prepared with a proposed solution."

One veteran teacher advocate says, "I've seen teachers in a room with the state commissioner of education. He's at the bar waiting to order a drink, and there's a group of teachers just hanging back. And I would say to those teachers, 'I know you want to be heard. Go over there and strike up a conversation with him.' To do that, teachers need to have what they want to say in their back pocket. You have two minutes. What's the one thing you're going to say that will be important?"

Recall Louisiana state superintendent John White meeting the English teacher at Starbucks—she asked for fifteen minutes, showed up with an important problem and a workable solution, and had thought about what would resonate with White. As a result, she helped change the direction of the state's Common Core implementation. Andy Coons, senior director for the NEA's Center for Great Public Schools, offers a telling example from his time as president of the Tacoma Education Association. Coons's teachers were on strike, and the governor had finally called Coons and the superintendent in. "The governor asked, 'Why are your teachers on strike?' I told her, 'It's about these eleven things. The top three are why we're on strike.' We went through the items. We had solutions and the superintendent had nothing. I got everything on that list."

There are three lessons here. First, don't be afraid to ask. Second, know what you're asking for. Be prepared to explain what the problem is and what you'd propose as a solution. Third, think about how to ensure that your solution will appeal to the person you're trying to convince and how it will actually work. Far worse than being told "no" is having someone who's eager to tell you "yes" only for you to fumble the opportunity.

KNOWLEDGE IS A POWERFUL LEVER

Cage-busters know what the facts are and what the rules actually say—not what people *think* they say.

Tammie Schrader recalls attending a meeting of her district's principals with their superintendent. She says, "Washington State was implementing a new teacher evaluation system that had an online evaluation tool that let you upload documents and pictures to demonstrate student growth." The thing was, the new system was complicated, could be time consuming, and required that a teacher be fairly tech savvy. As Schrader sat in the meeting, one principal mentioned that he was going to require all teachers to use the portal. Schrader just spoke up and clarified that the online tool "was intended to be an option, not a mandate." She recalls, "The principal looked flustered, then said, 'Okay,' sat back down, and that was that." A little knowledge can make all the difference.

A veteran elementary teacher who has served as a Washington Teaching Ambassador for the U.S. Department of Education, Greg Mullenholz says the most important thing he learned at the Department of Education is that "you've really got to know what the heck you're talking about. That's the first thing. A state commissioner doesn't want to hear some vague complaint like, 'This is bad for teachers because it's going to take away planning time.' You need to have something concrete to say; you need to be able to talk about what an evaluation system looks like and its particular weaknesses. If teachers don't know their stuff, the conversations can be, 'It's so cute that there's a teacher in the room'; but if you do, it becomes, 'Let's see what the teacher's take is.'"

Teachers often mutter that nobody is explaining policies and reforms to them. At the same time, state and district officials can feel like they're explaining but teachers aren't listening. The result can be a lot of talking past one another. Peter Shulman, New Jersey's assistant commissioner for teacher and leader effectiveness, says that "information is just not getting through to teachers." He recalls visiting one school piloting the state's new teacher evaluations. He says, "There'd been concerns that we were requiring an unreasonable number of observations, and the union steward asked how many were required. I said it was only three. He looked surprised, so I said, 'We sent out that memorandum three months ago.' The superintendent looked at the principal and said, 'Did you send it to him?' The principal looked at the vice principal and said, 'Did you?'" It's a familiar tale, but a frustrating one.

Shulman says, "Teachers complain that we've never explained something, and I'll tell them, 'Give me your e-mail, and I'll send you this memo which has been up on our Web page for twelve months.'" Now, it's easy for officials to think, "We sent a memo or posted the information on-line—we've done our job." And it's easy for teachers to think, "I'm busy, it's someone else's job to keep me informed." A lot gets lost along the way. Regardless of whose fault any of this is, cage-busters make it a point to seek out the knowledge they need.

Take the question of federal dollars. Jill Hendricks, executive director of federal programs for the Tulsa Public Schools, says a key to getting approval for the creative use of federal funds is teachers "collecting the research, citing evidence, and helping to make the instructional case." Generally, though, she says, "teachers don't do a lot of that. They take what's in place as a given, even though this limits programs, field trips, efforts to integrate math and English across the curriculum . . . Often, teachers don't know what they can do. For instance, I don't know of any teacher who's read the 'Designing Schoolwide Programs' guidance, which makes it clear that pretty much anything goes with schoolwide Title I programs. Teachers wouldn't need to read the whole thing to know that, just the [local education agency] part—it's probably no more than ten or twenty pages." But, she says, teachers haven't read it and therefore don't know what's possible.

A veteran congressional staffer says, "People come and tell me there's too much testing. It drives me up the wall. No Child Left Behind requires states to administer one test. That's it. Their state and districts do add a lot of tests, but I can't make states or districts take tests away. If you come in and tell me about things that I control, that's great. But teachers come in and tell me about things I don't control." Teachers are wasting time and energy when they complain to people about things those people don't control. Make sure you're bringing a problem to the person who can help solve it. Otherwise, you're wasting your time and their goodwill. Now, figuring out who controls a decision can be complicated, which is another reason cage-busters stay practical, concrete, and precise. Cage-busters hold off on taking their concerns up the ladder until they understand things clearly enough that they know just what the problem is and who can help address it.

Think about how you feel as a teacher when a parent comes to see you and then complains about the school's start time. You might sympathize, but it's not really something you can control. All you can do is refer the parent to the principal or district. If the parent continues to go on and on about start times, you might nod along to be polite, but what you're probably thinking is that you've got work to do and it would be nice if they went and talked to someone who could actually help.

Knowing what's what can help you get things done while avoiding unnecessary headaches. It can win respect from those who recognize that you know the deal. It'll discourage people from lazily telling you what they *think* you must do. And it helps you identify who can actually solve the problem, so that you're showing up in the right office with a solution they can do something about.

GETTING IT DONE

Teachers who identify problems, offer workable solutions, find allies, and manage up are well on their way to becoming cage-busters. At that point, there are plenty of tactics that can help.

Write It Down and Shop It Around. Writing down what you have in mind is a great way to discipline your thinking. Michelle Shearer says, "My advice to teachers is always to write it down, to put it on paper. Don't just spout ideas off in the teacher's lounge. A teacher I work with e-mailed me with an idea and I asked, 'What are you going to do with this?' She said, 'I don't know. I'm just talking.' I said, 'Get it on paper and start walking it through. Take it to the department chair, the assistant principal. If you really believe your ideas are good for kids, you've got to take them wherever they need to go.' Otherwise, nothing happens."

Writing it down can help teachers make sure their plans are practical and precise. Shearer says that when she and some colleagues were outlining the teachers' vision for student needs in their English language learners (ELL) program, "I noticed over and over that our proposal said things like, 'Teachers need this and teachers need that.' It was all true, but it was all emotion. The thinking wasn't clear. The process of getting very specific, particular, and granular with what problems we were trying to solve and why this would help was invaluable. The writing process helped us sort that out."

The Peanut Butter and Jelly Thing. Jacob Pactor, the Indiana high school English teacher we met in chapter 1, got involved in his local union because he judged that the contract wasn't helping to recruit and retain talented teachers. The teachers on the bargaining team were mostly veteran elementary school teachers with children, and they all planned on retiring from the system relatively soon. It occurred to him that "they would never realize that there was anything lacking in the contract because it suited them just fine." So Pactor and the negotiations chair started meeting informally with the superintendent. Pactor says, "People in power would like to think that ideas are theirs. So when we met, we discussed multiple ways to increase retention, any of which we as teachers were fine with, and asked them which they thought would be most effective." He explains, "It's like my mom making me a peanut butter and jelly sandwich before sending me off to school when I was six. She'd ask me if I wanted it with crusts or without crusts, and I thought I had the power because I could choose. But she set the terms, because she had already ensured that I'd want a peanut butter and jelly sandwich." Ultimately, they managed to shift dollars and boost compensation for new hires, helping to attract and retain new teachers.

Chipping Away Bit by Bit. Candice Willie-Lawes, the New York City special education teacher from chapter 1, describes herself as "a big believer in positive reinforcement and encouragement." When she found herself in a school that was "rigid and unforgiving," she "subtly suggested" changes. She says, "We didn't have recess, so I suggested we give recess at the end of a week to kids who'd been on exceptionally good behavior. We didn't do field trips, so I suggested we do a trip for students who'd read a certain amount of books as part of a reading program. I just suggested little things here and there. Even though I wanted to, I never stormed into my principal's office to say, 'You don't know what's good for kids!' But bit by bit I chipped away. By June, I felt like our students were getting a normal childhood experience." Willie-Lawes didn't pick fights. She changed things one subtle step at a time.

Give Them a Reason to Believe. Timothy Brewer teaches high school science at St. George's Technical High School in Middleton, Delaware. For nearly two decades, Brewer has been frustrated by how little time science students spend actually doing science. He says, "A lot of science teaching is, 'I'm going to stand up here and tell you stuff, and every three weeks we'll do a lab.' To master something, you have to practice it. I'd heard for years that kids can't get density. Well, yeah, if they only do it once. They can if you do it fifteen times." To free up time for lab work, Brewer restructured his course and moved routine instruction online. He says, "I told my principal that we're working on twenty-first-century skills. She said, 'Show me what the hell you think that means.'" He showed her what he had in mind. She told him, "Okay. As long as they're learning academic content, I'm open to it." So Brewer "showed her the rubric, how it maps to the standards, the content kids would learn, the project requirements . . . Then, she looked at me and said, 'Go for it.'" The deal included the principal bending a firm rule and allowing Brewer's students to listen to music in class. Brewer recalls the principal visiting his classroom, "And I saw the kids trying to pull the earbuds out of their ears without her seeing. She walked up to one kid and asked him, 'Did Mr. Brewer say to put those on?' The kid was scared and kind of nodded. She looked at him and said, 'Then put them back in.'" In winning over the principal rather than working around her, Brewer made sure that his classroom culture would be reinforced by the school leadership.

Try Sharing the Credit. Heidi Welch, a music teacher at Hillsboro-Deering High School in Hillsboro, New Hampshire, recalls, "I had a principal for whom every idea had to be his idea. Otherwise, he'd say, 'You know, this is not going to work.' That was the way it was, and I kept going in with my ideas and leaving frustrated." Eventually she learned to let him take ownership of the ideas. "I realized that I needed to go in and make it sound like it was his idea. So I'd walk into the office and say, 'Excuse me, what are your thoughts on this?' And then, once we discussed it, he immediately thought the idea was his." That, recalls Welch, was when things started to click. Welch may have been placating a self-centered boss, but a more charitable interpretation is that we're all more excited about ideas when we're invested in them, and she helped her principal feel invested.

There are a million ways to get things done. I've talked to hundreds of teachers about how they've changed what's possible and heard lots of good ideas. I could try to list them all, but there's no need. It would be boring, and, more to the point, it's the mind-set that matters. Cage-busters know that they'll always need to attend to the specifics of their own school and situation. If they just try to mimic what someone else did somewhere else, it'll probably fall flat. But if they start cage-busting with their eyes wide open, they inevitably wind up with colorful new stories of their own.

WASTED OPPORTUNITIES HAVE A COST

Failing to take advantage of opportunities hurts in two ways. One, it adds to the pile of unnecessary and avoidable frustrations that teachers encounter. Two, it fuels distrust among those who feel like they've gone to bat to create opportunities for teachers only to see teachers disregard them.

Now, teachers can have good reasons for passing on opportunities. Teachers *are* busy. They may have stepped up before and spent long hours working on a district initiative only to see leadership change and the whole idea be tossed on the scrap heap. They may feel like they have good reason to question whether the invitation is sincere. These are all valid concerns. And it's essential that leaders and lawmakers do their part (see "What Teachers Can Learn from Caged Principals"). But teachers need to do *their* part, too, which includes taking full advantage of opportunities when others are working to open the cage.

Language arts teacher Rebecca Snyder recalls her superintendent wanting to adopt a distributed leadership model. "The superintendent sent a call to the entire faculty seeking volunteers for the leadership initiative. Only a handful responded to that e-mail. He had to actually go and personally find and ask people so that every building and grade level would be represented.

I was surprised, because it was a way to have a voice and be part of a positive change." Yet, of 262 teachers in the district, hardly any opted in.

Delaware's Christopher Ruszkowski tells of another opportunity missed by his state's teachers. Delaware has an online library of assessments for nontested grades and subjects. Teachers who don't teach reading and math in tested grades have to use these assessments to demonstrate student achievement. Ruszkowski notes that teachers are highly critical of these tests. "They ask, 'Why was this in the seventh grade civics assessment or the tenth grade choir test? Why aren't the tests of higher quality?' So the secretary of education said, 'Okay, send us a better test. If you're creating great assessments, we'll approve them.'" The Delaware Department of Education braced for a flood of teacher-generated assessments, but, Ruszkowski says, "We received maybe thirty statewide. So we opened the window again for six months. We budgeted for an additional hundred submissions. Instead, we received a whopping two more." Ruszkowski says that one problem is how little teachers often know about these opportunities. He says, "It's amazing how little districts want their teachers to know about what the state tells them. You know, the state is a good enemy. Districts can say, 'The state is making us do teacher evaluations, blame them.'" And teachers often do, never even realizing what's possible.

Experiences like these make it all too easy for superintendents and policy makers—fairly or not—to roll their eyes when teachers clamor for input. Cage-busters make sure that when folks invite teacher leadership, teachers step up to the challenge. Imagine that a high school teacher has dozens of students who insist they want to do a community works project. The teacher spends a lot of time and energy setting it up and then, when the time comes, just one student signs up. Fairly or not, that teacher is probably going to be more skeptical of the next request.

MAKE YOUR PRINCIPAL A GREAT PRINCIPAL

We routinely hear that problem solvers had great principals. It's easy to *say*, "I wish I had a great principal too." What's easy to miss is that cage-busters help to *make their principals into great ones*. They do this by flagging

What Teachers Can Learn from Caged Principals

I'm often struck that teachers and administrators share similar frustrations, to the point where each group is sure the other "just doesn't get it."

School leaders, for instance, complain that they need more flexibility, more control over resources, and more freedom to manage staff. And they're enormously frustrated with "those bureaucrats in Central" who won't help them out. As one exasperated principal told me, "We're the ones in charge of the buildings; we're the ones closest to the kids. All those bureaucrats in Central are supposed to be there to help us do our job. How do we get those clowns to remember that?"

I always tell those smart, passionate, hard-working principals, "You're doomed to frustration as long as that's your mind-set." Why? Because one of the biggest frustrations of those "clowns in Central" is that the school leaders keep asking for "unreasonable" things—like a lot more control of money and staff. Those "bureaucrats" grumble that school leaders don't understand the need to coordinate busing, staffing, budgeting, curriculum, and the rest across a district full of schools—where some of the principals, in their estimation, can't be trusted. So they feel they can't let Principal A run free because the district will wind up in the headlines or in court if Principal B abuses that authority. And if those administrators try to create different rules for different schools, they'll quickly find themselves caught up in accusations of mismanagement, favoritism, or bias.

So who's right here? Everyone is. What's the relevance of this for teachers?

Well, I'll ask that principal who's complaining about Central, "How would you react if a teacher told you that your curriculum and schedule didn't work for them and they needed you to change it for them? And then, when you look askance, they told you that they're the ones with the kids and that you should support them and get out of *their* way?" Principals tell me this would drive them nuts. The interesting thing is how long it takes some of them to realize that this is how they're coming across to *their* supervisors.

If principals are focused on autonomy or flexibility, they're going to come up empty. That's because it's all about what *they* need. If those same principals start instead by pointing out a learning challenge and offering a solution that doesn't require more money or staff, they're much more likely to get help from above.

problems, offering solutions, being responsive, and making it easy for the principal to get on board. Try that first, *before* concluding you need a better principal. Terry Kaldhusdal puts it well: "Dealing with administrators is a lot like dealing with parents. If the only time a parent hears from you is when their kid is in trouble, they will avoid you. If the principal only deals with you when you need something, that's not a great way to build a relationship. But if you check in on them every now and then to let them know how things are going, they are happy to receive you."

Lots of administrators who may frustrate you are themselves frustrated, and you can either help them figure things out . . . or not. As one award-winning principal told me,

> The most frustrating thing about this job is that I don't get to focus much on my great teachers or the ones who are doing fine. Those are the ones who always say it'd be great if I gave them more freedom around professional training and scheduling. I'd love to. But the problem is the half-dozen or so teachers I've got who aren't very good, don't know that they aren't very good, and have an attitude problem. If I don't aggressively enforce start times, bell schedules, and meeting requirements, their kids will lose out, my associate superintendent will mark me down, and I risk having my job go up in smoke. The frustrating thing is that all my other teachers get caught in that. The worst is when my no-problem teachers get pissed at me, as if I'm trying to drive them nuts. If they've got better ways for me to handle this, I'd love to hear them.

When you get things done, it builds confidence, trust, and momentum. Education's laudable emphasis on culture can sometimes give the impression that consensus, collaboration, and buy-in is mostly about talk. Not so. You change culture by actions that shift expectations. As those change, school culture changes too.

4

Millions of Registered Voters— and Their Kids

[JON SNOW]: "It's true, isn't it? . . . What you said about the Night's Watch?"

Tyrion nodded.

Jon Snow set his mouth in a grim line. "If that's what it is, that's what it is."

Tyrion grinned at him. "That's good . . . Most men would rather deny a hard truth than face it."

—GEORGE R. R. MARTIN, *A Game of Thrones*

Help me . . . help you. Help me help you.

—JERRY MAGUIRE PLEADING WITH HIS CLIENT,
IN *Jerry Maguire*

IN 2013, RAFE ESQUITH, celebrated teacher and author of *Teach Like Your Hair's on Fire*, penned a *Wall Street Journal* column on why great teachers leave the profession. He wrote, "'The System' is now paying attention [to schools and schooling], but not the way we wanted. Instead of increasing resources, it's exerting more and more control, and preventing our best teachers from doing their jobs . . . Teachers with enormous experience and much to offer are being forced to shelve valuable lessons because they interfere with a testing schedule designed by someone who could not teach a class of students on his best day. Drop into a break room and you'll hear good teachers muttering bitterly, 'Those who can, teach, and those who can't, make rules for teachers.'"[1]

There is powerful truth to what Esquith wrote. But it's only a partial truth. After all, Esquith doesn't help teachers understand *why* the System responds as it does.

Let's start with the most basic of insights. Teachers are experts when it comes to teaching and learning and can be quick to observe that most policy makers are not. They're right. But it's rare that teachers then acknowledge that they're not experts in policy making, that there might be complexities and issues that *they* don't know much about. So it's useful to survey the world through the eyes of policy makers and to try to understand their concerns.

The 1984 film *Ghostbusters* is memorable on many counts, most of which don't have much to do with being a cage-busting teacher. There's one scene, though, worth recalling here. Malicious spirits have been running rampant in New York, and the Ghostbusters have been trapping them. It turns out, however, that their ghost storage facility violates Environmental Protection Agency guidelines. The Ghostbusters are arrested by an irate EPA official and dragged in front of the mayor, who Bill Murray's character, the slick-talking Peter Venkman, warns, "This city is headed for a disaster of biblical proportions."

> MAYOR OF NEW YORK: What do you mean "biblical"?
> RAY STANTZ: What he means is Old Testament, Mr. Mayor, *real* wrath-of-God-type stuff!
> EGON SPENGLER: Forty years of darkness! Earthquakes, volcanoes!
> VENKMAN: Human sacrifice! Dogs and cats living together! *Mass hysteria!*
> MAYOR OF NEW YORK: Enough! I get the point! And what if you're wrong?
> VENKMAN: If we're wrong, then nothing happens! We go to jail, peacefully, quietly. We'll enjoy it. But if we're *right* and we *can* stop this thing . . . Lenny, baby, *you* will have saved the lives of *millions* of registered voters.

The mayor dismisses the EPA official with a brusque, "Get him outta' here!" and then says to the Ghostbusters, "We've got work to do. What do you need from me?"[2]

Pop quiz: What are the magic words here? Answer: "Millions of registered voters." The job of elected officials is to work on behalf of the constituents who elected them. That's how democracy works. And if you want public officials to help you do your job, you need to help them do theirs. Doing so isn't actually all that hard. In fact, observant readers will note that the rules for cage-busting in the policy realm are a whole lot like those that apply in the schoolhouse.

WHY CAN'T POLITICIANS GET OUT OF SCHOOLING?

Talented educators regularly gripe to me about asinine accountability systems and terrible teacher evaluation schemes. They bemoan politicians who won't spend enough on schools, listen to them, or ask their advice. They ask why policy makers don't mind their own business and let the educators run the schools. What's easy to ignore is that those officials are responsible to all those millions of registered voters—and their kids.

I get the frustration. It's totally understandable. But I tell those teachers to see how things look to those policy makers. After all, public schools spend public dollars and hire public employees to serve the public's children. For better or worse, they're going to be governed by public officials. Those officials are going to set the policies that shape what educators can and can't do, how money is spent, how performance will be judged, and so on.

Now, you may say, "Hold up. Public officials haven't always done it this way." Well, that's actually incorrect. They always have. (Back in 1986, the National Governors Association declared in its influential report *A Time for Results*, "To sum it up: the Governors are ready for some old-fashioned horse-trading. We'll regulate less if schools and school districts will produce better results."[3]) But the reason that policy today *feels* more intrusive is because policy makers have been convinced that the old rules and regulations weren't getting the job done. So they've adopted new policies around accountability, teacher evaluation, and the rest in an attempt to make sure the public's kids are well served and public funds well spent.

Think about it like this. If you were an elected official and responsible for schools where only half of kids were reading at grade level, you might think you ought to do something about it. Now that doesn't mean your response would help. It could easily be wrong-headed. But your intentions would be good. And you wouldn't much appreciate it if you were denounced as an enemy of teachers or schools for trying to do the right thing. Cage-busters recognize that policy makers aren't acting out of malice.

If you're wondering why people who aren't experts on schooling get to make policy, it's simple: they're elected. You can wish that educators were free to spend public funds and run public schools as they see fit. But that's not how the System works. In any event, you can only make that argument if you also think police should be free to make up criminal law, doctors and pharmaceutical representatives to dictate health policy, and bankers to regulate banking. Otherwise, if you want a say in things like policing, health care, or financial regulation, then you need to be prepared to live by those same rules. Cage-busters are more inclined to deal with this state of affairs than to complain about it.

POLICY IS A CRUDE TOOL

Policy makers can make people do things, but they can't make them do them well. Policy is a blunt tool: it tells people what they must do or what they must not do. That works passably well if the challenge is collecting taxes or mailing out Social Security checks. But it works less well when it comes to schooling. The problem is that policy makers can't make schools or systems adopt reforms wisely or well. All they can do is insist that schools comply with punch lists—hire a parent liaison or set aside forty minutes a day for literacy instruction.

The trick is, most of what we care about when it comes to teaching and learning is about *how* you do things rather than *whether* you do them. Yet, equipped only with blunt instruments, policy makers are under a lot of pressure to make the world a better place. Worse, they *know* that their good ideas often go south, which makes them hesitant to trust those on the ground. Indeed, the more their ideas fall flat, the more distrustful they get.

That's why they're eager to find people who understand their aims, know what's happening in schools, and can help boost the chance that policies work as intended.

Policy makers aren't writing laws for people they know and trust; they're writing them for strangers whom they're entrusting with the public's kids. Randy Dorn, superintendent of Washington State's schools, is a former teacher, principal, and influential state legislator. Dorn says,

> I try to tell people, don't make politics so complicated. Politics is really relationships, just like schooling is. I always ask educators, would you give $10 to a stranger who walks up to you on the street? Because that's how a lot of people approach legislators. They show up and just ask for millions of dollars or laws that they'd like to see. If a stranger walks up to you on the street and says, "Can I have $10, my child needs it?" you don't know whether to trust them. You probably won't give it to them. But, if you've seen them and talked to them two or three times, and you feel you'll meet them a fourth time, then they're an acquaintance. Now you're a lot more likely to lend them the money. You know what a good advocate is? It's someone who knows their legislator, shakes his hand, and knows his first name. Because the legislator sees him as a real person who understands his needs.

Laws Get Written for the Lowest Common Denominator

Public schools have more than their share of rules. Teachers often ask me, "You talk to these principals, superintendents, and policy makers. Tell me, why do they think it's a good idea to make so many stupid rules?" Rebecca Mieliwocki, a seventh grade English teacher at Luther Burbank Middle School in Burbank, California, and the 2012 National Teacher of the Year, says, "All of this ridiculous administrivia just shows a lack of faith. I tell my administration it's ridiculous to have a checkpoint for every PD session. They tell me, 'You don't understand. Not every teacher is as committed as you are. We have to do this to make sure that you guys are actually getting together.' I told them it sounds like a personnel issue they should handle one-on-one. They said to me, 'Oh, Rebecca. If only you knew what it was like to be an administrator.'"

The same phenomenon that takes place in the schoolhouse also takes place in the statehouse. Here's the thing: rules are written heavy-handedly, with an eye to stopping obvious stupidity, and are targeted at the irresponsible . . . on purpose. Policy makers can't just make rules that only apply to the weakest link. As one key U.S. Senate staffer explains, "I see these educators who are doing great things out in schools and systems. I want to write the rules for them. But I can't. I have to write them for the lowest common denominator." Public officials are responsible for taxpayer funds and the quality of schooling. If someone hundreds of miles away, whom they've never met, misspends funds or harms a kid, public officials are held responsible and expected to fix it. If teachers are given freedom to spend professional development dollars, and a single teacher makes headlines for spending those dollars on a dubious seminar in Cancun, lawmakers will be expected to ensure that it never happens again. Multiply that by a hundred, and you may understand why lawmakers get so nervous—and wind up slowly constructing the cage.

Going back to the Enlightenment, the logic of democratic lawmaking was to ensure that laws were written and applied even-handedly, so that kings couldn't create one set of laws for friends and another for everyone else. When rules are applied across the board, they can't be based on trust or good intentions. Lawmakers can write policies for all schools, or schools that are failing to produce certain test results, but they can't start differentiating among schools based on which principals they like or trust.

An influential state legislator once told me, "Every time I visit a low-performing school, I hear that all the teachers are great, working hard, and doing everything they can. But then I look at the data, and we're spending more than most states and not getting the outcomes I'd expect. So my constituents expect me to do something. And if those teachers can't or won't tell us where the problems are, we [in the legislature] have to aim blind." Policies, rules, and regulations are one-size-fits-all by design. And they're written to keep in check the people who might be doing the wrong thing. That means that combating dumb rules, finding leeway around them, or getting them replaced is *never* just about saying, "This is a dumb rule." Why? Because it's a dumb rule for *you*, just like those rules were dumb for Rebecca Mieliwocki. But, if you're reasonably good at your job, like Mieliwocki is, the rules *aren't being written for you.*

It's the same reason that teachers generally don't write rules with an eye to their eager students but, instead, with a focus on those who may be disruptive. It ought to also resonate with any teacher who's sought protection from a lunkheaded administrator. TNTP president Tim Daly puts it bluntly: "Teachers want policies that protect against administrators who are bad actors. That's because they fear the worst and imagine themselves in a situation where they need that sort of protection from a malevolent moron. But those same teachers hate it when those same principles are applied to them." It's okay to hate it, but it's vital to understand why it's happening—because that'll help you figure out how to change it.

Cage-Busters Make Their Peace with Policy

Cage-busters understand that policy makers have it pretty rough. Governors, legislators, school board members, and federal officeholders are all interested in making things better for kids and responding to voters. Yet, they have only the most rudimentary tools with which to do any of this.

As Tammie Schrader, whom we met in chapter 3, observes,

> I've had the opportunity to sit in the U.S. Department of Education. I see them listening, being thoughtful, and really trying to make good decisions. I don't think they're sitting there saying, "Let's get teachers" or "Let's screw them over." But they don't know what they don't know. And what they just can't know is how that policy will play out in a classroom. The feds might craft a smart, sensible policy. But then the state gets that policy, and they have a whole team of people that tries to decipher and apply it. Then that information goes down to districts, where folks try to decipher and apply it. Then it goes to principals. By the time it hits my classroom, it looks like something that makes no sense at all for kids.

Policy makers find all of this just as frustrating as teachers do. They're eager to work with educators who are demonstrating success and can help them figure out workable solutions. Now, good policy makers should understand the limits of their role, know when to back off, and not imagine it's their job to "fix" schools or dictate to educators. And I tell them that. But this book isn't for them. It's for teachers. After all, cage-busters focus on what they can do rather than what they wish others would do.

THE CAUTIONARY TALE OF NO CHILD LEFT BEHIND

Let's be clear on what I am and am not saying. Educators can and should, for instance, push back on flawed accountability systems. But they need to be clear that they're offering workable alternatives and not just complaining about the premise that teachers should be accountable. It may be useful to consider why school accountability has been handled so clumsily since No Child Left Behind. The impetus was not a neoliberal cabal or sheer idiocy but something simpler and far less conspiratorial.

Starting in the 1990s, liberal lawmakers like Senator Ted Kennedy and Congressman George Miller grew frustrated that increasing education spending didn't seem to be making a difference for kids. They were particularly concerned that the federal Title I program might not be doing much for the low-income kids it was intended to help. And they felt that state leaders and superintendents showed a lack of urgency when it came to digging into all this or doing something about it.

In 1994 President Bill Clinton pushed for some minimal transparency requirements around student outcomes. As part of the Elementary and Secondary Education Act (ESEA) reauthorization, he wanted states to annually assess one elementary grade, one middle school grade, and one high school grade in reading and math and to issue a report card with the results. There were to be no consequences, and he offered new federal funds to support the effort.

How did educators respond? The associations and education school cognoscenti exploded in outrage. They explained how hard it is to appropriately assess students, the problems with standardized testing, and why the whole proposal was unnecessary and troubling. In the end, a federal program offered funds to states that wanted to voluntarily adopt Clinton's report card idea. Yet, when Clinton left office in 2001, only a handful of the states that had taken the money had actually done what they'd promised in return. By the time ESEA was reauthorized in 2001 (as NCLB), the traditional voices had blown their credibility. So what happened? The policy makers basically roared in annoyance, turned to would-be reformers who offered actionable suggestions instead of excuses, and imposed something much harsher than what educators had rejected in 1994.

Union leaders say that they've learned this lesson. As NEA president Lily Eskelsen García puts it, "When my members are complaining about these dumb teacher evaluation systems, I challenge them. I tell them, 'What the politicians are doing is stupid and crazy. But we can't just say that. We need to come up with solutions.' If we're the party of 'no,' shame on us. We have to be the party of doing better." She pauses, then adds, "Though it is fun to point out how stupid their stuff is."

There are two big lessons here. First, policy makers are more concerned about ends than means. They want to see good schools, improved student outcomes, and dollars spent wisely. They're less interested in the details of how that happens. If you show up with ideas that *they believe* will help produce the desired results, you're pushing on an open door. If educators had stepped up in 1994 with ideas for smarter outcome metrics or accountability systems, the story of the next two decades would have been very different. Second, teachers have to earn the trust of lawmakers. Right now policy makers don't trust that teachers are reliable guardians of the public interest, and that trust is the first step in getting policy makers to listen carefully to what teachers have to say. This is why the moral authority that flows from policing the profession is so foundational. (See "Seven Tips for Dealing with Lawmakers.")

THE ACCOUNTABILITY THING

Teachers need to clearly and vocally embrace the principle of professional responsibility if they are to get a fair hearing from policy makers. Now, this doesn't mean cage-busters should feel obliged to accept any particular approach to accountability. The University of Pennsylvania's Richard Ingersoll notes that teachers have legitimate concerns: "The push for accountability has not been wrong, but it's been one-sided. It's Management 101. You don't hold employees accountable for things they don't control." This one-sided deal came about because lawmakers didn't trust educators. To help lawmakers remember their Management 101, cage-busters embrace two precepts: you have to define success, and there have to be consequences for failure. If you're willing to do just those two things, you'll get a hearing.

Seven Tips for Dealing with Lawmakers

When problems can't be solved closer to home, cage-busters know they have to deal with legislators and state officials. Teachers may not have a lot of experience dealing with these folks, making it easy to misstep. On this score, a veteran Capitol Hill staffer offers some candid advice. In her years as senior education staffer for one of the nation's most influential lawmakers on education policy, she's seen hundreds of teachers walk through the doors. Here, she offers some straight talk on how to work with lawmakers and their staff.

1. *You don't need a lobbyist.* "Sometimes people assume you need a lobbyist to make an appointment, but people in Congress work for you. Just call and make an appointment."
2. *Do your homework.* "Know whom you're talking to. What major pieces of legislation have they written? You only have to know enough so that you understand your audience. I worked for a senator who was a champion for kids with disabilities, yet people would come in complaining about the difficulties of accommodating special needs kids. They had no idea who they were talking to. If they wanted someone who would help weaken those provisions, they needed to go somewhere else."
3. *Tell me about things I can change.* "Think beyond the story you want to tell. Find the link between your concern and my job. I can't help people with things that I don't control. Come in and tell me about things that I can change; otherwise, I feel like I'm wasting your time and you're wasting mine."
4. *Don't blame the kids.* "Often teachers say, 'I'm on board with accountability. I don't mind assessment, but you don't understand the kids I serve.' This is blaming the kids. All the international data and research data tell us that kids can indeed learn. If you see the kids and their potential, how can you be presenting them as the problem? So, go back and think where else is the system breaking down, because it can't be the kids." (Note: If you think this sounds unfair, I hear you. I think professionals should be responsible for doing their work well—not necessarily for producing the results that public officials wish to see. But this is how some very smart legislators and staff think about things. So, be prepared to address those concerns and offer tough-minded alternatives.)

5. *Bring data.* "Data is hugely influential. Your voice and story matter and are powerful, but data doubles your impact. Telling me you're a great teacher is one thing, but showing me your scores is another. It's much more compelling when a teacher says, 'I've moved kids nine percentage points a year for the last three years and here's an important lesson for policy,' than a teacher who comes in and just says, 'I've taught for forty-three years.' Your voice is more powerful when I see you've done some work to show it's fact, not opinion."

6. *Articulate what should happen.* "It's on the teacher to articulate what needs to change and how that change will solve the problem. That takes some work. It's not easy from the teacher's seat to know whether it's the law or implementation that is the problem. But when you've figured that out, then I'm really interested. Until you do, it's hard for me to know if I can help."

7. *Remember, lawmakers deal with lots of issues, which means decisions are often made by staff.* "A member of Congress has to make decisions on twenty-seven different issues. On a given day, my boss may have to vote on nuclear disarmament, environmental regulation, changes in juvenile justice programs, and student loans. In any given piece of legislation, 90 percent of the decisions were made by staff. Bills are passed by Congress that not one of the 535 members has actually read. So, keep that in mind when meeting with staff."

Whether thinking about Washington or their state legislature, cage-busters do well to keep these tips in mind.

AFT executive Marla Ucelli-Kashyap says of the union, "We're getting more practical. We have to self-regulate or there will be externally imposed regulations that we hate. Having something imposed from outside is generally far more painful than reforming your own practices." Think of it this way. When we read about a scandal involving a handful of police, there's often a call for more oversight of the entire police force. Civic leaders may demand that the police be prevented from using certain tactics or be held accountable in new ways. Police can view oversight as counterproductive, especially for all the good officers subjected to more reporting, paperwork, and pressure. But it can be hard for observers to tell the good officers from the bad ones, so we insist on blanket policies. Teachers who want out from under simple-minded accountability systems need to self-regulate in a way that reassures policy makers that the "good cops" are in charge.

Consider the veteran teacher who wrote to me saying, "I embrace accountability. But I can't imagine quality accountability involving anything but teams of experienced professionals evaluating schools, teachers, and student processes. I cannot imagine conceding that high-stakes tests should factor into an evaluation of my teaching effectiveness or my school's effectiveness. I'm afraid outcomes are impossible to measure in this field. Does this mean my voice can have no weight?" Well, if he offers an alternate strategy for ensuring quality, he'll get a hearing. But if he winds up saying little more than, "Trust us," I'm afraid he's going to be disappointed.

Absent Professional Trust, There Are Just Three Kinds of Accountability

When lawmakers trust professionals, they give them a lot of leeway to determine how they go about their business. Think of how a mayor deals with the police in a community where the cops have a pristine reputation. That mayor is going to pretty much let the police chief make the calls, unless something happens to fracture his trust. That's why establishing professional trust is so powerful. The way to establish that trust is by convincing policy makers that you're watching out for the public so that they don't have to. When that trust is absent, public officials feel obliged to step in. And when they do, it turns out they only have three ways to pursue accountability, each with its own problems.

Lawmakers can hold public services accountable via input regulation, outcome accountability, or consumer choice. As much as they wish there were other approaches, there aren't. Input regulation dictates how services should be provided (e.g., textbooks should be purchased every seven years). This is what we bemoan as "red tape." Outcome accountability doesn't regulate how the work is done as long as providers deliver the requisite results. This makes it possible to peel away red tape but requires that schools be evaluated based on clear, universal metrics (like test scores) and that there be consequences for poor results. Consumer choice leaves decisions about quality to individual families. That alleviates the need for red tape or specified outcomes but raises concerns that parents may be uninformed or make bad choices. These models can be mixed and matched, but, at day's end, these are the options.

Most educators would naturally prefer a model of professional self-regulation to any of these. The trick is that educators don't currently enjoy the requisite trust. That kind of trust must be earned; it can't just be demanded. Cage-busters acknowledge that reality, and work to forge that trust.

BIG P VERSUS LITTLE P POLICY

Jeanne DelColle, a history teacher, spent a year at the New Jersey Department of Education after being named the state's 2012 Teacher of the Year. While there, she coordinated monthly policy discussions between teachers and state officials.

> Some teachers complained about using student achievement for evaluation. I told them, "We took Race to the Top money and the ESEA waiver, so student achievement has to be a portion of our evaluation. If you don't like student growth percentiles, do you like value-added models?" Of course, they hated value-added even worse than they hated student growth. So, I said, "OK, if you don't like student growth, and you don't like value-added, what do you suggest?" The response was crickets . . . I don't think a lot of them understood that, once we took the money, using student achievement was a federal requirement. They thought it was something the state did on its own. I said, "Look, before pointing fingers, make sure you know your information." You have to make sure that you know who's making the decision and what you want changed. Otherwise, how do you know whom to talk to or if it's in their power to do what you're asking?

When talking policy, it's important to distinguish between what I tend to call *Big P* and *little p* policies. On the one hand, Big P policies are formal provisions that present stubborn and hard-to-change barriers. These include things like teacher tenure laws, curricular mandates, and seat time requirements. Big P policies are often statutes, meaning they've been passed by a legislative body like the Congress or a state legislature or are legal rulings that have been handed down by federal or state courts.

Little p policies, on the other hand, are local policies, accepted practices, or district conventions that can be more readily altered. They include things like school staffing, class schedules, dress codes, disciplinary norms, teacher evaluation, and hiring practices. Much of what teacher leaders, principals, and district officials say they "can't" do anything about is of this ilk. Little p policies are often enacted by the school board and can be changed as readily. Or they prove to be nothing more than system routines. All of this is much easier to change than teachers might imagine.

In fact, there are really only three kinds of issues when it comes to dealing with little p obstacles. The first has to do with rules and regulations. Laws aren't self-executing, especially in a realm as complex as schooling. Therefore, federal officials, state employees, and district staff devise rules to put spending policies or staffing requirements into effect. These rules often turn out to have a lot of wiggle room. The second has to do with norms and routines. Often when someone says, "I can't do this in my school," what they really mean is, "That's not the way we do things in my school." The third has to do with politics. Someone will say, "Sure, that's *theoretically* possible, but it's not *politically* possible." Parents wouldn't like it, the union would disapprove, and so on. Okay. Fair enough. That means, if it's important, the challenge is to change some minds or get your allies involved.

Determining whether a given concern is a little p policy is often the key to knowing whether quiet politicking, a memorandum of understanding, or creative thinking is enough to solve the problem. This is where knowledge can make all the difference. I recall working with one district where a team of administrators and teachers was trying to ramp up the caliber of professional training. The problem: they said that the contract specified that they only had three full days and so many half days to work with each year. Some teachers were refusing to report for additional days, even when offered their daily rate. The collaboration was at a standstill because the contract seemed to give all the power to foot-dragging colleagues. Here's the thing. The contract *didn't* say what they thought it did. The actual wording of the contract was quite elastic regarding the permissible amount of paid professional development. What they thought the contract said was actually just the routine the district had adopted years before. Educators could change that routine. The problem was they had taken little p policy as Big P policy, ceding too much power to the weakest link.

Distinguishing Big P from little p policy makes it possible to do some crucial things. It helps you know when you've been imagining barriers that aren't really there. It helps you make sure you're going to the right people and the right place when you're trying to solve a problem. And it helps you see how many of the supposed "policy" headaches in K–12 are actually of the little p variety. (See "How to Argue and Win Every Time" for additional tips on how to get things to go your way.)

PEOPLE WANT TO HEAR WHAT TEACHERS HAVE TO SAY

Believe it or not, teachers have a sympathetic audience: people care what teachers think. In 2013, the annual Gallup poll on schooling found that more than 70 percent of Americans have "trust and confidence" in public school teachers.[4] Ross Danis of the Newark Trust for Education notes that reformers are eager to find ways to connect with teachers because "parents tend to get most of their information from teachers."[5] After all, the public knows that teachers are closer to the classroom than anyone else. The question is what teachers choose to do with this influence. Greg Mullenholz, the former Washington Teaching Ambassador we met in the last chapter, says, "What fascinated me was this perception that folks at [the U.S. Department of Education] would look at us and think, 'They're just teachers.' But the high-level folks actually had a lot of respect for what we had to say. We would meet with them regularly to discuss the feedback we were getting from teachers in the field, and they'd use it to inform what they were doing."

Joe Fatheree reflects,

The real game changer for me was being named Illinois Teacher of the Year. That honor opened up a myriad of new opportunities and helped me understand what it really meant to be a teacher. Case in point, I was invited to attend a policy meeting shortly after being recognized. Several prominent policy makers and business leaders were at the table. During the course of

How to Argue and Win Every Time

Cage-busters only argue when they have to. When they do have to, though, they keep it practical, precise, and concrete. Attorney Gerry Spence offers some terrific tips on doing this in *How to Argue and Win Every Time*.[6] What does Spence know about this stuff? Well, he hasn't lost a jury trial since 1969 and has never lost a criminal case. He offers suggestions for framing a "power argument."

- *Prepare until we have become the argument.* "Prepare until you know every scale on the hide of the fish. Having prepared, next understand that good preparation is like writing a script for a screenplay. Proper preparation requires one to tell the story."
- *Give the argument in the form of a story.* "Remember, fables, allegories, and parables are the traditional tools of successful argument. Every movie, every soap, every sitcom, most lyrics in popular songs, all operas and plays, most successful television commercials are in story form."
- *Tell the truth.* "Being who you are is powerful. Saying how you feel is powerful. To be open and real and afraid, if you are afraid, is powerful. The power argument begins and ends by telling the truth. Truth is power."
- *Avoid sarcasm, scorn, and ridicule. Use humor cautiously.* "Hold back insult. No one admires the cynic, the scoffer, the mocker, the small, and the petty. Giving respect to one's opponent elevates us . . . Remember: Respect is reciprocal."
- *Action and winning are brothers.* "The worst of head-on attacks is often better than the most sophisticated defense . . . The great champions of the world take control. The great generals attack first, and attack again. Take the initiative. Do *something*."
- *Admit at the outset weak points in your arguments.* "You can expose your weaknesses in a better light than your opponent, who will expose them in the darkest possible way. An honest admission having come from you not only endows you with credibility, it also leaves your opponent with nothing to say except what you have already admitted."

> • *Understand your power. Give yourself permission to win.* "Remember, arrogance, insolence, and stupidity are close relatives."
>
> Cage-busters only argue when they have to. But when they do have to, they make it a point to argue wisely and well. Spence is a terrific resource for doing just that.

the conversation a question was posed as to how teachers would respond to a certain piece of legislation. A U.S. Cabinet member looked down the table at me and said, "Okay, we need to hear what Joe has to say." Everyone at the table looked my way and waited to hear my thoughts. It was at that moment that I really understood how powerful a teacher's voice could be and how willing influential people were to listen.

Opportunities abound, even if you don't feel ready for them. Jay Hoffman was appointed to Vermont's standards board for professional educators, where he's focused on professional growth opportunities. He says, "I've been well received, and I hardly know why. I know about three more days of things than the other folks in the room, but they've been solidly behind my proposals. It's amazing." He didn't have to become a standards expert to make a difference. He just had to know a bit more than everyone else. Hoffman adds another bit of hard-earned wisdom. He says, "Call your local legislator cold and say, 'Hey, I'd like to get together with you.' Teachers have more credibility than they might think. Don't worry about being blown off a few times. It's the nature of what they do. They're pulled in a thousand different directions. Stick with it and eventually you'll get an audience. It's just a matter of being a hound dog." The trick is, once you get that meeting, be sure you listen, don't complain, show up with something to say, and have solutions to share.

Maria Fenwick, who's taught and worked on teacher policy in Massachusetts, says, "When teachers don't get a response, they should not take it as, 'Oh, nothing happened.' They should regard it as an invitation to follow up. Policy makers will hear a great idea from a teacher, think, 'I love this,' and then go back to the policy world where things aren't always cut-and-dried. Following up can keep it going. And follow-up isn't that hard. It's an e-mail or a phone call. It's not a big production." Wendy Uptain, a former kindergarten teacher who heads up teacher engagement for the Hope Street Group, says, "We talk about meeting legislators like it's a first date. Set up a meeting and make it a short and sweet introduction. Introduce yourself and ask for some suggestions and advice. Listen. Don't race to offer recommendations on how to fix something or tell them you need more money. Ask if there's anyone else you should talk with. Use e-mail to keep in touch. They're much more likely to take you seriously because you're not just someone from out of the blue."

Now, teachers often tell me, "If politicians want to make education policy, they need to spend a lot more time visiting classrooms." It's true that this would be terrific. Just keep in mind that they have lots of other demands on their time. They've got cops who want them to visit the precinct, nurses who want them to visit public health clinics . . . you get the idea. They're obliged to suffer through lots of Kiwanis lunches, charity dinners, and community forums. And if they're in the state legislature they also probably need to hold down a full-time job.

Moreover, it's not always clear what a classroom visit will accomplish. Are you hoping the legislator will change her mind on testing? How will that work exactly? The visitor will see what happens in your classroom, but how do you see that translating into her changing her mind on some big policy question? Often, there's no reason to think it will. If you're trying to forge a relationship, know that a thirty-minute visit (which requires lots of additional travel time for the visitor) will probably entail only a moment or two of you talking to the official, whereas a short office meeting can provide more real interaction. It's fine and sensible to call for classroom visits, but don't let that distract from what you can control.

WHAT TO SAY TO POLICY MAKERS

When educators do get the chance to talk to policy makers or to speak up in public hearings, they often do so in ways that are self-defeating. If you understand where policy makers are coming from, it gets a lot easier to focus on what might influence them.

This means three things in particular. First, don't demand more money. Everybody asks lawmakers for money. If policy makers had more money to give, they'd give it. But mostly what they hear from teachers is that schools need more. (This is true even in places where districts are spending more than $20,000 per student each year.) Second, emphasize shared concerns. In other words, presume that they also care about the kids and approach them in that spirit. Third, offer solutions and let them know how they can help, other than by forking over more bucks.

Wendy Uptain offers some useful advice drawn from the experience of her program's teaching fellows. She says, when engaging policy makers, "Be sure to end your questions with a question mark! People often stand up and give an impassioned speech instead of actually asking anything. It turns everyone off. When you get up to ask a question, make sure it's a question. Do your research. Be sure that you can speak intelligently to someone well versed in the issues. And propose solutions that work *beyond* your classroom. If you show a policy maker that you have your eyes set beyond just the four walls of your classroom, they'll listen accordingly."

I remember meeting a group of accomplished North Carolina teachers who'd been disheartened by the state's decision to abolish tenure, eliminate hundreds of millions of dollars annually in pay for advanced degrees, and use only a small portion of the savings to create a tiny annual bonus for a quarter of the state's teachers. The teachers were angry. I totally got that. But, here's the deal. Those legislators also had valid concerns. They were concerned that tenure too often protected the undeserving and that paying for advanced degrees was subsidizing course-taking that didn't improve instruction. Disagreement on these things was not a good reason to dismiss legislators as misinformed or hopeless.

Those legislators may not want to pay for education degrees, but that doesn't mean they're wedded to cutting teacher pay. If you take the policy maker's concerns seriously, agree that the current system doesn't do enough to reward excellence or address mediocrity, and propose a viable alternative, you can alter the debate. Rather than arguing whether to pay for the old credentials, the question can be *how* those dollars might best attract, retain, and energize great teaching. Framed that way, it's tougher for anyone to argue that the money should simply go away.

Don't Get Discouraged If They Happen to Disagree

When decisions don't go your way, it's easy to grumble, "They never wanted to hear what I had to say anyway," and decide that it was all a waste of time. But people can listen carefully and still disagree with you. People value different things, have competing concerns, and see the world in different ways.

Reflecting on his tenure as chancellor of the New York City Schools, Joel Klein has said he could have done a better job communicating. He's also noted, though, that many who accused him of not listening really mean that they just didn't like his decision. Klein has said of a long meeting with one critic, "We sat down for three hours. He told me exactly what he thought and I said, 'I really understand you. I even understand where you're coming from. I just disagree.' And he said, 'You don't listen.'"[7]

Lisa Clarke, a social studies teacher from Kent-Meridian High School in Kent, Washington, and a Washington Teaching Ambassador, says she disagrees with key federal policies, "but I wanted to be there to understand it. When I became a Teaching Ambassador, I saw there were smart, kind people who really want the best for students, just like I did. I realized just how complicated it is. Before I met these folks, it was easy for me to just dismiss people I disagreed with." She says, "The thing that's really disturbing are the accusations of bad faith on both sides. That does great harm. But I'm not sure that I would have realized this if I was still in the classroom full time."

Okay, you think, maybe that applies when people really are trying to do the right thing. But what about those evil people that *you're* dealing with? The thing is, believe it or not, that pretty much everybody is trying to do the right thing—at least as they see it. Heck, even the president of one NEA state affiliate explained, "We're one of the most Republican states you can see. That can pose challenges for us. But behind closed doors I find we can have our disagreements and still come together, and we can work with them. Maybe it's not everything we'd like, and they do some things that we don't like. But, with the exception of a couple folks, the legislators are open and constructive."

You know how you're sure you're right about policy X? Believe it or not, those who disagree with you are equally sure *they're* right. If you take time to meet people, listen carefully, and grasp their concerns, you'll find more points of commonality than you might expect.

Check Your Stereotypes at the Door

Treat policy makers and advocates with the same courtesy that you'd like from them. Give them a chance before you make assumptions. Justin Minkel, a second grade teacher in Springdale, Arkansas, and a blogger for *Education Week*, tells a terrific story about checking your assumptions. He says, "My dad's a construction manager. He had a racist worker once who told him, 'Don't put me on crews with any Mexicans. I hate Mexicans.' My dad promptly paired him up with Luis. At the end of the day, when my dad asked how it went, his worker reported, 'Luis is okay. I can work with him. But I still hate Mexicans.' The next day he found himself on a crew with Tomas. By the end of the week, he said, "I still hate Mexicans . . . except for Luis, Tomas, Miguel, Jose, and Juan Carlos. My dad pointed out, 'Those are the only Mexicans you know.'"

This all came to mind, Minkel says, when he attended a convening of the National Conference of State Legislatures: "On the last day of the convening, I told the legislators they'd shattered my stereotype of politicians. I said, 'You're not the stereotype.' They laughed, and someone called out, 'You're not, either!'" Minkel says, "I had my assumptions about lawmakers when I walked into the meeting and they had their own assumptions about teachers. The stereotype of teachers as lazy, reform-resistant, bottom-of-the-class union goons just doesn't jibe with the reality of dedicated, skilled professionals that most parents experience. But many teachers do our own share of stereotyping—making sweeping statements about 'soulless administrators' or painting anyone from the Gates Foundation as a helmeted clone in the Empire."

Minkel found his preconceptions pleasantly off-base. "We learned that sometimes the middle-aged white Representative from Tennessee cares deeply about equity, and the union-busting rep from Alabama is desperate to bring students in his state the kinds of schools they deserve. We disagreed about plenty of policy. But everyone listened more than we spoke and respected the integrity of the speaker even when we disagreed with their position." Now, muses Minkel, "It's possible that one of the teachers took the plane home and said, 'Well, I still think legislators are teacher-hating empty suits, except for Representative Brooks, Senator Wiger, Senator Ruiz . . . ,' and maybe a legislator made it back to his district and said, 'Well, I still think teachers are lazy union goons with a martyr complex, except for Rod, Jessica, Cheryl . . .' But, more likely, we learned to see one another a little more clearly."

The Problem with Demanding "More Money"

Every single day, someone is asking policy makers for more. Cops, firemen, park officials, librarians, youth services directors, transit directors, public housing officials, college presidents, public health providers are all saying, "What about us?" And they all want to know how anybody can oppose more funds for *their* valuable service. No matter how much money there is, there's only so much to go around—and there's never enough for everyone.

Policy makers are used to the dance. Group A comes in and says they need more, and lawmakers (or, more often, their staffers) smile and say they'll see what they can do. Then Group B comes in and they do the same dance. At the end of the day, the staffers look at each other and sigh, as one said to me, "Come on people, *think* about it. If we had more money to give, we'd have already given it to you." So, if you join that dance, you waste time and energy. Worse, you burn valuable goodwill. You're better off focusing on those things where you're on the same page.

And here's the neat trick. Build trust. Convince policy makers that you're spending money wisely and well. And guess what? They'll *show* you the money.

Remember Tammy Laughner from chapter 2? Her superintendent was threatening to cut off funding to her program, so she appealed directly to Indiana's Republican state superintendent Tony Bennett. Bennett told her that he'd have her back. Bennett said, "When I went to see Project RESTORE in action . . . I swear, it's enough to make a bleeding heart out of anyone. So when I heard from Tammy that the [district] superintendent intended to cut a line item from her budget that would have sunk the program, I wrote the [district] superintendent a letter saying, 'If you zero-out the budget for this program, I will personally allocate state funds to provide the resources that it needs, and I'll issue a press release explaining why I had to do what I did." Tammy's funding was left untouched.

POLICY FAVORS THOSE WHO ARE PREPARED

Decades ago, political scientist John Kingdon penned the classic volume *Agendas, Alternatives, and Public Policies.*[8] In it he argues that every so often forces conspire to create "policy windows" during which it's possible to win the votes to pass new laws. Being informed, at the table, and equipped with a plan can make all the difference when those windows open.

Kip Hottman, a high school Spanish teacher in Kentucky, recalls visiting the state capitol on a snow day with an eye to learning more about policy making. His first stop was a state senate education committee meeting, where a senator was championing a bill calling for computer programming to be counted as an alternative world language. The committee passed the bill. Hottman says, "My friend turned to me and said, 'Your whole world just changed in eight minutes.'" Before, Hottman says, "I'd never even thought about policy." Now, returning home, he e-mailed fellow teachers in the World Language Teachers Network to see if anyone had heard about the development. Within minutes, he recalls, "My e-mail blew up." Two days later, Hottman heard from the Kentucky World Language Association asking if he'd be interested in working on advocacy issues.

Hottman e-mailed the senator who sponsored the bill, taking care not to vent. He started by saying he respected the senator's points regarding the importance of computer programming. The senator agreed to sit down and discuss Hottman's concerns. The bill ultimately died in the statehouse. Meanwhile, Hottman ensured that he'd be at the table when this question is revisited in future years.

Policy usually moves at a glacial pace. At times, though, it can move quickly and unexpectedly. If you've built trust and are involved, you might be surprised at how big a difference you can make.

DON'T STAY IN YOUR CORNER OF THE FOREST

Remember, policy is a crude lever. It's not nimble or easily targeted. And its impact depends on how it's implemented. For these reasons, trying to change the law can be a lousy way to solve problems in schools or systems. This is why cage-busters tend to start small, tackling those problems in their school or system that drain time, passion, and energy, and *then* work their way up. That way, when they wind up talking to lawmakers, they're talking to them about solving specific problems that they can't solve in their school or system.

In truth, schooling is so complex that how education policies play out tends to be more a matter of practice than of words on a page. This means that you can still shape and improve policies long after they've been formally adopted. The early stages of policy involve politicians writing the statute— amid all the political noise and bright lights. But that process only sketches the broad outline of the law. From there laws are given life by hundreds or even thousands of decisions made by federal, state, and local officials. Those decisions are made out of the spotlight, can be easy to influence, and often have more practical impact on classrooms than the formal text of the law itself. This means teachers can have an enormous impact on policy by working with those state and local officials, and can do that without having to spend a lot of time in statehouses or chatting with elected officials.

When cage-busters feel put-upon by policy, there are a few useful mantras they keep in mind. One is that it's not personal. Laws get written for everyone . . . that's just the way it works. Another is that it's hard to change laws; it's much easier to change rules or how those rules are applied. A third is that "policy" frustrations are frequently as much about implementation as about the policy itself. And teachers can do a whole lot on that score without needing to change the law.

Finally, recall a bit of wisdom gleaned from Winnie-the-Pooh, who knew, "You can't stay in your corner of the Forest waiting for others to come to you. You have to go to them sometimes."[9] If you think lawmakers and public officials are getting it wrong, that's cool. But don't just complain about it. Reach out, listen, build trust, identify problems, propose solutions, and see what happens. You might be pleasantly surprised.

5

Tackling Everyday Problems

If you don't watch it people will force you one way or the
other, into doing what they think you should do, or into just
being mule-stubborn and doing the opposite out of spite.

—Randle Patrick McMurphy in Ken Kesey,
One Flew Over the Cuckoo's Nest

I'll tell you what leadership is. It's persuasion—and
conciliation—and education—and patience. It's long, slow,
tough work.

—President Dwight D. Eisenhower

"TEACHER LEADERSHIP" is a good thing. Cage-busters are all for it. In practice, though, it can add up to little more than pleasant words. It's rarely done much to tackle those things that sap teachers' time, passion, and energy. That's why cage-busters start not with leadership but with solving those problems. Along the way, they may wind up being teacher leaders. But that's a happy accident.

Too often it can be easy to get the formula backward—to focus on talking about leadership, rather than freeing teachers from the cage. In 2013, Iowa launched a teacher-quality initiative that encouraged districts to designate 25 percent of their teachers as "teacher leaders."[1] This kind of thing is well intentioned, but schools have long had department chairs, grade-level leaders, mentors, and a slew of other teacher leader roles. These jobs are usually more an exercise in bureaucracy than cage-busting. More titles won't help. Michael Dunlea, whom we met in chapter 3, says, "Someone can give you a stamp of approval that says, 'You spent 180 hours sitting in a leadership program, so now you're a teacher leader,' but, meanwhile, you sat at home while these problems were going on and did nothing to solve them."

Cage-busting is about mind-set and skills, not titles. Bad meetings or dumb uses of data can bring to mind the old, wry line, "Everybody complains about the weather but nobody *does* anything about it." *That's* where cage-busters step in. Consider the Teacher Leader Model Standards crafted by the Teacher Leadership Exploratory Consortium.[2] The standards say that a teacher leader helps "colleagues work collaboratively to solve problems, make decisions, manage conflict, and promote meaningful change."

The trick is that teacher leaders say they're often unsure how to get started actually *doing* any of this. Worse, sweeping aspirations can be a recipe for frustration, as teacher leaders find their animated efforts leading to little practical change. When that happens, teacher leaders can sour on the whole enterprise and retreat back to the classroom cage. *Cage-busting is not teacher leadership. Instead, it's doing the things that make teacher leaders successful.*

Cage-busting teacher leadership starts by tackling the familiar realities that lead teachers to retreat to their classrooms: dismal experiences with data, soul-sapping meetings, frustration with families, mind-numbing professional development, and faddish technology adoptions. That's the kind of teacher leadership addressed in this chapter. Now, let's be clear: cage-busting leaders don't *stop* with this list, they *start* with it.

WHY TEACHER LEADERSHIP IS OFTEN A CRUDDY DEAL

Teacher leadership can feel like a cruddy deal. Teachers sigh that it often means more work with not much say-so or satisfaction in return. The best case can involve spending time and energy on stuff that doesn't help you. The worst case is that that you're distracted from your kids and classroom. Jeff Hinton, a retired Marine who teaches high school history in Clark County, Nevada, says of teacher leadership that "at a certain point it gets pretty ridiculous. It's the 'just one more thing' approach to education. It may just be one thing, but think how many 'just one things' teachers have in a day. Each person comes along and says, 'This'll only take a few minutes.' You add it up, and it's overwhelming."

Consider the teacher who leads a collaborative effort to launch a new tutoring program and whose reward is being told, "Hey, there's something else I'd really like you to take on." As one teacher put it, "I'm sick of being volun-told I'm taking on these assignments." I think of the terrific teacher who built a successful International Baccalaureate program in North Carolina, attracting students and posting exceptional results. He received little praise and no support (or additional pay). What he did get was a steady stream of directives from his principal about what else he ought to do to expand the program and attract recognition for the school. When he succeeded at nearly doubling the size of the program, the program's results declined, leading the principal to repeatedly make her displeasure known. The teacher wearily shakes his head and says, "I love IB and I love our students. But if I'd known then what this would demand of me, I'm honestly not sure I'd have started the program."

Teachers across Utah have volunteered to be part of the Educators Taking the Lead program to help implement a new teacher evaluation framework. When asked what teachers get for participating, Sharon Gallagher-Fishbaugh, the president of the Utah Education Association, says, "Absolutely nothing. They are stepping forward, and the irony is that they are doing all of this for nothing."

These norms effectively punish extraordinary effort, encouraging all but the foolhardy to duck and keep their heads down. As Roxanna Elden, author of *See Me After Class*, says, "A teacher who wants to be a cage-buster really has to decide for herself what she'll spend the unpaid time on. For example, I don't volunteer to be on a lot of committees. You have to figure out ways to say no sometimes. Being the person who says yes to everything can become a cage in itself."

Cage-busting can help teacher leaders create the schools and systems to which they aspire. Cage-busters start by tackling some of those places where dysfunction can seem as much a part of the profession as the curriculum or the classroom.

GETTING "COLLABORATION" RIGHT

In K–12, we talk a lot about collaboration. And we should. Collaboration is a good thing. However, it's a term that's used so casually that it can become shorthand for "be nice." The problem is that teachers are often in grades, departments, schools, or systems where they're working with people who don't collaborate back. As AFT director of field programs Rob Weil says, "Collaboration for collaboration's sake is a waste of time. To pat each other on the back, say, 'We get along, we're friends,' what good is that if it's not improving the system? There's a lot of that out there."

Collaboration needs to be a two-way street. Well-meaning experts can proffer advice that winds up leaving teachers stuck in the cage. In *The First-Year Teacher's Survival Guide,* best-selling author and English teacher Julia Thompson advises that when dealing with "difficult colleagues," teachers should "recognize that you share a common goal: the education of the children entrusted to your care. If you hold this goal in mind, you have little choice but to work well together, because the alternative could result in failure, for students and for you."[3] The caged response is to be nice and hope things improve. Cage-busters choose another course. Cage-busters eschew vague talk of "collaboration" for a more precise and practical notion—that of the "coalition of the willing." Cage-busters want to work with people who want to work with them. And they know that just putting out good vibes and hoping for the best probably isn't going to get it done.

What does it look like to build a coalition of the willing? Courtney Fox, a first grade teacher at Mount Pleasant Elementary School in Wilmington, Delaware, says, "Fifteen years ago, our principal brought coaches into the school to showcase the Responsive Classroom technique. A few of my colleagues and I embraced it, forming a small committee and a book club. You can't just force it upon people. A lot of times, it's just, 'You should do this,' and people don't understand the reasoning or have a personal investment. Those efforts don't succeed. We did the exact opposite."

Fox and three of her colleagues started meeting every week before school, and each invited one other potentially interested colleague to join them.

> We knew that personal connection was huge in getting this going. When you try to start something, it doesn't have to be launched schoolwide. A

lot of times teachers put up a poster and invite everyone, and then no one comes. My colleagues and I would meet beforehand and say, "What's our agenda today? What do we want to have people leave here with?" We were clear on our mission and goals. We got people invested by doing our leg-work to look for strategies that we knew would work and getting people to commit to small, easy things at first. People would say, "We go to meetings all the time and nothing comes to fruition, but you hold us accountable for doing something when we leave here. When we check back in, we feel like there's movement" . . . We now have twenty-four of us talking before school every week. We send people to get more formal training. We've solicited foundations and usually sent four to five teachers to training every year, at a total cost of around $4,000. I can't think of any other programs in our school that have been sustained for fifteen years. But our group has lasted through four or five administrators. They've each come in with their own agendas, but ours is the group that the teachers have never let go away.

Fox and her colleagues didn't just collaborate. They found like-minded colleagues, made disciplined use of time and energy, and built a collabora-tive that now includes 80 percent of the school's teachers and that has re-shaped the school's culture. Mount Pleasant is in one of Delaware's poorer districts, but the teachers in the program stick around, and they have got-ten their school named a Delaware Recognition School in the process.

There are a few things to keep in mind when trying to create a coalition of the willing. One, it's easier with people who agree on the mission. A big challenge in most schools is honest disagreement about things like disci-pline. Finding agreement can be wearying, especially as it's rarely clear that one approach is obviously right. Agreement makes it possible to avoid exhausting conflicts, reduces friction, and makes new teachers more likely to stay. University of Arkansas professor Patrick Wolf and three colleagues report that "schools that recruit for mission seem to be able to retain teach-ers for 10 or more years," while other schools have more turnover and a tougher time recruiting.[4]

Two, the most straightforward approach to getting agreement may be starting a new school or program from the ground up, recruiting like-minded colleagues. Another approach is Fox's: not worrying about school-wide change and instead starting with those who get it. As former NEA collective bargaining honcho Bill Raabe observes, "Let's say three-quarters of the teachers at a school want to do something, and a quarter don't want to. I'd start looking for creative options to get started. You might try changing the schedule or professional development for a period of time. You can see how it works, with some kind of incentive for those who want in. You can go to the union and ask if there are ways to waive provisions that are in the way."

Three, using little p policies to shape school norms can make it easier to forge agreement. Use these policies to make the culture work *for* you rather than *against* you. For instance, a mutual consent hiring process that allows faculty at a school to interview and choose new colleagues can ensure that new teachers are a good fit. Peer assistance and review can make it easier for teachers to deal with colleagues who aren't doing their share. This can nurture and reinforce agreement, making teacher workrooms feel less like a neutral corner and more like the inner sanctum of a tight-knit team.

SO, WHAT EXACTLY DO YOU *DO* WITH DATA?

Most teachers have some idea of how to use data to diagnose student needs, gauge progress, and adjust instruction. But most discussion of data tends to stop there. Unfortunately, even good assessment data is often of limited utility for cage-busters, because they are interested not only in refining a lesson but in rethinking how the school works. Using reading and math scores to inform instruction is fine, but limited.

Knowing what to re-teach or how to adjust a lesson won't provide insight into how much time is being wasted, which policies are hampering instruction, or if students are actually doing their homework. While the data needed for that can't be found in state test results, it can be found. For instance, in a pioneering study, Brown University professor John Tyler has examined how teachers use the online data system in one mid-sized district. He found that they logged in once a week and, over the course of the entire school year, spent slightly more than one hour looking at the data. The reasons that teachers offered for making so little use of the data included a lack of time, training, and support.[5] This kind of analysis requires a concerted effort to ask the right questions and find a way to collect the relevant information. This means thinking not just about test scores but also about the routines and behaviors that produce them,

Today, it's rare that anyone focuses on the data that teachers need to cage-bust. This is true even in organizations that generally evince a cage-busting mind-set. For instance, in 2014 the Data Quality Campaign held a national event in Washington, DC, to highlight a new brief titled "Teacher Data Literacy: It's About Time." The brief has smart things to say and offers suggestions on how to make data less "overwhelming" and more useful for improving instruction.[6]

The report features a graphic labeled "Ms. Bullen's Data-Rich Year" to show how teachers can benefit from rich student data. In the fall Ms. Bullen can chart Joey's progress to show his parents how he's doing. In the winter the principal can identify which instructional techniques are working and which are not. In the spring the principal can help Ms. Bullen reevaluate how she fared. And in the summer Ms. Bullen and her colleagues can use data to identify "promising practices." The vision that emerges is a thoroughly caged one. In each case, data use is monitored by the principal and applies only to classroom practice. There's no point where the teacher is stepping up to use data to examine school norms, challenge her principal, or rethink how professionals go about their work. Cage-busting with data requires more than formative assessment and good intentions. It requires at least five things.

- *Don't allow data or research to substitute for good judgment.* When presented with promising programs or reforms, ask the simple questions: What are the expected benefits? What are the costs? How confident should you be that promising results are replicable? In fact, data can be as important for illuminating challenges as for its ability to dictate solutions. After all, one popular justification for cage-dwelling inertia is, "We're already doing the best we can; there's really no big problem here." A lack of data enables that kind of inertia. Good data can blast right through it.
- *Be sure that you're collecting data with an eye toward solving problems.* Student achievement data is vital, but it doesn't tell you how well time is being used or how well the school is communicating with parents. To figure out what's going on behind the test scores, you need to ask

the right questions and figure out how to measure what matters. A useful tool here is action research, which I usually dismiss as one of those awful ed school conceits. In the hands of a cage-buster, however, action research can be a powerful tool for identifying opportunities, illuminating barriers, and solving problems. It can ensure that convenient metrics aren't narrowing your thinking. If you don't know what share of kids are fluent in a second language, that's a great action research project. If you don't know how often teachers are e-mailing, calling, or visiting parents, there's another. Action research is a way to dig down and identify opportunities to do better.

- *Metrics need to measure what matters.* Always be sure that you're not working for your metrics but, rather, that they're working for you. Be clear about the outcomes you'd like to see in a classroom, schoolhouse, program, department, or district. Cage-busters don't just default to state achievement data. That data is valuable but limited. State tests generally can't tell you if students are mastering a second language, excelling in science, volunteering in the community, becoming good citizens, or getting engaged in the arts. Cage-busters focus on what they think is important, not on what someone else happens to measure.

- *Solutions that work in one place may not work somewhere else.* As LeAnn Buntrock, director of the Woodrow Wilson MBA program in educational leadership, puts it, "One thing I see often—and it just drives me nuts—is when you go into a school and the leader tells you they have a discipline problem. So, they say . . . we are going to institute a school uniform policy. And that's just fabulous if student dress is what's causing your discipline problems. But if you look at your data, you might notice, 'Well, actually, most of our discipline referrals take place when kids are getting off the buses. So we need to have more teachers there when kids are getting off the buses.' It comes down to figuring out the root cause of the problem."[7] Make sure you're using data to identify *your* problem.

- *Think of time and dollars as data, too.* Knowing where time and dollars go can be a powerful tool for finding solutions (see "School Budget Hold 'em"). Jason Kamras, chief of human capital for the District of

Columbia Public Schools says, "In my fourth year in the classroom, I was teaching seventh grade and some students were coming in with third or fourth grade skills. They simply needed more time. I could have said, 'There's not much I can do. I don't control the schedule.' But I went to the principal and said, 'How about creating an extra period for seventh grade math?' He gave me a copy of the budget in Excel and said, 'Knock yourself out. If you can come up with a plan, great.' It was the first time I saw the spreadsheet and how much schools got charged for teachers, custodians, and so on." Kamras explains how "to create the extra math class, we cut one elective and made up for it by adding afterschool activities with external partners. After one year of the 'double math,' we reduced the number of students performing below grade level by 40 percent." Time is a very real cage. People think they can't do much about it, but often they can if they're creative. The first step to figuring out what might be done is getting clear data on where things stand.

FLIPPING THE SWITCH WITH FAMILIES

Cage-busters know they can't change rules and schools by their lonesome. They need allies. And parents can be powerful force multipliers. It's easy for teachers to regard parental support as nice but largely beyond their control. In fact, schools and systems have frequently wound up treating parents as a necessary nuisance. As journalist John Merrow observes, "If you ask professional educators in a public forum whether they view parents as assets or liabilities," they'll always insist parents are "our greatest asset" and "invaluable partners." However, asks Merrow, "what if you caught them off guard, late at night after a few drinks, say? Or, better yet, what if you simply examined how most schools treat parents?" Half-hearted back-to-school nights and parent involvement committees show, he says, that "most administrators and many teachers hold parents in low regard" and "push parents away in subtle and not-so-subtle ways."[8]

Cage-busters know Merrow's right, and they think that's nuts. They approach parental engagement with fresh eyes and a sense of possibility. Seth

School Budget Hold 'em

The analysts at the Boston-based Education Resource Strategies (ERS) argue, "It is more important than ever to make investments where it really matters."[9] But in working with dozens of districts they have discovered that "the opposite is occurring: We see multiple examples of district operations and practices that perpetuate" questionable spending decisions and make it tougher to meet the needs of their students. None of this is news to the cage-buster. The problem is that teachers aren't necessarily equipped to wade into these questions.

For assistance, teachers can look to a terrific resource from the good folks at ERS, a game called School Budget Hold 'em. The game is designed to provide an engaging way to think about how resources are being allocated. As ERS staff note, administrators often just "make minor adjustments to the previous year's budget, hoping to preserve existing positions and perhaps purchase some new materials. They often separate budgeting from school planning." School Budget Hold 'em empowers players to determine how they might better spend limited funds.

Cards are arrayed into two columns: savings and investments (e.g., spending). Players click "play" on a card to put it into the mix. For instance, a player could select "increase student activity fees by $50 per student in Secondary schools" (for a budget savings of 0.3 percent) and "eliminate cost of living adjustments and replace with market based adjustments when revenues allow" (for a budget savings of 0.8 percent) in order to "give $10k stipend to your top 15 percent" of teachers for playing an increased leadership and coaching role (at a budget cost of 1.0 percent). The three moves, together, would save 0.1 percent of the district budget. If the player then wants to "add Pre-K for 50 percent of Kindergarten students" and offset it by "partner[ing] with community groups to provide 50 percent of summer school programs," they then need to trim the budget elsewhere by another 1.4 percent.

The exercise is custom-built for cage-busters. It can sharpen thinking about problems while surfacing concrete, precise, and practical solutions. It can help teachers ditch vague wish lists and help them weigh real trade-offs. It's worth playing a few rounds. You can find the game online at www.erstrategies.org/hold-em.

Andrew, a special education teacher who founded New York City's high-performing Democracy Prep charter schools, famed for off-the-chart parent and student activism, says, "You really only have three choices if you're stuck teaching in a low-performing school. One, you can fight the system and risk being fired or not making progress. Two, you can close your door, forget about everything, and work on making your classroom awesome. Three, you can get those people who want the same things that you do to put pressure on the school and system. More than anyone else, that's parents and students."

Karen Mapp, senior lecturer on education at Harvard University, puts it perfectly: "Family engagement shouldn't be a chore or seen as an add-on to the 'real' work of teaching and learning. Done right, it flips the improvement switch. You may only have a few hours a month with parents. But if you win those parents over in that time and connect them to their children's learning, it can be a powerful accelerant. Viewing parents as a partner and not as an enemy can mean you don't have to work so hard at turning around a school. Family engagement is a strategic component of whole school reform." Now *that's* a cage-busting mind-set: it's not just that involving parents makes good sense; it's that these efforts can more than repay the time, energy, and passion that teachers devote to them.

Mapp tells of a conference in Boston where the ATLAS Communities Project was highlighting family-school partnership efforts at a Philadelphia elementary school. Karen Jackson, the school's principal, had worked with her staff to create a welcoming climate in the school and to build trusting relationships with families. Previously, almost all communication home had been discipline related. At the conference, a parent who had had a combative relationship with the school stood up to give her testimonial. While clearly nervous to be onstage, she said, "I'd lay down on the trolley tracks for Ms. Jackson and the teachers at the school. They reached out to me and treated me as a partner in my son's learning. I'm afraid to fly but came here for Ms. Jackson because I wanted to tell you my story." Mapp says, "There wasn't a dry eye in the house. It was a powerful example of what happens when parents and school staff are partners."

In chapter 3 John Solet talked about struggling to boost parental involvement. He recalls one father who left a lasting impression on my perception of parents. This guy was a solid 300 pounds and lived off the land as a shrimper. He was this big, old Native American guy. He'd come to school barefoot, just yelling at everyone. Administrators would basically lock their doors. Eventually his son needed an intervention. It was shrimping season, and the boy had stopped coming to school. I did a home visit. I'd heard the horror stories, so I parked like six blocks from his house and walked the half-mile gravel driveway to his trailer. He opens the door and says, "What the hell do you want?" I said, "We need to do something about Paul or the courts may get involved." And he says, "I'll help Paul if you can help me out." He says, "The only thing I really want is to learn how to read to my granddaughter. If you can help me get my GED, I'll do everything I can to make sure he goes to school every day." That floored me. He was giving the administration so much trouble because he couldn't figure out what the documents said and was too embarrassed or didn't have the skills to explain himself. I spent some time helping him, and it paid off. His son started coming to class regularly. Word got out to the community that I meant business. It made my work a lot easier.

Is this cage-busting or just working overtime inside the cage? That's a judgment call. It depends on whether Solet was magnifying parental and community support enough to repay his time and energy. The key is ensuring that the reward for connecting with parents isn't just more work.

Cage-busters don't think teachers can or should try do this all by themselves. They push for their schools to help. During 2013–2014, the Washington, DC school system had fifteen schools in the second year of the Family Engagement Partnership. Teachers conducted home visits and participated in Academic Parent-Teacher Teams, with the Flamboyan Foundation covering the cost of materials, coaching, professional development, and curriculum. After the effort's first year, an initial evaluation by researchers at Johns Hopkins found promising results. More than 90 percent of parents said it improved their relationship with their child's teacher and that they were better able to help their child at home. Meanwhile, more than three-quarters of teachers said it helped get families more engaged and made them feel more supported.[10]

Seth Andrew says that Democracy Prep has taken the energy that parents usually use to push their personal demands and redirected it.

It's a judo move. Instead of directing their energy at teachers or principals, we've directed it at public officials and moving the larger system. The
first thing we did was to teach parents how the system works. We've got a
number of schools "co-located" with other New York City schools. Over
time, parents in our co-located buildings regularly complain about the
food. They are right to complain. It's bad. It's unhealthy. There's hair in
the food. But they don't understand that we are one of three schools in the
building and that because we're in a Department of Education building
we're required to use the district's provider. Once they understood the food
isn't something we control, we helped them figure out how to push the but-
tons of the portfolio office downtown. They got their way. The system let
Revolution Foods come in and offer the kids an alternative, and we got the
outcome we wanted—but couldn't have done it on our own.

Andrew offers another take on getting the parents involved, explaining,

Democracy Prep never mails anything, and we rarely backpack stuff to parents. We never mail a report card. We tell parents, "You must come pick it
up." Ninety to 95 percent of parents come at the first availability. There are
always a few stragglers you need to call, but eventually our kids make them
come. Now, for that, you need a classroom culture where the kid says, "Mom,
I need to know my grade." Most teachers try to use parents to mobilize the
kids. They tell the parents, "Make sure your kid is here on time or reads at
night before bed." The paradigm shift for us was when we realized we had
much more leverage on the kid than the parents. So, you'd have the kid saying, "Hurry up mom, I'm going to be late to school," "I need you to turn off
the TV so I can do my homework," or "I need you to leave the living room so
I can read—because I share the bedroom with four other kids." That totally
reframed our approach to getting the parents to cooperate. The kid is more
likely to be the change agent. Most teachers in America are spending inor-
dinate amounts of their time and energy on parent communication, at an
insanely low payoff. If you spend those same hours each month trying to get
your kids excited, that's going to be a much bigger payoff. Just keep in mind
that you've got thirty to fifty hours a week with the kids, but maybe one to
two hours a month with the parents. It took us a while to get that. We'd
spend all this time saying, "We only had 20 percent of parents show up last
night" and stressing out that "those parents are so disengaged." It's when we
started focusing on the kids first that things started to cook.

Whether you're inclined to focus on parents or students, the logic is the
same. Cage-busters look for ways to make sure that schools amplify their

time, passion, and energy. Enlisting families is a powerful way to do just that.

PUTTING AN END TO AWFUL MEETINGS

Plenty of teachers grumble that they sit through too many useless meetings. When you ask them what they've done about that, they just shrug. They've come to regard those meetings as an unpleasant fact of life. The thing is, tedious or disorganized meetings are not just a waste of time; they're actually destructive. They signal that teachers' time isn't valuable. They waste a chance to work together and solve problems. In fact, researchers have reported that "perceived meeting effectiveness" explains more than one-quarter of employee enthusiasm and about one-fifth of job satisfaction.[11]

Casie Jones, whom we met earlier, recounts, "For a couple of years, we had a teacher ambassador program where teachers from every building would meet. It was an opportunity for teachers to have a say as the district's policies were in transition. What could have been this powerful platform turned into a complaint session, with teachers saying, 'We don't have enough resources' or 'This isn't fair.' It's good to feel passionately, but there was a sense of whining. Those teachers didn't realize that they defeated themselves."

Bad meetings are not a force of nature. Teachers can do something about them. We met Jeanne DelColle, who organized meetings between teachers and officials at the New Jersey Department of Education. She says, "I set down ground rules in the very beginning to keep the conversations on track. From the very first meeting, I said, 'Number one, we are here to troubleshoot and problem-solve, not to moan or whine. If you're here to complain, this isn't the group for you.'" You and your colleagues can decide whether meetings are going to be productive . . . or not. It's your place to decide whether you'll tolerate it when administrators run dull, rambling, or overly long meetings or whether you and your peers will speak up, identify problems, and offer solutions.

Harvard University education professors Kathryn Parker Boudett and Elizabeth A. City have penned a book that can help with all this. In *Meet-*

ing Wise, they note, "Terrible meetings are suffocating. They make people feel bored, frustrated, and sometimes downright angry. If there is an agenda, it's not followed, or it's hijacked—and that's tolerated. Meetings run long, and everyone complains afterwards—but not to the people in charge . . . During bad meetings, participants' minds are consumed by endless chatter: Did we really need a meeting to cover this? Is she really going to make that same point she always makes *again*? Are we really going to pretend that what we decide here matters?"[12]

Boudett and City offer terrific suggestions as to what teachers can do about all this (see *"Meeting Wise"*). They urge those leading meetings to think of them like great classrooms, where "participants are actively engaged in challenging tasks, using their minds, solving problems, and communicating. In meetings, the facilitator is like a skillful teacher who plays different kinds of roles . . . And in both, all participants know the norms of behavior that they are expected to follow."[13] Careful planning produces meetings that are organized, focused, and efficient.

Laura Strait, the California elementary teacher we met in chapter 3, says, "My old school had co-planning time, but it was mostly just teachers venting about students. Here, PD is geared to what we're doing in the classrooms. Surveys ask what we liked and what we need. There's an exit ticket that asks teachers to name one thing that can be improved." Strait says the school has avoided negativity by working hard to establish norms and then maintaining them. "The sessions are for problem solving, not venting. Venting comes up, but we have to bring ourselves back to center. We say, 'Let's review our norms, get it back on track, and hold each other accountable.'" She notes, "Teachers can make it easier for the principal. Teachers need to be clear that we're all in this together, so it's not just the principal. Teachers can help the principal, role-playing it out and letting her know what to expect."

There are some practical ways teachers can push school and system leaders to pay more attention to the costs of bad meetings.

- *Get precise about costs in time and money.* It's hard to tackle a problem until you see the problem. Bad meetings are such a part of the familiar wallpaper of our lives that we can fail to notice them. A useful way to change that dynamic is to get concrete about the time and the cost of staff meetings. A weekly 45-minute professional learning community (PLC) for fifty administrators and faculty amounts to 27 hours per staff member per year, or about 1,350 hours of staff time. Put another way, factoring in employee benefit costs, that's probably $50,000–100,000 in personnel time. Are those meetings the best use of that time? Of those funds? This can be a great way to launch a serious discussion about what's getting accomplished and what should change.

- *Collect the data.* Administrators and teachers alike often have only a shaky grasp of how much time is spent in meetings, how productive those meetings are, or what the associated costs are in time and money. Getting your hands on this kind of data and sharing it can make a huge difference. Some organizations spend a lot more staff time in meetings than do others: some devote as little as one-fourteenth of their personnel budget to meetings and others as much as one-sixth.[14] If you're frustrated by meetings, you're probably not alone. A study of managers across a variety of organizations found that more than one-third of them thought meeting time was unproductive, and two-thirds said the meetings failed to achieve their goals.[15] Get the data on your school and put it to good use.

- *Do the little stuff.* Having fewer meetings or more focused meetings can help. But veteran educators and staffing experts offer up additional tips. One is to take care to schedule it for the amount of time you need. One veteran educator explains, "If you schedule a meeting for sixty minutes, it takes sixty even if everyone is just moving at half speed. So think about the scheduling; don't just default to Outlook." Another tip is to take a page from Courtney Fox's playbook and only invite the people who want and need to be there. Big meetings tend to drift, especially when people have personal agendas or feel forced to attend. And make sure you know what the goal of the meeting is and that it gets accomplished. Good meetings reach decisions or move things along. Insist on that.

Cage-busters don't leave quality control to the principal. They work with colleagues to establish norms, support the principal's efforts to enforce those norms, and hold one another to a high professional standard. None of this is any different from what good teachers do every day in their classroom. It's just that teachers know they're in charge in their classrooms but can lapse into thinking of themselves as captives, rather than co-captains, when it comes to the larger school.

RETHINKING THE DEAL WITH PROFESSIONAL DEVELOPMENT

Teachers voice a lot of frustration with professional development. Veteran math teacher Gary Rubinstein puts it elegantly in *The Reluctant Disciplinarian*, observing, "School in-service classes are times of role reversal: Teachers become students (loud and uncooperative). Administrators become teachers (boring and demanding) . . . In-service topics range from the utterly useless to the totally useless. One year my colleagues and I spent three hours learning the subtleties of new grade sheets, with advice like, 'When you bubble, use a number two pencil, and be sure to erase any stray marks.' At my friend's school, teachers recently received 'risk management' training . . . with advice like, 'You can prevent slipping on rainy days by thoroughly drying off your shoes when going indoors.'"[16]

Though teachers spend ninety hours a year in professional development, the Boston Consulting Group reported in 2014 that just 29 percent of teachers are highly satisfied with their PD.[17] Done right, PD and support can amplify—rather than drain—time, passion, and energy. But Stanford University professor Linda Darling-Hammond and several colleagues have observed that the "training [educators] receive is episodic, myopic, and often meaningless."[18] This is doubly discouraging because, while teachers say high-quality PD is valuable and energizing, lousy PD demoralizes teachers and undermines their sense of professionalism. University of Washington professor Morva McDonald points out that bad PD actually undermines the profession: "Most professional development doesn't highlight that teaching itself is intellectual work. We don't structure training to reflect how professionals learn."

Asked about PD's unimpressive track record, teachers tend to voice a sense of helpless resignation—that this is just the way it goes. This is true

Meeting Wise

In *Meeting Wise*, Kathryn Parker Boudett and Elizabeth A. City offer tips for turning mindless meetings into useful ones.[19] They observe, "In lots of schools and conference rooms, time is being wasted. While the research base on the use of time is not deep, one finding is clear: *quality matters more than quantity* . . . The important question is not, 'Do we have enough time?' But 'Are we making the best use of time we already have?'" They offer ways to ensure that meeting time is used wisely and well.

- *Think before you sit.* "Watch where you sit, and whom you sit next to, since this could affect both your and others' ability to participate . . . Try sitting in a new seat once in a while. When we mix things up, we find it almost always offers a new perspective on the conversation, and it can sometimes shift the group's participation dynamics in a positive way."
- *Be fully present.* "When you're in a meeting, be there 100 percent. There are no doubt plenty of other things you could be doing with the time, some of which may feel more urgent or appealing. But if the meeting's purpose is worthy, give it your full attention. You, your fellow meeting participants, the facilitator, *and the children whose education depends on you* deserve that."
- *Build on the ideas of others.* "There are times in meetings when people are tripping over one another to get their ideas out. In this situation, it can be particularly helpful if participants commit to building on others' ideas . . . basically, whatever someone says, you don't judge it, but instead try to build on it."
- *Challenge ideas, not people.* "Sometimes it takes courage to challenge someone you disagree with, and sometimes it doesn't, but in either case, separate people and ideas. A subtle change in language can make the challenge feel less personal, which makes it safer for everyone to engage."
- *Provide constructive feedback.* "Challenge yourself to figure out how to share your ideas for improvement. Maybe you provide feedback privately. Maybe you get people together and offer a suggestion from the group . . . If participants tolerate bad meetings, the price is high. Kids lose."

They offer a pointed reminder, "By the way: debriefing with a colleague who has no role in designing the next agenda or facilitating the next meeting doesn't count as 'feedback.' That kind of conversation is usually more like complaining or venting or processing. When you think about it, how many gripe sessions out in the parking lot actually translate into constructive suggestions?" There's a big difference between complaining and problem solving. Acting can foster a culture where time is valued, aimless meetings are frowned on, and meaningful engagement is a norm.

even of savvy teachers. Casie Jones says, "Honestly, a lot of the PD provided in Memphis is a waste of time. A lot of it was put on by people trained to say things they didn't truly understand, because it was so new. It was just a black hole. We have to get in sixty-seven hours of PD credits, so we'd think, 'Let's find the biggest thing we can and suffer through it.'" Cagebusters reject that hopelessness wholly and completely. They *don't* do this via vague calls for professionalism. They do it by seeing the problem, putting forward sensible solutions, and working to make those real.

Start by being honest. In my experience, most teachers privately complain about their PD. Yet, when given a chance to weigh in, they say everything is fine. The 2012 Metlife Survey found that 73 percent of teachers rate their professional development as excellent or good.[20] The 2013 Scholastic Survey found that 60 percent of teachers who teach math or ELA said their Common Core State Standards (CCSS) PD was "extremely or very helpful." (At the same time, 71 percent of teachers say they need "quality CCSS-based professional development!")[21] It's possible that Rubinstein, Darling-Hammond, McDonald, and most teachers I talk to have it wrong and that teachers really do love their PD. But I doubt it. I think, as we discussed in chapter 1, that teachers have gotten so used to dysfunction that they've learned to mutter, "Fine, fine, it was fine," while rolling their eyes and counting the minutes until they can return to their classroom refuge.

So, what do cage-busters *do* about lousy PD? They get precise about the problem. Is the PD too erratic? Off point? Poorly designed? How much time is being spent on PD, and how many of those minutes are utterly wasted? Once they're clear on the problem, they work to address it. Julia King, a seventh grade teacher at DC Prep Charter School, describes how her school approaches PD. She depicts a mind-set that any teacher would relish: "There's intensive advance planning for all professional development. Any PD we give is reviewed by many members of our school team. I'll be presenting PD in two weeks. When I submitted my draft a few days ago, I only did it after an hour-long conversation with my peers. I'm getting mentoring in how to message things, present context, and find ways to make people want to buy in. All of our PD is expected to value teachers' time and kids' time. Any professional development we do is planned, evaluated, and then discussed afterwards. The expectations are high."

Cage-busters work with similar-minded colleagues to devise possible solutions. They don't get stuck on what's supposedly permitted. They ask, "What would be the best for our students? What would help teachers in this building do our best work?" For instance, a lot of teachers believe that intensive coaching can make a real difference. But peers and administrators are stretched so thin, and the classroom refuge so culturally ingrained, that teachers usually get observed only a handful of times a year. What would it take for teachers to have access to weekly coaching sessions, whether that involves a live observation or reviewing a recorded lesson with a mentor?

Curtis Chandler, a staff developer in Hutchinson, Kansas, argues that there's more flexibility to customize PD than teachers may realize. He says, "In my small rural district, we wanted to get tech savvy but the district didn't have the funds for PD. So we called one tech guru, who agreed to come, and recruited practitioners from the district who were already there. We called it Tech Camp and held it during a few days over the summer. Most of the time, the only obstacle is that the district has to approve it as PD. It's more a question of paperwork than anything." He says it's not hard to get district approval, advising, "Start by saying to your administrators, 'Wouldn't it be great if we offered something over summer that wasn't mandatory?' So long as people are willing to head it up and handle logistics, most administrators are open to it."

There are several practical ways to push for more useful professional development.

- *Make feedback transparent.* Schools and systems routinely collect surveys from teachers at the end of PD sessions, but the results can go unheeded and unused—which leads teachers to provide pro forma feedback. Ask school and system leaders to provide a forum where teacher feedback can be publicly shared and discussed. If the feedback seems unduly positive, ask about that. Most importantly, though, merely seeing the results taken seriously can be a powerful way to get colleagues to start offering serious feedback.
- *Push for teachers to be empowered and to be responsible for results.* One-size-fits-all PD rarely meets anyone's needs. That's why many employers have sought to give employees more control over their PD. Leading organizations of all kinds have developed customized offerings based on development needs and job responsibilities, empowered employees to choose those that seem most useful, and then expected employees to be accountable for demonstrating improvement. Work with your district to embrace this kind of approach.
- *Get serious.* Sitting for a few hours or a half day in a cafeteria while someone reads from their PowerPoint is a bad way to get better at *anything*. We usually improve through mentoring, practice, and feedback. So push your school and system accordingly. Shift PD resources into high-quality coaching, boost the time devoted to each point of focus, and make sure teachers have the time to get their hands dirty.

Cage-busters don't try to do this alone. They work with like-minded colleagues to take a stand for excellence. They reach out to administrators and ask, "How do we tackle this problem together?" If disappointed by the response, they explore alternatives. What they doesn't do is imagine that desultory PD is inevitable or deem a pedantic PLC to be "good enough."

VIEWING TECHNOLOGY AS A TOOL

Technology is too often hailed as a miracle restorative. Enthusiasts have made over-the-top claims about the transformative power of iPads, laptops, the Internet, television, videotapes, radio, and the gramophone. Each time, teachers are encouraged to forget about the last wave and to get excited about glitchy new software and shiny devices. For all that, nothing of importance seems to change. Here's the thing: it's not the technology that matters but *how we use it*.[22] The key is to think of technology not as a solution but as a tool. Most times, technology's biggest payoff is helping us do familiar tasks faster and better—freeing up talent, time, and dollars for better uses. If teachers with one-to-one devices can, each day, spend 10 minutes fewer entering data and grading quizzes, 10 minutes fewer passing and collecting tests and papers, and 10 minutes fewer walking students to the library or accessing student data, they will save 80 or 90 hours a year. That's essentially another *15 instructional days* that they can devote to instruction, mentoring, or anything else.

Special education teachers spend several hours per student each year creating IEP goals, developing intervention plans, and assessing progress—and then more hours tracking and updating these each reporting period. Jamie Pagliaro, chief learning officer at Rethink, a company that provides online support for special education, says Rethink's data-collection tools, printable materials, and library of video-based demonstrations can reduce paperwork and reporting time by 20–25 percent—saving dozens of hours a year.

The practical headaches associated with classroom technology can be a deal breaker. Matt Pasternack, a former teacher and now an executive with the e-learning company Clever, recalls surveying hundreds of elementary and middle school teachers about their experiences with school software. Eighty percent of teachers said they would use software more if it took less time to log in, but they reported that *just over 25 percent* of the class time spent using software is wasted due to problems with "setup, troubleshooting, or login." The average teacher spent 61 minutes a day using software in elementary school. This means that the average elementary teacher experienced 15 wasted minutes a day. That's more than 40 hours a year of wasted time, more than a full week's instruction.[23]

When it delivers, technology can make it possible to do things that used to be difficult, or impossible. Matt McCabe, who teaches AP World History at Pritzker College Prep in Chicago, used technology to provide his Advanced Placement students with more writing support. He explains, "We needed our kids to do more writing. We've got about sixty kids, and there's not enough time to give them the individual attention they need." Since the school was going to do a pilot iPad adoption anyway, McCabe suggested using iPads in AP History and linking them to digital tutoring. "We recruited about sixty adult tutors, and each provides an hour of feedback a week. Students now write essays on a two-week rotating cycle. We've seen a massive improvement in student writing. Since we implemented the program 52 out of the 168 students have scored a 3 or higher on the AP exam. That blows away the results of any other nonselective school in the city." McCabe says, "If we go to our principal with a thought-out idea and roadmap of the costs, he's likely to make it happen."

Teachers can do more than they think to shape how their schools and systems approach technology. Cage-busters know the drill: identify problems, offer solutions, be concrete, and get colleagues on board. Meanwhile, millions of teachers are using free new digital tools like MasteryConnect, ClassDojo, LearnZillion, and EdModo that can help with formative assessment, classroom management, lesson planning, and instructional support. The cool thing is that once enough teachers in a school or district start tapping into a technology, they can bring leaders along for a ride. Tom Vander Ark, founder of Getting Smart, says, "There's a tipping point with these free providers. Once you get about 40 percent of teachers in a district using something, it's easy for the leadership to get behind it. We've seen that in a bunch of districts. The district will start to support it, to buy premium services that let teachers access data and use additional features." When cage-busters think these tools have promise, they encourage and organize their colleagues to help that process along. As always, there's strength in numbers.

Now, it's sometimes suggested that embracing the possibilities of educational technology (or seeking more efficient use of teacher time) is somehow anti-teacher. That seems a strange stance. After all, is it anti-doctor to support the use of X-ray machines? More generally, recall what AFT's iconic president Al Shanker said on the subject of technology a quarter-century ago: "What we need to do in schools is go through a process of rethinking . . . Schools need no longer assume that the only way to learn is through lecture and blackboard. Students can learn through a video-tape, audiotape, computer, an older student or a community volunteer."[24] Technology allows us to rethink how educators teach. The question for the cage-buster is whether teachers will be leading that effort, or complaining that policy makers, vendors, and reformers are making a hash of it.

PUTTING THE MEDIA TO GOOD USE

When teachers speak up about problems, solutions, and professional responsibility, they can use media to amplify their message. Engaging the media or writing for public outlets isn't as difficult as you might think. Truth is, the media is hungry for teacher voices. Stefani Cook, a business education teacher in Rigby, Idaho, recalls sitting on a panel on the Common Core for the local media. Afterward, she relates, a local TV reporter said he was glad to have a teacher contact and asked if he could call her in the future. She muses, "So often, teachers are not at the table for decisions . . . just because people don't know whom to invite."

The media can also help mobilize the public to defend and sustain programs you have built. Tammy Laughner says that the first time the district tried to cut funding for key personnel in her Project RESTORE, Matt Tully, the local reporter who had penned a five-part feature on it for the *Indianapolis Star*, tweeted about it. Laughner says, "Immediately, a bunch of people in the city got on Tully's bandwagon. They started flooding downtown with calls, saying, 'Why are you messing with this program?' And one of the assistant superintendents said, 'I don't know what these guys want but let's give it to them.' And we got it."

Blogs, social media, newspapers, radio, and TV can serve as valuable platforms. Alex Fuentes, a biology teacher at Cesar Chavez High School in Washington, DC, grew vexed with the high rate of teacher turnover at her school and the message from leadership that retention was a problem for school leaders to solve, not teachers. After Teach Plus training helped her see the media "as an avenue for teacher voice," she decided to take her concerns public. She drafted an op-ed for the *Huffington Post*. Knowing this could be sensitive, she first shared the piece with her principal and CEO. They read it and told her to go ahead. The piece prompted the school to start convening teacher forums and to establish a teacher advisory committee on boosting retention. She made it easy for her principal to be supportive, and her principal responded in kind.

Indeed, established teacher-writers I've spoken to, including *Education Week* bloggers Justin Minkel, Larry Ferlazzo, and Marilyn Rhames, say they haven't had any significant grief from administrators—despite penning regular, widely read, and sometimes controversial commentary. Rhames even tells of becoming friendly with the former superintendent of the Chicago Public Schools because he reached out after reading what she had to say. Teachers who publish informed, reasoned commentary have few horror stories and report that it can do more to open doors than they had ever imagined.

Brian Crosby, the English teacher in Glendale, California, whom we met in chapter 2, has penned two books and writes a column in his local paper. He shares some hard-won wisdom: "I try not to be acrimonious. If I'm sitting across from someone, and they're using untethered rhetoric, I don't respect them. I wouldn't listen. It can be a hard line, but I'm careful not to overdo the hyperbole or to come across as a mealymouthed politician type who says nice things that don't mean much." It can be a tough balancing act, but that's a tone that'll get you heard. (For more advice on all this, see "Making the Media Work for You.")

PROVIDING LEADERSHIP THAT MATTERS

Teacher leadership is not necessarily cage-busting. And it can be terrific even when it isn't. But a cage-busting mind-set equips teacher leaders to do more than help their colleagues be slightly better denizens of the cage.

Teacher leadership often feels more like a burden than a boon because leaders wind up with more on their plates and little to show for it. Opportunities to sit on important committees or to advocate for policy change can provide an exciting opportunity to be heard, but they also mean more

Making the Media Work for You

In *The Teacher of the Year Handbook: The Ultimate Guide to Making the Most of Your Teacher-Leader Role*, Alex Kajitani, the 2009 California Teacher of the Year, offers a slew of tips that can help any teacher leader.[25] Kajitani has achieved national acclaim for his Rappin' Mathematician persona and has cropped up everywhere, including the *CBS Evening News*. His smart suggestions include good advice on how to leverage the media.

He writes that teachers might not believe that the local news cares about their work, but "the media love a good education story! You know that little spot at the end of the evening news, where they plug in something uplifting or inspiring each night? Yep, they are looking for people just like us to fill that spot!" He says that connecting with the media "is not as intimidating as it sounds." He recommends getting the names of education reporters for local newspapers, radio, and TV stations and "drop[ping] them a note to introduce yourself and to offer a story suggestion. I've found that when I'm sincere about the work I'm doing—and keep my focus on the work, rather than on me—reporters have been friendly and responsive."

For teachers ready to take this on, Kajitani offers some tips to help look and sound like a pro.

- Less is more. Keep things clear and on point.
- Match your wardrobe to your message. He admonishes, "If we want to be paid and respected as professionals in society, we can do our part to show them that we *are* professionals."
- Do your homework.
- Always, *always* ask for a copy of the video or segment once you're finished. Kajitai advises, "Be sure to watch it, share, and send the producer a thank you note!"
- Smile!
- Speak in soundbytes. He writes, "Keeping your answers short and simple is the key to sounding great. Remember: *EVERYTHING you say is 'on the record.' If you don't want it broadcast or printed, don't say it.*"
- Connect. Kajitani writes, "If possible, get to know the person who will be interviewing you on camera before the cameras are rolling."

- Be real. He advises, "When you speak, the goal is to be confident and articulate, but not every word that you utter will be beautiful and profound. Be the person that you are: authentic, real and realistic."

  Savvy cage-busters know that, for most teachers, social media is a lot more important than television. Kajitani urges teachers to create blogs or contribute to sites such as the the *Huffington Post,* AOL's *Patch,* Examiner.com, *Edutopia,* or *Education Week* but also cautions teachers to think about their image when posting—all good advice, whether you're focused on your neighborhood or your nation.

work. Significantly, they may not lead to the kinds of concrete in-school changes that directly repay teachers for their time, passion, and energy.

It's natural for teachers to want to take on roles where they can offer lawmakers advice on teacher evaluation or the Common Core. And doing so is good and sensible, so long as you remember that cage-busters focus more on solving concrete problems than on abstract debates. Cage-busters start with what's in front of them—time that's wasted, meetings that demoralize, PD that's pointless, and parents who aren't engaged. They begin by problem solving at their school. When told that some problems can't be solved at the school, they ask, "Why not?" If they have to, they then try to solve those problems at the district.

When problems are supposedly beyond the district's reach, they ask for proof. If the obstacles are real, they start thinking about state and federal regulations and policies. This does three useful things. One, it ensures that teachers are talking to the people who can actually solve the problem. Two, it helps them make sure that they know precisely what problem they're hoping to solve and what they'd like someone to do. And three, it means that each exertion on their part is about solving a real problem and isn't just in service of someone else's grand agenda.

6

The Union Question

The teachers unions have more influence over the public schools than any other group in American society. They influence schools from the bottom up, through collective bargaining activities that shape virtually every aspect of school organization. And they influence schools from the top down, through political activities that shape government policy. They are the 800-pound gorillas of public education.

—TERRY MOE, *Wall Street Journal*

It is not in the interest of [union] members to have incompetent teachers in their midst, passing along poorly educated students to the next teacher.

—DIANE RAVITCH, *The Death and Life of the Great American School System*

IT CAN BE TOUGH to broach the union question without getting sidetracked. Teacher unions are a lightning rod. Defenders argue that unions are unfairly maligned and denounce critics as enemies of public education. Meanwhile, union critics attack teacher unions as political strongmen who defend sexual predators and care mostly about membership dues. Indeed, when Rod Paige was U.S. Secretary of Education, in a moment of frustration, he denounced the teacher unions as "terrorist organizations." Happily, the cage-buster need not wade into this broader debate. Cage-busters can like or loathe unions. What matters more is that teacher unions are a powerful force that can reinforce the cage—or be used to bust it. Cage-busters leave the grand pronouncements to others and focus on the concrete changes that help create the schools and unions they desire.

Maddie Fennell puts it well. She argues, "You need union leaders who are there for problem solving rather than the comfort of adults." Fortunately, this approach is more feasible today than the headlines might lead you to believe. If you back away from the heated politics, broad points of agreement are clear. After all, in 2011 the NEA's influential Commission on Effective Teachers and Teaching endorsed peer evaluation to expedite the dismissal of ineffective teachers, said seniority should not be the determining factor in teacher retention, and called for differentiating compensation.[1] AFT president Randi Weingarten says, "Tenure, done right, is a tool for teachers to be able to stand up for children and exercise judgment. It's a tool to attract and retain the best and brightest so that they can take the educational risks needed to create great schools. But we need to fix what's broken. Tenure is not supposed to be a job for life, a cloak for incompetence, or an excuse for managers not to manage."

Meanwhile, in 2014 the influential "reform" organization TNTP, which has been a leading champion of increased teacher accountability, rejected calls to abolish tenure. In *Rebalancing Teacher Tenure: A Post-Vergara Guide for Policymakers*, TNTP argues, "Many people view changes to teacher tenure as a choice between two extremes: keep existing laws exactly as they are or get rid of tenure entirely. We think that's a false choice." TNTP recommends lengthening the tryout period for teachers, linking tenure to performance, focusing tenure hearings on student interests, and ceasing to tolerate egregious misconduct.[2] Democrats for Education Reform (DFER) has been deemed anti-union, but DFER president Joe Williams has argued, "We don't think teacher unions are going anywhere. Nor should they . . . From coast to coast we have seen so many poorly-run public school systems with obnoxious, buzz-kill bureaucracies that we are often thankful that someone is on the ground making sure teachers don't get screwed by the public education machinery."[3]

Surveying all of this, a cage-buster sees plenty of common sense and common ground. He wonders how the sensible mass of teachers has allowed discussions about tenure, pay, evaluation, and the rest to get hijacked by extremists. The answer: educators didn't address concerns, lawmakers responded with clumsy tools, disgruntled educators lashed out in anger, and things cartwheeled out of control. Cage-busters have the power to turn this around because they know a potent secret: unions are ultimately what teachers make them.

TEACHER UNIONS 101

Most of the nation's 3.5 million teachers belong to a union. The two major teacher unions in the United States are the National Education Association and the American Federation of Teachers. The unions negotiate for teachers on issues of salary, benefits, and working conditions; advocate on policy; and provide members with services like professional development and legal protection. Twenty-six states are "closed shop" and require educators to be part of the teacher union in order to teach; twenty-four states have right-to-work laws that make membership optional.[4]

Founded in 1857, the NEA has 3.2 million members nationwide. Besides teachers, the membership includes administrators, higher education faculty and staff, education support professionals, and retired educators. The NEA is governed by a Representative Assembly that consists of more than nine thousand delegates elected by local and state affiliates. The delegates are responsible for electing the organization's executive officers. The NEA, headquartered in Washington, DC, has term limits, ensuring that no president can serve more than six years.

The AFT, an affiliate of the AFL-CIO, has 1.5 million members. Founded in 1916, the AFT is concentrated most heavily in northeastern cities, including New York City, Washington, DC, Chicago, New Haven, and Baltimore. In addition to teachers, AFT members include paraprofessionals and school-related personnel, higher education faculty and staff, government employees, and health-care employees. Also headquartered in Washington, DC, the AFT's leadership includes a president, secretary-treasurer, executive vice president, and a forty-three-member executive council.

Between them, the NEA and AFT generate more than $2 billion per year in revenue, with most of that coming from membership dues.[5] Those resources have permitted both unions to be powerful political players. The NEA and the AFT consistently rank among the nation's most influential unions and among the biggest donors to political candidates.[6]

Besides the NEA and AFT, there also exist a number of smaller unions and teacher associations. For instance, the Texas Classroom Teachers Association (TCTA) represents fifty thousand teachers and educational staff across Texas. The TCTA and similar groups in other states provide professional services and legal protections without engaging in the broader activities or policy advocacy of the AFT or the NEA. There are also local-only teacher unions across the country. The Roscommon Teachers Association is one such example, having decertified from Michigan's NEA affiliate and recertified as a local union.

HOW WE GOT HERE

Teacher unions, as we know them today, have not always been with us. Back in the nineteenth century the NEA was a professional association and its membership included administrators and supervisors. Indeed, it wasn't until the 1960s that the NEA first started to operate as a recognizable union. That was in response to the AFT's success at collective bargaining. The pivotal moment occurred in 1960, when a United Federation of Teachers (UFT) strike prompted New York City mayor Robert Wagner to let teachers collectively bargain (meaning their union could bargain with the district to set wages, benefits, and working conditions on behalf of the teachers).

Until the 1960s, districts had generally enjoyed a free hand in setting teacher compensation and work conditions. Without legally enforceable contracts, teachers lacked protection against administrator favoritism and abuse. And administrators did some truly awful stuff. They engaged in personnel practices that would be illegal under today's equal employment opportunity laws, including plenty of cases where administrators blatantly discriminated on the basis of gender, race, religion, and marital status.

Unions tackled the worst abuses around work conditions, due process, benefits, and more, claiming a series of big wins in the late 1960s and early 1970s. By the mid-1970s, with nearly 90 percent of teachers in either the NEA or the AFT, teaching had become America's most unionized occupation. Harvard University professor Jal Mehta has noted that "wages, pensions, and benefits did improve but at a cost to their [teachers'] professional self-image and moral power." The result, Mehta says, is that teachers came to be seen as one more "interest group."[7]

In a famed 1985 speech, AFT president Al Shanker presciently argued that if teachers were seen as an interest group, they'd pay for it. He told the New York State United Teachers, "Collective bargaining has been a good mechanism, and we should continue to use it. But now we must ask whether collective bargaining will get us where we want to go." He called for new steps, including the creation of a national exam to limit entry into the profession, giving students more freedom to choose their public school, having impartial panels of teachers to judge colleagues accused of incompetence, creating career ladders, and restructuring schools so as to better attract talented new teachers into the profession.[8]

Shanker biographer Richard Kahlenberg recounts Shanker's belief that "just as the AFT had revolutionized teaching by introducing collective bargaining 25 years earlier, it was now time for a 'Second Revolution,' in which teachers would 'take a step beyond collective bargaining' to improve education. 'Limiting action to collective bargaining made teachers appear unprofessional,' [Shanker] said. 'We tend to be viewed today as though we are acting only in our own self-interest, wanting better salaries and smaller classes so our lives can be made easier. That image is standing in the way of our achieving professional status.'"[9]

This is a sensitive subject, so let's be clear. Plenty of policies governing teacher tenure, pay, and work requirements may have made sense when they were adopted decades ago. But that doesn't mean they necessarily make sense today. Cage-busters judge arrangements with fresh eyes and a precise, practical focus on solving problems. They look skeptically at assertions that a given idea is "pro-teacher" or "anti-teacher." Instead, they assess proposed changes to tenure, evaluation, or pay by asking whether they will help attract, retain, and support terrific educators. They look at old norms governing seniority, teacher roles, or the school day to see if altering them will help teachers make better, smarter use of their time, passion, and energy.

UNIONS AREN'T MONOLITHIC

Unions are not monolithic. They can vary dramatically from one place to the next.

Unions can play a constructive role. Dan Montgomery, head of the Illinois Federation of Teachers, points to his time at Niles Township High School as an example of what unions can do. Montgomery says, "Niles has produced three Nobel Prize winners. Superintendents came and went, but the stabilizing force was a strong union and a united, hard-working faculty. Pretty much every significant committee includes a majority of teachers. Teachers have power and act responsibly." When there was a burst of plagiarism, they "adopted a simple policy that held teachers accountable if they didn't spot it. There was a cultural cohesion that had a lot to do with the union."

Unions can also play a destructive role. David Upegui teaches science at Central Falls High School in Rhode Island. An alum of Central Falls, Upegui had been pursuing a PhD in epidemiology at Brown University when he earned a teaching credential, tutored students, and was recruited to teach at his alma mater. He tells of how on his first day, at a schoolwide meeting, the union president said, "We don't believe this man deserves a classroom here because he didn't go through the same hiring process as everyone else." Upegui had two students win gold medals in the Rhode Island College Science Olympiad, and he earned an Amgen Award for Science Teaching Excellence (which netted the school a $10,000 grant). None of that placated the union leadership, which continued to harass him. Upegui says, "I had a hard time transitioning from Brown, where I was expected to do great work, to a place where the union defended and perpetuated mediocrity. I keep thinking, 'If you stand in front of a chalkboard every day and don't do what you're supposed to be doing, you shouldn't be teaching,' but this is the stuff the union defends."

Even when unions seek to be constructive, there are practical challenges. Elizabeth Evans, who served as director of the Illinois Network of Charter Schools before founding VIVA Teachers, says, "I work with some unions that are definitely interested in investing in professional practice as well as their members' workplace concerns. But realities require that they're set up for collective bargaining first . . . So this turns into that telephone game, where you start with a message that makes sense, and by the time it gets to a teacher, it's incendiary or irrelevant or simply never gets there."

The bottom line, argues the AFT's Rob Weil, is that unions are not all the same: "There's a lot of variation in [union] locals. There are places where the union and district are working together well, and there are places where they are beating the hell out of each other." Jason Kamras, the chief of human capital for District of Columbia Public Schools, agrees. He says, "Every city has a unique dynamic. In some places, unions are a significant obstacle to change. In others, they're indispensable partners."

Cage-busters eschew sweeping generalizations, recognizing instead that unions are ultimately what members choose to make them. NEA vice president Becky Pringle says, "When I talk with members who've run into resistance from their local leadership, my advice is to learn how that organization operates and how you can influence it." Cage-busters embrace Pringle's advice. Then, if disappointed by the results, they explore their options.

AREN'T UNION LEADERS ENEMIES OF CAGE-BUSTING?

Precision matters. Cage-busters reject both vague assurances that union leaders are eager to do what's best for students and claims that they don't care about the kids. Cage-busters find it far more useful to think of union leaders the same way they think about school leaders or policy makers—as people who face a lot of demands but may well prove reasonable if given a chance.

Teacher complaints about union leaders can sound a lot like those they voice about administrators. Arielle Zurzolo is an executive director with the teacher-led group Teach Plus, a former charter school union leader, and a liaison on a Teach Plus-NEA partnership. She observes, "The NEA is so siloed within its own organization. There's an unwritten code of whom you can talk to and how you can reach out to them. There are just these hierarchical structures and power dynamics that are nearly impossible to navigate." It's no surprise that teachers can get frustrated dealing with this.

Meanwhile, union leaders can sound like frustrated superintendents when they say they're eager to hear from members who may be reluctant to speak up. AFT president Randi Weingarten says, "A lot of people feel helpless, up and down the line. Just get involved. Just do something. Sometimes it's the baby steps and simply creating trust. The problem is that when people do finally decide to step forward, they often start with what's wrong and what they don't like, as opposed to finding common ground."

Right or wrong, NEA and AFT leaders feel like their organizations have changed substantially in recent years. Segun Eubanks, director of teacher quality for the NEA, says, "The change at the NEA has been significant. There's now a broad understanding that teacher voice and teacher accomplishment ought to go together. Ten years ago, we couldn't have had a productive partnership with Teach Plus and some of these other organizations. The world has changed and unions need to change with it. There's more recognition that 'We must embrace the fact that teachers are differentially effective.' That can seem matter-of-fact to outsiders. But some of us are like, 'Wait a minute. That's a big change.'" AFT's assistant to the president for educational issues, Marla Ucelli-Kashyap, says, "We polled our members and they told us the number-one thing they want is help doing their job better. The union has to be that professional support. Yes, you want someone to advocate for your rights and defend you if you're wrongly accused. But professionals want to be good at what they do and recognized for their work. So, much of what we're doing now is helping provide teachers with what they need to be more effective."

The notion that things may be changing gets some support from Matt Kramer, co-CEO of Teach For America. For a long time, says Kramer, few TFA alumni showed much interest when it came to leading within teachers unions. More recently, though, he says, "We've started to see promising stories of TFA members and alumni getting involved. Unions have an important role to play, but it is critical that teachers get involved so that the union can represent the perspectives of the large majority of teachers. When our people get involved, they see the ways they can make a difference, they step up, and we're seeing changes. The unions have been held captive by a fringe element. But that's changing in some places."

In 2014 the teachers at UNO charter schools in Chicago voted to unionize. Larry Campbell became the first president of the newly formed United Educators at UNO, an affiliate of Chicago's Alliance of Charter Teachers and Staff union. He recalls, "We went around talking to teachers and asking them what they wanted. Sure, they wanted the basic stuff, like pay and working conditions. But far more important to them was the stuff that would help them advance professionally—to have the opportunity to act and be recognized as professionals." With that in mind, he says, "Our union charter created a 'solutions committee'—a joint teacher-management committee that promotes a collaborative solutions-oriented relationship. It offers a forum for teachers to talk to management about things we wanted to work on but didn't want to bring to the bargaining table or file a grievance over. A good example is our curriculum mapping. If it had happened a few years ago, the administration would just have given us a new curriculum. But we had this forum and teachers who wanted to design their curriculum, and the administration was happy to collaborate. There's a lot of stuff that teachers and management have in common," he says, and the solutions committee seeks to make it easier to tackle those shared concerns.

In 2012, policy think tank Education Sector reported that 43 percent of teachers thought unions should boost their focus on "teacher quality and student achievement," up from 32 percent five years earlier.[10] But most teachers still wanted their unions to "stick to traditional union issues such as protecting teachers' salaries, benefits, and jobs." Moreover, whatever teachers want, they're not yet seeing evidence that unions have successfully taken up the cause of professionalism. While 70 percent or more think unions protect teachers from being unfairly fired and that they effectively negotiate salaries and benefits, less than half think unions provide support to new teachers, keep teachers updated on instruction and curriculum, or provide high-quality training.[11]

Cage-busters see great opportunity in the chasm between what unions *can* do and what teachers often see their unions doing today. If unions are to embrace a different mind-set and role, it's up to cage-busters to make that happen.

WHY MESS WITH THE UNION AT ALL?

Unions are the primary vehicle for voicing teacher concerns and influencing policy. Trying to discuss educational practice or teacher empowerment without talking about the union is like discussing the beach without mentioning the ocean.[12] Jennifer Martin, an English teacher in Montgomery County, Maryland, has observed that she needed to engage in her local union in order "to have any real impact on the issues."[13] At the same time, unions have incentives to steer away from issues that divide members and toward those (like benefits and working conditions) on which there is broad agreement. Unions are also usually dominated by their veteran members. This tends to make unions fairly reactive, focused on protecting teachers from disruption. But it doesn't have to be that way.

As the University of Pennsylvania's Richard Ingersoll observes, "There's no reason why unions couldn't get out front on proposing models of pay-for-performance that work. Teachers aren't lockstep against factoring performance into compensation. But most of what policy makers and reformers put out there isn't even intelligent. When I say this at NEA or AFT leadership meetings, they kind of wince—but they're also open to it. They're just cautious, and for good reason. They've seen a century of dubious efforts. That's where I'd love to see some cage-busting union leadership. But remember that leaders follow the membership in any democratic organization. They can lead, but they need members who want them to lead." Teachers need to demand *and support* cage-busting union leadership.

Unions have the resources to identify and cultivate talent and bring people into leadership and policy roles. In 2011, the AFT launched the Teacher Leaders Program, which identifies and trains participating teachers to take a more active role in their schools, unions, and communities. It began as a pilot program in five communities and by 2014 had expanded to roughly twenty districts. The program provides orientation and support for interested locals, including technical assistance and stipends for participating teachers.

The NEA has launched a handful of teacher leadership and teacher voice initiatives. In 2014, the NEA, along with the Center for Teaching Quality (CTQ) and the National Board for Professional Teaching Standards, launched a pilot Teacher Leadership Initiative in six states. Much of the program takes place online over CTQ's virtual Collaboratory. The NEA is also engaged in a leadership training and partnership program with Teach Plus in the Future of the Profession Fellowship. In that effort, about fifty teachers a year are selected and given the chance to learn about advocacy and interact with policy makers through gatherings in Washington, DC, and monthly Web-based trainings. The program culminates with the fellows briefing NEA leaders on their recommendations regarding the future of the union and the profession.

Unions have the muscle, money, and members to make things happen. The NEA's longtime contract guru Bill Raabe says that when it comes to bad professional development, "unions can demand the kind of PD that makes a difference. I tell unions to come to [the national NEA] and seek money in order to show districts what good PD looks like. If teachers aren't getting it from their district, have your local go to the national and see if someone can help you design your own plan. There's nothing to stop unions from using dues money to provide PD. In fact, unions can go to the district and offer a deal—they'll take responsibility for the district's professional development and be responsible for the results."

A compelling illustration of union influence is the role that the AFT's Al Shanker played in launching the charter school movement. Believing that schooling needed to shed the factory model if teachers were to be regarded as more than assembly line workers, he first presented his vision of charter schools in 1988 in a landmark address at the National Press Club. In speeches and articles that followed, Shanker envisioned groups of teachers proposing research-based school designs. If approved by boards composed of school board and union officials, the teachers would be empowered to launch their own schools. The Citizen's League in Minnesota ran with the idea, and in 1991 the first charter law was enacted in Minnesota.[14] More prosaically, in 2011 researchers Saul Avery Rubinstein and John McCarthy examined six districts where collaboration with AFT affiliates had preceded sizable academic gains. They observed that, in most cases, the collaboration had received assistance from the AFT's Center for School Improvement, leadership training at AFT's Union Leadership Institute, or support from the AFT's biannual QuEST conference.[15]

Since 2009 the AFT's Innovation Fund has invested in dozens of projects across the country. Investments have included ShareMyLesson.com, a hugely successful online platform that allows teachers to share and access lesson plans. The Fund has supported the creation of a Minneapolis charter school authorizer, giving teachers the chance to put the autonomy and power of chartering to work. Ann Bradley, who runs the fund, says, "Our efforts are collaborative with the districts. These are systems that are trapped by practices—by things that are just habit." The Innovation Fund has the dollars and muscle to push beyond those habits.

"Unions are democratic organizations," says Paul Toner, who served two terms as president of the Massachusetts Teachers Association (MTA). "If members aren't happy with what the union is doing, they should try to get elected. Then they'll control the tools, power, and capacity that unions have and can use them to do what they think is right." When you walk away in frustration, you leave the machinery to those who remain behind.

TRUST IS EARNED, NOT GIVEN

Cage-busters know that influence depends on trust and that unions are sorely lacking on that score. The AFT's Rob Weil puts it bluntly: "Respect and trust is stuff that's earned, it's not given. That's a hard lesson for a lot of people to learn. They want you to trust me first, and then I'll do it. We have a system that hasn't embraced teacher leadership. Teachers in schools today mostly don't understand what leadership means or the responsibility that comes with it. We have to say we want the respect and the accountability that comes along with it." Utah's Sharon Gallagher-Fishbaugh explains that, as a union president, "To talk effectively about your concerns, you have to acknowledge culpability for some problems. And certainly the unions have some culpability."

Trust is earned by demonstrating a good-faith commitment to addressing problems. Gallagher-Fishbaugh reflects, "It's so frustrating when I hear people say, 'You can't trust teachers to evaluate teachers because they will just give them passing marks.' The research shows that, in peer-to-peer evaluations, the educators are harder on each other than administrators are." The consequence of accumulated distrust is a public perception that teachers are soft on their peers. Changing that starts with action.

Montgomery County, Maryland, provides a terrific example of how this can work. With 144,000 students and a reputation for excellence, Montgomery County is generally recognized as a pretty terrific place for both students and educators.[16] In the late 1990s, Mark Simon, then the president of the Montgomery County Education Association, and superintendent Jerry Weast designed and implemented Montgomery County's heralded peer assistance and review (PAR) program (see "Montgomery County's PAR Program").

CONTRACTS CAN BE MORE FLEXIBLE THAN YOU THINK

Over the years, books like *United Mind Workers* have made the case for more flexible, professional contracts.[17] The challenge is that contracts, like policy, are generally the product of distrust, and it's hard to change the contracts before building that trust. As Maddie Fennell says, "We write one-size-fits-all contracts, often because someone's doing something wrong and we write the contract to stop that. Most teachers don't understand why that language is in there. They just say that it doesn't make any sense. And nobody ever teaches 'The History of Why Language Is in the Contract.' So we get stuck."

When parties don't trust each other, it's natural to write in language that the other guy will have trouble sidestepping. Thus, contracts include work rules that govern the number of minutes that teachers can be required to work with students, the number of students a teacher will instruct, when and how teachers will submit lesson plans, and directives

Montgomery County's PAR Program

For over a decade, Montgomery County, Maryland, has assigned every new teacher to its peer assistance and review (PAR) program. Veteran teachers can be referred by their principal. If a principal refers a teacher, an evaluator visits the campus, talks to the principal and the teacher, observes the teacher, and recommends whether intervention is appropriate. Doug Prouty, president of the Montgomery County Education Association (MCEA), says that most referrals lead to teachers being enrolled in PAR. Teachers are not allowed to appeal a referral.

PAR teachers are assigned a consulting teacher. Selected through a competitive process, consulting teachers spend three years, full-time, in the role. After their term, they return to their school-based assignment. PAR is overseen by a panel of eight principals and eight teachers; it's chaired by the vice president of the MCEA and the vice president of the principals' association.

The sticky part is that teachers are evaluating peers with an eye toward their potential dismissal. "But we don't have too many qualms about that," says Prouty, because PAR ensures that teachers are no longer entirely at the mercy of their administrator. When the PAR panel reviews each case, Prouty says, "there are two sets of data to look at. Those data are most often in agreement, but even when they're not, the process is fairer and more transparent."

Annually, about 750 teachers are involved in PAR. About 600 of those are new hires, and another 100–150 have been referred for underperformance. In a given year, the panel typically recommends about 40–70 teachers for dismissal. Most of those are new teachers, but 10 or more are typically probationary or tenured. While tenured teachers can appeal to the school board, the state board, and even the state court of appeals, the PAR panel has never had a dismissal overturned. Prouty notes that another 25–30 veteran teachers quit each year when informed they're being referred to PAR. The process moves quickly enough that determinations are made by May 1, encouraging teachers facing dismissal to retire or make a move, thereby avoiding drawn-out conflict or formal school board action.

Prouty says, "In some places, union members say they'll never accept this. They see it as a dereliction of duty by the union. We tell them that we've seen positive results in student achievement and that teachers, even if not renewed or dismissed, get the support they need. It helps members decide whether the choice to become a teacher was the right one."

PAR has helped MCEA build its relationship with the district and earn a hearing on other fronts. Superintendent Josh Starr says, "PAR has been a foundation of our evaluation system. We collaborate with our union, especially on the thing that's most important, which is who's in front of our kids. That trust extends to other areas of our work with the union. Within six months of my being here, the union president said we needed to incorporate student surveys into teacher evaluations. I said, 'Great . . . I don't need to figure out workarounds.'" That's how teachers get input on the front end.

Prouty says, "In terms of selling this to members, most know, in their building, one or two teachers who aren't doing what they need to do. If you're a third grade teacher and you know a second grade teacher isn't doing what she should be, it means you have to work harder and can be blamed for what children didn't learn." He says, "There are still teachers in my membership who think the job of the union is to protect you no matter what, but they're fairly rare at this point."

Action changes culture. After more than a decade of PAR, most teachers have gone through it or grown accustomed to it—and the district's culture reflects that reality. Prouty says, "By taking responsibility for the quality of teaching and learning, we benefit. We're seen as accountable professionals, like doctors. It's clear that we're not in the business of protecting someone just because the school system hired them."

PAR is a case of putting the power of the union to good use. "To a certain extent," says Prouty, "you have to approach your union by assuming that people want to do the right thing. That's usually true. If you find an issue that is meaningful, work together on it and solve it; it builds a level of trust between the union and the system. That lets you do more and more together."

regarding everything from bulletin boards to Hepatitis B immunizations. The result has left both teachers and administrators feeling stymied. This is aggravated because, amidst the pile of particulars, there's often uncertainty about exactly what contract language means or requires. The result is that people feel tripped up not only by the actual contract but by what they *think it means* or *have heard that it says.*

Cage-busters don't allow themselves to be stopped by rumors or assumptions. If someone claims that the contract prohibits something, ask them to point out the relevant language. If they can't, the contract does *not* prohibit it. Even if they *can* find relevant language, don't take their interpretation as the last word. As Lori Nazareno pointed out a few chapters back, Denver's contract restricted the number of minutes a teacher could teach a week—but not in a given day. Bill Raabe, NEA's longtime director of collective bargaining, explains, "Often what people think is in the contract isn't there. People just don't realize what they can do. They often believe the contract says more than it does."

Even when contracts have restrictions, Raabe says, "it's often an urban legend that, if we look to do something different from what the contract says, the union will stand in the way. The first thing that teachers need to do is assume that the union and district will support good ideas, rather than assume they'll get in the way. Instead of focusing on a strategy or what's possible, teachers will just say, 'We've seen that our union or our district doesn't have any flexibility around X.'"

Raabe says teachers vastly underestimate the opportunity for faculty at a given school to waive provisions from the master contract: "Some contracts specifically allow teachers at a school to waive provisions if a sufficient number want to. When contracts don't have any waiver language, most people think that they're stuck. In my view, it's just the opposite. If waivers aren't addressed in the contract, presume they're possible. If a group of teachers at a building gets together and wants to do something that only affects their campus, the union will usually support waiving it."

Moreover, teachers don't need to regard existing waiver opportunities as a given. For instance, the 2012 contract negotiated in Newark, New Jersey, made it possible for teachers to waive almost anything in the contract with a vote of 51 percent of the faculty at a school. The waivers require a sign-off from the principal, superintendent, and union president, but they make it easy for a simple majority of teachers to enlist a coalition of the willing. Any district could adopt that kind of waiver language—if teachers push for it. District leaders certainly have no reason to object.

"Now, it's different if teachers want to do something like modify transfer policies," explains Raabe, "because that affects other schools. But things that only affect PD, time, curriculum, how you assign teachers within your school . . . those are the kinds of things you clearly can waive irrespective of whether contract language explicitly allows you to. The truth is you can waive anything if the district and union agree. I'd advise teachers in schools who say, 'We want to do this but the contract doesn't say we can'—I'd tell them, 'Put together your rationale, what you want to do, the difference it'll make for practice and for kids, and make the case to the union and the district."

PUSHING THE UNION FROM THE INSIDE

Union leaders are elected. This means they need to heed the views of voting members. Cage-busters hoping to push the union need the strength of numbers if they're to succeed. As our friend Maddie Fennell notes, "When you push on the union as an individual, it's very, very, very difficult to win. Union leaders won't move on something one teacher wants but will move on things a group of teachers or a building wants."

Former Massachusetts Teachers Association president Paul Toner says, "A lot of younger or new members who support reasonable change often tell me they feel like the union leadership isn't representing their views, or that their local or state association is standing in their way. I always tell them, 'You should be running for union office.' You can complain about the union, but it's a democratic organization. Right now, by not participating actively, they're ceding the field to the angry people. To be a leader, you have to show up—to the debates and the votes."

Toner explains how he won elections by 2-to-1 margins even as he won plaudits from outsiders for being forward thinking. He says, "On teacher evaluation, we engaged our board and members and used member polling to develop a proactive, sensible evaluation framework that was not all about test scores. We went around the state meeting people, working the press, and forging good relationships with policy makers, legislators, and superintendents. I had that polling data and one-to-one conversations with members, so I knew that it wasn't just me off by myself but that the members were with me."

Toner recalls that the MTA leadership was ready to oppose a statewide initiative that would limit seniority-based layoffs—until they saw that 75 percent of members agreed that performance should count for more than seniority. He asks, "Why would we spend millions fighting an initiative that most of our members didn't oppose?" The union went to the table and negotiated a legislative compromise. Because Toner supported the principle of teacher evaluation, the MTA got a big say in its design, yielding a model that both teachers and "reformers" have generally lauded. He says, "We had polling data from the NEA showing that most teachers think student performance should be a part of the evaluation of teachers but that it shouldn't be *the* measure. So we negotiated that." When unions embrace the principle that performance matters, they wind up with a big say in *how* things are done. And, as noted earlier, when it comes to schooling, it's usually the *how* that matters most. (See "Rock the Union" for a nice example of pushing the union from the inside.)

DON'T BE AFRAID TO CHALLENGE THE UNION

I frequently hear from teachers who feel that the union doesn't reflect their concerns. My question for them is the same one I ask any teacher frustrated by their principal: *What are you doing about it?*

Rock the Union

In 2013 the NEA partnered with Teach Plus to launch the Future of the Profession Fellowship. It's a yearlong program in which fifty teachers are chosen to advise the NEA on how to strengthen participation among newer teachers. The group crafted a document titled "Rock the Union: An Action Plan to Engage Early Career Teachers and Elevate the Profession."[18]

The report urged, "We want the NEA to become the club we want to join . . . We want to know that our union puts students first." The group said the union's priority should be helping teachers answer the question, "How do I become a better teacher and improve my students' learning?" Instead, they lamented, "all too often union meetings, contract policy, newsletters, trainings, and support offered, such as lawyers and grievance advice, do not help us answer this question. In fact, when many of us attend union meetings we don't hear the word 'student' uttered at all."

The group charged, "It is difficult to navigate union structures to figure out where decisions are made or how to participate in areas that match our interests . . . It is unclear how to advocate for change within the union or to use the union as an avenue to advocate for improved change." The group also blasted "a 'wait your turn' mentality that early career teachers often come up against" and lamented that "most of us have experienced our divergent opinions dismissed as wrong and/or naïve."

The fellows sketched some recommendations to the national NEA leadership. They called for "A fair, rigorous evaluation system with teachers leading the process; differentiated compensation; effective, collaborative, and teacher-led professional development; rigorous, selective teacher preparation; and career pathways that acknowledge, celebrate, and reward excellence." The document also recommended five organizational changes to the NEA:

1. Increasing the share of its budget spent "proactively improving teaching and learning" so that it would equal the share "dedicated to defending the union against attacks"
2. Designing programs that would help state and local affiliates identify and support "high-potential union leaders to implement change" that would advance the profession
3. Implementing new governance arrangements that would focus on "early career teachers" and boost the prominence of issues these teachers care about
4. Using technology to "modernize existing processes" by doing things like adopting an "online voting option for elections and contract ratifications"
5. Launching "an integrated 'Rock the Union' communication initiative" to spread the word about "innovative and important NEA initiatives"

You may like these recommendations, or not. But this is what it looks like to push a union from the inside.

Mike Stryer started teaching high school social studies in Los Angeles after nearly two decades in international business. In his second year, when the old union representative resigned, he was elected as a building representative to the United Teachers of Los Angeles (UTLA). Stryer remembers attending his first UTLA governing assembly, expecting to talk about curriculum, assessments, and working conditions. Instead, he says, "we launched deep into a push for a vote to denounce the condition of Bolivian tin miners. Now, I'm sure that's important, especially in Bolivia, but we had a 35 percent dropout rate. It made me realize why a lot of teachers are completely turned off by the union. It didn't represent classroom realities, the needs of teachers, or the needs of students. I tried to stand up and speak, but it was a lonely experience. I knew there were thousands of teachers [who] had my sensibilities and shared my opinions, but I was the only one talking."

Stryer eventually helped launch NewTLA, a group of UTLA members seeking to change the direction of their union. NewTLA recruited teachers to run for the UTLA House of Representatives. Stryer says, "We got 75 teachers who hadn't been involved before to run and get elected." With only 300 teachers in the UTLA House of Reps, the potential impact was significant. NewTLA met fierce pushback, however. Stryer says, "I was called everything under the sun. Folks were saying, 'You have a hidden agenda, you're a privatizer.' Just the other week I was called a 'Kool-Aid-drinking Nazi propagandist.'" Stryer and his colleagues pushed the UTLA to embrace a multiple measures approach to teacher evaluation, incorporating student outcomes. Anticipating a fight, Stryer says, "I studied the contract and the bylaws. It allowed us to bypass the leadership and take a referendum directly to the members if we got 500 members to sign a petition. Few people even knew you could do that. The result would become official policy. So we gathered the signatures and got it approved with 56 percent support. That made it the 'official policy' of the UTLA for negotiations." This isn't pro-union *or* anti-union; it's taking the union as it exists and finding ways to change norms and solve problems.

The great thing about cage-busting is that once you open the cage door, others can follow you through it. The Los Angeles example provided a model in 2012 for a group of Boston Teachers Union members to form BTU Votes and to push to democratize their union. Historically, BTU's bylaws required that teachers had to go downtown to vote in union elections, between 8:00 a.m. and 6:00 p.m. This effectively disenfranchised those who couldn't slip away from school in order to trek across town. One close observer noted that "the people who voted were mostly retirees, because they were the ones with time to get to the union hall during that time." Low turnout allowed a small cluster of veterans to dominate union affairs. BTU Votes pushed to amend union bylaws in order to permit mail-in voting. They needed 10 percent of union members to sign a petition in order to force a vote. BTU Votes recruited one hundred teachers and got one-third of the BTU membership to sign on. On its second try, the proposal got the two-thirds vote required to change the bylaws. Mail-in voting is now routine, boosting participation by more than 15 percent.

Teachers have more power than they may imagine, but they have to use it. Stryer says, "Do your homework. Details matter. When we did the direct initiative, we made sure every little thing was correct so it couldn't be thrown out. Money could have helped, but it wasn't necessary. This was all social media and word of mouth. It really only takes a few people. We were able to do this in *Los Angeles* with a core group of five!"

SOMETIMES YOU NEED TO START YOUR OWN TEAM

Well-intentioned efforts may not be enough. After all, unions are big, stodgy organizations. They can be tough to change. One strategy for doing so is to join other dissatisfied teachers and seek strength in numbers.

Teach Plus

Celine Coggins launched Teach Plus in Boston in 2009 because, she says, "at the time, when we talked about performance-based pay or teacher leadership union leaders could say, 'Teachers don't want that,' as if teachers were monolithic. And no one could really challenge or question them when they said that. I thought it'd make sense to bring teachers together, especially younger teachers, and see what they said."

Teaching in Worcester, Massachusetts, Coggins had been frustrated by the limited opportunities for teachers to grow on the job or to influence big decisions about schooling. Her views solidified during a stint working for the Massachusetts commissioner of education on teacher quality issues. She raised the requisite start-up funds from the Boston Foundation when she argued that "Massachusetts has cornered the market on using research to influence education policy, but what could really boost this work is getting teachers involved." She recalls, "There was huge teacher interest from the outset. We'd targeted sixteen teachers for our policy fellowship and had seventy-five applications after three weeks of word-of-mouth." Coggins says,

> We work between the policy world and the teaching world. We try to help teachers educate themselves on the issues, weigh in, and make sure their opinions are heard. We've got fifty Teach Plus–NEA fellows offering a vision for the future of the profession and of the association. These are voices that can otherwise remain silent because teachers don't know enough about the issues, the process, or how to get heard. We're helping them think about things they can do tomorrow in their union or can introduce at the general assembly if they only collect fifty signatures. We try to help make it clear how to influence their unions and systems . . . When teachers think about unions and city councils, most of them think those are a waste of time and that it's all just talk. Connecting the dots helps them get over that. We allow those teachers who have gotten involved, or run for union office and had the old-guard machine against them, to share their experiences.

Coggins offers an important caution as well: "If you're going to put a bunch of teachers in a room with people who do 'policy,' though, they need to be prepared. Sending teachers in there and saying 'have a voice,' when they don't know the details or understand the context, is a disservice. When teachers are in a meeting with representatives of the U.S. Department of Education to discuss teacher evaluation and a teacher complains, 'I have mold in my classroom,' and we've had that happen, that's a wasted opportunity."

By 2014 there were more than seventeen thousand Teach Plus members in the Teach Plus Network. The network holds events for teachers, hosts webinars, and sponsors national working groups on topics like assessment and teacher pay. Teach Plus also sponsors policy fellows in Boston, Los Angeles, Chicago, Memphis, Washington, DC, and Indianapolis. Coggins says that the goal is to keep fellows focused on "things they can do tomorrow."

Educators 4 Excellence

Educators 4 Excellence (E4E) started in New York City with a handful of teachers tired of feeling ignored by the district and their union. Cofounders Sydney Morris and Evan Stone taught in New York City, in the largest elementary school in the state. Each day, they had an hour-long commute on the 4 train from the East Village up to the school in the North Bronx. During those long train rides, they shared frustrations and discussed what they could do about them. Sounding a theme that's all too familiar, Morris says, "In room 402, I could close the door and focus on my students. In that room, I had lots of responsibility, autonomy, and control. Yet, beyond those four walls I had little say in any decision that affected my students or me as a professional . . . We knew our union was a critical lever for change and so we started by trying to get more involved, but it didn't always seem like there was much opportunity for new ideas or open discussion."

Morris and Stone were moved to start E4E after learning that in the United Federation of Teacher's 2010 leadership election, 40 percent of the votes cast were by retirees and another 25 percent by nonclassroom personnel. "Classroom teachers were actually a minority of the folks who voted!" Morris says, adding, "Only 18 percent of those teachers who could vote actually did vote. We'd hear from colleagues about how incredibly frustrated they were by the conditions of their profession, but they weren't engaging in the most important vehicle for their voices to be heard."

Stone, Morris, and a dozen colleagues regularly met on the weekend, for a beer on Friday or to lesson plan on Saturday. Stone says, "There were four from our school and a few others we knew from Teach For America." The group agreed to pen a declaration of beliefs that became the foundation of E4E. Stone says, "We had teachers from seven or eight schools, some new and some with a decade or more of experience, but we all had the same frustrations: a lack of meaningful feedback, of tools and supports, of aspirational career pathways. The goal was to lay out our visions and beliefs and see if other teachers felt the same way."

The declaration called for a system that "recruits, retains and supports the highest quality teachers" by offering higher starting pay, for "high-level professional development and support," and for "an evenhanded performance-based pay structure to reward excellent teachers." It advocated eliminating "last in, first out" layoffs and ensuring that tenure is a "significant professional milestone." And it demanded "plac[ing] student achievement first" when making decisions about schools or spending.[19]

The reaction was striking. Stone recalls, "We went from a dozen teachers to a few hundred who had signed on pretty quickly. But as we grew, there was also opposition who tried to paint us as 'just a group of young, Teach For America, anti-union teachers.' This was surprising to us, because not only was it not true, but we were active members of the UFT and simply wanted to have productive, forward-thinking conversations with our colleagues and our leaders. At times, it was tough, especially when others engaged in petty attacks . . . But we kept growing because we offered like-minded teachers camaraderie and a safe space for solutions-oriented dialogue. It wasn't one teacher standing up, but many standing together."

By 2014 E4E encompassed more than fifteen thousand teachers across the country and had chapters in New York City, Los Angeles, Chicago, Connecticut, and Minnesota. In addition to its advocacy and policy work, E4E offers a Teacher Leadership Program that enables teachers to learn about education policy, network with colleagues and policy makers, and fight for policy change.

Both Teach Plus and E4E have sometimes been denounced as "anti-union." Cage-busters find that a strange way to describe union members working to change the stance of their union. Unions are what their members make of them. Pushing to change a union's position isn't anti-union; it's what engaged union members are supposed to do.

THERE ARE TIMES TO SEEK ANOTHER WAY

Just as schools or districts may prove recalcitrant no matter how diligently you try to bust that cage, the same can be true of unions. At such times, cage-busters may opt out and choose to seek another way.

The Association of American Educators (AAE) started in 1994 with the goal of being an alternative to the NEA and AFT. The AAE, which has twenty thousand members nationwide, bills itself as "the non-union professional educators' organization." Alexandra Freeze, AAE's senior director of communications and advocacy, says Gary Beckner launched AAE when, in seeking to attract the next generation of teachers to the union, "he found a need for a true professional organization like the American Bar Association. As a competitor to the unions, we offer teachers individual liability insurance, professional development, and legal support, but we don't collectively bargain, have a PAC, or give money to partisan politics."

Larry Sand founded the California Teachers Empowerment Network (CTEN) to offer teachers information independent of what's being offered by unions or districts. Sand started out as a classroom teacher in 1971, got laid off due to a lack of seniority in 1975, worked for Al Shanker, and then returned to teaching in California in the 1980s. He says, "I was always a go-along-to-get-along kind of guy. I was not a cage-busting teacher. But, as time went on, I began seeing more and more that was wrong in the system. I saw bad teachers who couldn't get fired. I saw good teachers being paid less than mediocre teachers. I saw all these stupid policies in place.

"Finally, in 2005," Sand says, "we had a 'paycheck protection' initiative in California." He liked the idea that teachers should have to opt in to contribute the political portion of their union dues. But "that initiative, Prop 75, went down to defeat. It left a bad taste in my mouth. I realized there are a lot of teachers like me who don't like what the associations are doing but that the union activists pretty much have a lock on the union." That same year Sand attended the NEA convention—"It was an eye-opener. There was little room for dissent." Disenchanted, he sought out Gary Beckner, head of the AAE, who helped Sand raise the funds to launch CTEN. Sand recalls, "We got names for our contact lists by sending a letter during the Prop 75 fight that told teachers their dues were being raised $60 a year over three years for this political advocacy."

Sand says that CTEN "inform[s] teachers how unions are spending their money and how they can leave the union. Teachers don't talk about that. You tend to lose friends if you resign from the union." Sand is not the only union watchdog of this ilk. The most notable watchdog may be Mike Antonucci and his Education Intelligence Agency. Antonucci's blogging and reporting have earned him a reputation as perhaps the leading observer of the AFT and the NEA. Individuals like Sand and Antonucci hope to move the unions not by persuasion or collaboration but by flagging concerns from the outside.

Now, just as some union critics may regard some of this chapter's earlier discussion with skepticism, so may pro-union teachers similarly regard the perspective of AAE or CTEN. And that's cool.

REMEMBER TREEBEARD'S ADMONITION

Remember Treebeard's admonition from chapter 1? You know, that "nobody is altogether on my side"? That applies big time with the union question. Cage-busters aren't pro-union or anti-union. They're for forging schools where their time, passion, and energy are valued and amplified. The question is never whether a cage-buster is for the union; it's always *whether the union is for the cage-buster.*

The focus on whether someone is pro- or anti-union is not only beside the point, but it can get downright silly. As Celine Coggins relates, "One thing that's been challenging is that some of our big accomplishments get reported in the media as 'anti-union,' even when they're led by Teach Plus fellows *who are also leaders in their union.*" Cage-busters can't do much about simple-minded reporting. But they can take care not to be distracted by lazy labels.

After all, as AFT's Randi Weingarten puts it, "we can all agree on what the end goal is. We want safe, welcoming, collaborative schools with great teaching and learning. We want schools to be a place where parents want to send their kids, educators want to work, and kids are engaged." So what can teachers do collectively, and individually, to help accomplish that? Cage-busters make it a point to judge everyone, "reformer" and union leader alike, on what they're doing on that score—not *what they're saying* but on what they're doing.

Just as it's not helpful to impugn the motives of policy makers or tell them they're idiots, the same is true with your union leaders. The cage-busting teacher regards the union with clear eyes. She sees it as a hammer that can be wielded to build the cage or to bust the cage. Cage-busters seek opportunities to solve problems and reimagine their schools and the profession. Unions *can* be a powerful mechanism for doing just that.

7

Square Pegs and Round Holes

Well, I suggest you gentlemen invent a way to put a square peg
in a round hole. Rapidly.

—Gene Kranz, in *Apollo 13*

Maybe it's wrong-footed trying to fit people into the world,
rather than trying to make the world a better place for people.

—Paul McHugh

CAGE-BUSTERS DON'T just want "better" schools or teaching. They
want schools where teachers and students can do their best work. That can
require big changes, because the job description for the twenty-first-century teacher leaves something to be desired. Jeff Hinton, retired Marine
and high school history teacher in Clark County, Nevada, says, "There are
teachers who are passionate about teaching, love what they do, and want
a bigger seat at the table without necessarily going into administration.
We need opportunities for leadership, time to mentor, and involvement in
the evaluation process. But we're so locked into old-line thinking that this
never happens. In the military, it's different. There, you're used to people
climbing ranks and the subdivision of labor. In schooling, teachers are
trapped in our little cages."

By her third year of teaching, Sydney Morris, co-founder of Educators
4 Excellence, says, "the question of professional growth really started to
hit a nerve. I looked down the road and wondered if, in twenty-five years,

I'd be doing the same exact thing without ever having the opportunity to expand my reach and broaden my impact?"

Chris Poulos, a Spanish teacher in Redding, Connecticut, says that Megan Allen, a former Florida Teacher of the Year, puts it just right when she observes, "When it comes to being a teacher leader, I feel like a square peg being forced through a circular hole." Poulos spends half his time at his school as an instructor and coach and half as a state education agency's first Teacher Leader in Residence. He says, "A big problem is that there aren't any defined roles for teacher leaders. When I talk to people about my role, they ask, 'What do you do?'"

Cage-busters wonder whether being a teacher should necessarily mean spending six hours a day in a classroom with twenty or thirty kids. They ask hard questions about what teachers *do* and how schools and systems can help them do it better. Cage-busters hold a variety of views on how to reshape the profession and about what teacher roles, responsibilities, evaluation, or pay should look like. That diversity is good and healthy. The mark of the cage-buster is not a particular stance on things like career ladders or differentiated pay but the belief that educators should have much more leeway to create great schools and systems.

Sometimes cage-busters believe they can do their best work in their current school or system, and sometimes they feel like the better course is to launch a charter school, a new organization, an education tech venture, or something else. That's not a bad thing. In fact, it's a terrific thing *if that's where their passion lies*. But this should be a choice and not an act of desperation. After all, cage-busters don't just accept the world, complain about it, or retreat from it; they reshape it into a place where they and their colleagues can do their best work.

NOT "JUST A TEACHER"

For more than a century, it's been largely assumed that teachers will do pretty much the same job, in the same room, for the same number of children on the first day of their first year and on the final day of their last year. This has deprived teachers of the chance for professional growth. It has left them with little positional authority. It has limited their opportunities to reap broader professional respect, public recognition, the perks of success, or outsized compensation. In a nation where most fields elevate their stars, schools have done their best to stifle them.

Zak Champagne, the Florida mathematics teacher we met earlier, won the Presidential Award for Excellence in Mathematics and Science Teaching in 2006. "I'm so frustrated with this 'just a teacher' notion," he says. "I got tired of being told time and time again that I was too good to be 'just a teacher.' They meant it to be a compliment, but it was the most offensive thing someone could say." Even so, he says, "it got to where I couldn't take advantage of those opportunities within the constraints of the classroom. There was no way to teach and still do all the work I wanted to do. We've been trapped by the idea that there's only one track—teacher to assistant principal to principal. Some teachers will want to be principals, but that's not for me."

Trying to address this problem without cracking the cage can lead to flawed, patchwork fixes. Says Julia Rafal-Baer, who oversees Teacher and Leader Effectiveness efforts for the New York Department of Education, "We've learned that districts find it really challenging if the state is telling them that they need to call everyone a 'teacher leader' or a 'master teacher.' It can come off as condescending or create tension. If a veteran teacher is working with a younger teacher who's been dubbed a 'master teacher' because of state-required titles, it can unnecessarily complicate things."

Again, as noted earlier, what matters is not the title "teacher leader" but what those leaders *do*. And squeezing new titles and roles into the cage doesn't do much to address the "just a teacher" problem. The way to empower the profession is not by endorsing a particular, flavor-of-the-month proposal for career ladders or merit pay but by thinking like a cage-buster—What problem is being solved? Where is teacher time, passion, and energy being wasted? How might schools be staffed and organized so to better address those problems? And what should all of this mean for evaluation, professional growth, and pay? (See *"Teacherpreneurs"* for more thoughts on all this.)

Teacherpreneurs

What might it look like to reinvent the profession? For a terrific resource, check out Barnett Berry, Ann Byrd, and Alan Weider's book *Teacherpreneurs: Innovative Teachers Who Lead but Don't Leave*.[1] Berry, a former social studies teacher and RAND Corporation researcher, is founder and CEO of the Center for Teaching Quality. Byrd is an executive with CTQ and a National Board certified teacher, and Weider is a professor emeritus at the University of South Carolina.

Berry, Byrd, and Weider argue that today's vision of teacher leadership is far too pinched and that "the challenges facing our public schools cannot be met with all teachers serving in the same narrow roles designed for a bygone era." *Teacherpreneurs* asks how schools can empower terrific teachers to lead, grow, and build without having to leave the classroom. The book profiles eight cage-busting teachers from CTQ's Collaboratory, a group of accomplished teachers who've stayed in the classroom while taking on new roles. The profiled teachers have done things like start their own teacher-led school, design new performance pay systems, host a public television show, and create peer review programs.

After each chapter, the authors provide a brief template for activities; encourage the reader to ask, "Now What?"; and offer suggestions for identifying goals, acting on them, and sharing what they've done. For example, following the chapter on barriers that teacherpreneurs can face, there is a guided activity for seeking anti-barrier solutions that can help readers break out of familiar routines.

Teacherpreneurs offers a rich set of uplifting, inspiring, and extended portraits. The authors share the story of José Vilson, who entered a school where teachers had been beaten down by nay-saying administrators and "led a small revolution in how teachers in his Washington Heights school work with one another." It's a terrific tale of cage-busting writ large.

Teacherpreneurs is written by practitioners and is full of inspiring, first-person tales. If you're reading this book and want to know what it really looks and feels like to be a cage-busting teacher, it's time to pick up *Teacherpreneurs* or check out CTQ's online resources at www.teachingquality.org.

The Double-Helix of Structure and Culture

The teaching job as usually practiced has a lot more in common with early-twentieth-century manufacturing work than with most twenty-first-century professions. Teachers have little control over their calendar or schedule, staffing or hiring, or daily responsibilities. This isn't news. Nor are the suggestions for doing something about it. So it's a mistake to imagine that proposed reforms are *bound* to work now that a new generation is proposing them. As always, what matters is less *what* is done than *how* it's done.

It's not like the need to rethink teacher roles, pay, evaluation, or autonomy are new ideas. Al Shanker, Ted Sizer, Deborah Meier, Adam Urbanski, and plenty of others were promoting ambitious proposals a quarter-century ago. Many good ideas, from career ladders to peer review, have been tried only to yield meager results. Why? A crucial reason is that most of these attempts flew in the face of existing policies, practices, and contracts—they crashed into the cage. New duties were piled atop old. Titles came with little real authority or compensation.

As we saw in chapter 5, "professional" opportunities for teachers have frequently been divorced from any serious room for professional growth, autonomy, or leadership. Emily Davis, a Spanish teacher in Florida, says of the teacher advisory council at her school, "It was just putting a check in the box. 'Teachers are at this table. We talked to teachers.' But the flow was missing . . . there was never that action." Meanwhile, real school leadership is typically the province of those teachers who take on the most challenging students, mentor new colleagues, and serve as sounding boards for the administration and do so without titles, recognition, or compensation—in other words, reflecting all the perversities of a caged profession.

Doing better isn't just a matter of titles, exhortation, or professional development. The chief talent officer for Connecticut's Department of Education, Sarah Barzee observes that changing what teachers do "runs up against structures of traditional schools. If we're going to do more than tinker around the edges, we need to create a structure, climate, and culture that can support new roles. This has got to be systemic. It can't just be individual teachers, because there are competing priorities and interests.

If you're an excellent teacher and I'm your principal, I want you in my building. But, for you to expand your reach and inform policy, you need release time that takes you out of the classroom. I see why the principal might not want that. That's why there have to be systems and structures." And it's cage-busters who must champion those systems and structures.

UNBUNDLING THE TEACHING JOB

Teachers are asked to do a little bit of everything. They are asked to design lessons, facilitate discussions, deliver lectures, craft tests, grade essays, monitor homework, call parents, design individualized programs for students with special needs, mentor colleagues, patrol the cafeteria, discipline infractions, and on and on. The unstated assumption is that teachers are, more or less, going to be equally good at all of this. As a result, plenty of perfectly competent educators struggle just because it's hard to be good at everything. By leaving rules, roles, and routines intact, most improvement efforts wind up asking teachers to do everything better and trust that the right PD is all that's needed for things to work out.

The cage-buster sees things differently. If the traditional teaching job makes it difficult for teachers to excel, the cage-buster asks why we can't rethink that job. The cage-buster embraces the notion of a career ladder in which educators can grow and take on new responsibilities. But cage-busters aren't satisfied with ladders that have all teachers following the same basic path, from novice teacher to master, with little regard for individual strengths or interests. The cage-buster wants career ladders that fully reimagine the job and that are ripe with new possibilities to nurture excellence, professionalism, and meaningful cooperation.

Taking Specialization Seriously

Over the past century the medical profession has taken a very different course than has schooling. In 1900 there were no medical specialties. But advances in research and technology led doctors to take on more defined roles. In the early twentieth century surgery emerged as the first modern specialty. Since that time, less expensive and less extensively trained paraprofessionals (like registered nurses and physical therapists) have come to support highly trained physicians in increasingly systematic and sophisticated ways. Today there are about two hundred recognized medical specialties, allowing cardiovascular surgeons or pediatricians to focus on applying their particular expertise without feeling obliged to do a bit of everything or keep abreast of developments in unrelated specialties.[2]

Indeed, you rarely see a thoracic surgeon or anesthesiologist unloading an ambulance, working the copier, or delivering Jell-o to patients. Medical practice has been reconfigured so that skilled professionals can do more of what they do best. And, for all of medicine's problems, the results have been huge in terms of health outcomes. None of this is to suggest that medicine has gotten specialization and teamwork just right. But health care does offer plenty of useful ideas, including models of how highly skilled professionals can work in concert with support staff.

Educators can make much more ambitious use of tutors and community members, just like doctors do with nurses and orderlies. One intriguing model is Citizen Schools, which partners with middle schools in seventeen cities and has tapped community members to teach structured afterschool enrichment courses on subjects from brain science to rocketry. The Boston-based Match Public Charter High School and the Apollo 20 schools in Houston have demonstrated the benefits of integrating structured, full-time tutoring into their instructional program. Reading Partners, which serves more than 130 schools across several states, trains volunteer tutors to provide the supplemental reading instruction that many students need. A gold standard 2014 evaluation found that the initiative significantly boosts reading comprehension, sight-word efficiency, and fluency.[3] Cage-busters don't romanticize specialization but they do see lots of opportunity to think more expansively about the possibilities of new roles and modes of collaboration.

Taking Hybrid Roles Seriously

Hybrid roles allow teachers to remain in the classroom while playing to their strengths or taking on new responsibilities. These roles might include delivering online instruction, supervising instructional teams, or much else. The result is a job that lets teachers make fuller use of their talents and increase their impact. All of this can also make it easier for schools to justify substantial boosts in pay for accomplished educators.

Plenty of teachers say they are enthused about the new possibilities. In 2012 the annual MetLife survey reported that 51 percent of teachers are at least somewhat interested in finding ways to combine classroom teaching with other roles in their school or district.[4] Brooke Peters, co-founder of the Odyssey Initiative, has written about Maine's Reiche Community School and its use of hybrid roles. At Reiche, Kevin Brewster teaches kindergarten in the morning and serves as school leader in the afternoon. Brewster explains, "Having a classroom of students keeps me grounded in the work of the class. For policy decisions, I know how it's going to affect my students and my time."[5]

As Jeff Hinton says, "I'd like to see this idea of teacher leaders who have these hybrid roles in schools happen. I would teach a few courses in the morning and then have the rest of the day to plan things like common units, mentor new teachers, or be involved in the evaluation process." Hinton argues that accomplished teachers are better positioned than administrators to supervise curriculum and instruction. "I'm the expert on my students, on my content, on pedagogy. We didn't earn advanced degrees or get National Board certification to be lectured by administrators who probably weren't very good teachers anyway." (See "Five New Models of the Teaching Job" for some specific ideas of possible hybrid roles.)

Taking Teams Seriously

We talk a lot about teams in schooling. But *team* isn't usually just another word for "people doing stuff together." On good, disciplined teams—whether a polished football team or an accomplished symphony—all members are not presumed to be equally skilled or equally important. Indeed, teams are typically built around the strengths of the most talented members, with recognition and pay reflecting those different contributions. Good teams take advantage of diverse skills and seek to design roles that let each teammate do more of what she does well.

New York–based New Classrooms offers a nice illustration of what it looks like to put the team mind-set to work in K–12. By working with schools to integrate teacher-led, small group, software-based, and online instruction, New Classrooms helps make it possible to dismantle the familiar classroom cage and base instructional decisions on what teachers do well and on individual student needs. Rather than every teacher marching a class of twenty-five students through an identical scope-and-sequence, differentiation is woven into the very fabric of the school day. This enables teachers to share responsibilities and do more of what they do best. A given teacher might take the lead on fractions instruction, while other teachers can decide how to divide responsibility for tutoring or large group instruction. For such changes to deliver on their promise, though, it's vital that roles and pay be reimagined.

The fact that some teammates can make a bigger contribution than others, based on their ability and experience, is just a given. It's not a basis for judging character or self-worth, but it is a reasonable way to think about responsibilities and compensation. The cage-buster buys the notion that harder-working and more skilled team members should be compensated accordingly. *But* she recognizes that there are lots of ways to act on that insight—some of them wise and many of them less so. Accepting the principle that excellence should be rewarded *creates no obligation* to endorse stupid systems just because they're nominally merit based.

Five New Models of the Teaching Job

There are many ways to reimagine what teachers do. In working with districts to develop an "opportunity culture," North Carolina-based Public Impact has helped develop several visions of new roles that seek to magnify the contribution of terrific practitioners. Consider five models sketched by Public Impact's Bryan Hassel, Emily Hassel, and Sharon Barrett.

- *Multiclassroom leadership.* Instead of just serving as grade-level or department leaders, lead teachers would be personally responsible for the student outcomes of other teachers on their team. They'd be empowered "to select and evaluate peers" and would oversee a cluster of classrooms take on the kind of "accountable

continued

mentoring—with the leader ultimately responsible for team out-comes—[that] is very common in other professions."

- *Specialization.* Elementary teachers would specialize in their "best subjects or subject pairs," while a high school writing teacher might be freed from responsibility for the whole language arts curriculum. Meanwhile, having paraprofessionals handle paperwork, custodial duties like recess, and some routine instructional tasks would allow teachers more time "to reach more students, collaborate in teams, and focus on the most challenging elements of instruction."

- *Time/Technology swaps.* In blended schools, where students spend a chunk of time learning digitally each day, teachers can "teach more students, for higher pay, without reducing personalized, higher-order instructional time." Schools can use technology to increase the reach of terrific teachers while reducing the number of students that a teacher has at a given time. In some versions of this approach, the very idea of the "classroom" is re-imagined, with students working in ever-changing groups.

- *Class-size changes.* Another option is to enable terrific teachers to teach more students in return for additional pay. How to craft such plans "is a nuanced decision for the teacher and school and would depend on the students' ages and other needs." One version would increase class sizes across the board while using the savings from a smaller staff to provide increased training, compensation, and paraprofessional support.

- *Remote teaching.* While students may prefer an in-person teacher to any kind of remote or digital alternative, "some schools have critical shortages of teachers in some subjects—higher-level math and languages are common—or shortages of *excellent* teachers in many subjects." Webcams and interactive whiteboards can allow teachers to teach remotely—from the next building or from a conti-nent away—ensuring that every student has access to a competent teacher.

These models are possibilities, not recipes. It's fine to reject any (or all) of them. Cage-busters are focused not on promoting any particular model but, instead, on how to design a profession in which educators can do their best work. For more on all these ideas, check out www.opportunityculture.org.

CAGE-BUSTING BEYOND THE CLASSROOM

Many teachers confess to feeling guilty about changing schools or changing roles. They shouldn't. Cage-busters see the classroom as a place of possibility, not a prison. Sometimes the cage-buster's best bet is to find a role in which he can do his best work. Elliot Sanchez founded Louisiana's mSchool, a tech startup providing computer-assisted math tutoring, after he taught and tried his hand at district and state roles. After all that, he says, "I felt like if I wanted to do my best work and make a real difference, I had to do it outside of the state and district system. And, to be honest, I had no idea what that would look like." But he focused on problems, solutions, and finding his way forward—not on anyone else's preconceptions of what educators are supposed to do.

Cage-busters celebrate those who choose to seek new possibilities, inside or outside of the classroom. Jason Kamras, the chief of human capital for the DC Public Schools, started out teaching middle school math and in 2005 was named the National Teacher of the Year. What prompted him to leave the classroom? Kamras says, "I was able to do some very exciting things with 150 kids every year. But, as a classroom teacher, there's a fairly finite impact you can have even when you're really trying to innovate. There were things I wanted to change that I couldn't from Room 112. So when a couple of cage-busting district leaders asked me to join them, I went for it." Because they think in terms of possibilities, cage-busters are open to new opportunities when they arise.

EMERGE: Solving the "Getting Kids to College" Problem

As a fifth grade teacher in Houston, Rick Cruz never intended to launch an initiative to help at-risk kids go to great colleges. But as he watched his fifth graders enter middle school, he saw that he "had talented students who lacked the means or social capital to advance." Cruz had gone to Yale and recalled talking to a colleague about what it had been like to be a minority student at an elite college. During their chat, he floated the idea of a program that "would identify students with stellar academic potential and prepare them to successfully apply to and persist in selective colleges."

My mentor was the district's chief academic officer [CAO]. I told him, "I have this idea of creating a program that would mirror what private consultants do for wealthy high achievers." He set me up with a principal at a high school where I could run the program . . . Just being able to say, "The district's CAO stands behind this" opened doors. The principal was receptive but told me he doubted we'd get 10 kids who were interested. Turns out we had 125 kids apply. When the principal saw that he asked, "What'd you promise them?" We selected fourteen students for that first group. We started by introducing them to the schools out there. We explained to them that these schools have generous financial aid policies—that students can go if they get in, and that it's usually *cheaper* to go to these private schools, with need-based aid, than to community college. Then something clicked.

EMERGE begins each year with a boot camp on how to write a personal statement and submit a strong college application. Students are mentored by graduates of selective schools, receive intensive SAT and ACT prep, visit college campuses, and get a feel for college life. The program starts with local colleges, but, says Cruz, "we take students up to the Northeast, where they travel through Boston, New York, Philadelphia, Providence, and New Haven. They stay in the dorms at Columbia and Tufts and interact with students and professors at Harvard and Yale." Within a year, Cruz's initiative caught the eye of Houston superintendent Terry Grier, who offered Cruz the chance to take the program districtwide.

Grier promoted Cruz to assistant superintendent for college readiness, allowing him to shift from a small nonprofit effort at a couple schools to a role where he could help more than two hundred thousand students across three hundred schools. At first, Cruz hesitated. "I was nervous about the internal politics. I knew I'd be really young and would be perceived as inexperienced. I also didn't know whether I'd be able to operate as effectively within the constraints of a large bureaucracy." Cruz told Grier his concerns. As Grier tells it, "I promised he'd have 100 percent support. I told him he'd have all the authority he needed, with no boundaries, no bureaucracies. I said he wouldn't hear the word 'no.'" (Note that Cruz got this assurance *before* taking the job, when he still had leverage.)

Early on Cruz faced a massive bottleneck. He reported to a senior district official who was blowing him off. This went on for months, until Cruz bumped into Grier in a hallway and the superintendent asked how things were going. Grier told Cruz that, effective immediately, he'd be reporting directly to him and that there were no "nos." Grier says, "The guy above Cruz was frustrated and jealous. Rick's only mistake was to keep trying to work through channels rather than coming to me right away." Then there is the seniority thing. Cruz wasn't yet thirty when he was promoted. That can be a recipe for resentment. But, as Cruz says, "in a lot of professions you're up or out before thirty. A lawyer can be a partner in a big firm by thirty." The cages wrought by hierarchy and seniority are a mind-set, not an inevitability.

Cruz says, "We started off with just volunteers. Now we have five full-time program managers and are working in fourteen high schools. We'll be adding schools and students in the years to come. We've partnered with Yale for a summer EMERGE Program." In 2014 EMERGE graduated sixty-three seniors, each of whom was admitted to a school ranked in the top 100 nationally by *U.S. News & World Report*, and almost all were accepted by institutions promising to meet 100 percent of their financial need. In 2014 EMERGE alums were accepted at Brown, Columbia, Harvard, Princeton, MIT, Stanford, and Yale, among other colleges. Backed by Cruz's team, the graduating class received over $250 million in scholarship and financial aid offers—a district record and an increase of more than $60 million from the year before.

LearnZillion: Solving the Teacher Isolation Problem

Eric Westendorf started teaching in Indonesia. On returning to the United States, he taught in New York and then North Carolina. After graduating from Stanford Business School, he served for five years as assistant principal, principal, and then CAO at E. L. Haynes, a Washington, DC, charter school. Westendorf says, "We got to a place where we were doing all the things people write about. We were recruiting fantastic teachers. We had a culture of no excuses and high performance. We were collaborating outside of regular school hours. We were doing data-driven instruction. We were letting go of those people who weren't performing. But I still felt like we were a long way off. It came down to the fact that teachers, even in this collaborative environment, were mostly working in isolation."

He tells of a terrific sixth grade teacher who had a great technique for teaching division of fractions. As principal, he had time to see it, but his teachers didn't. He says, "We paid lip service to observing one another, but we all had crazy schedules. So there was no way to really spread pedagogical content knowledge or routinely see the practice of colleagues. That's where LearnZillion came from. The idea was to solve a problem. The problem was how teachers could more readily learn from their colleagues. I started by asking, 'What if we could capture teacher expertise and share it with others in a simple way, where teachers don't have to leave their classroom to see it?'"

With a former Stanford classmate, Westendorf built a Web portal where teachers could share materials, resources, and instructional videos for math and English language arts instruction in grades 2–12. He says, "We'd cobbled together Google Docs and YouTube videos so teachers could use that in their classrooms. What made the difference was that we had a minimally viable product. We won $250,000 from the Next Generation Learning Challenge and got started." Today, LearnZillion offers thousands of Common Core–aligned lessons along with instructional resources, "director's cut" videos explaining the lessons, customizable materials, and more—all of which allow teachers to borrow and learn from talented colleagues.

Westendorf advises, "Don't spend all your time dreaming up something ideal. Just try your idea. As soon as you do, you start learning stuff. I thought, at first, once I had teachers create a few lessons, it ought to be easy for them to churn out new ones. But no one created new lessons for a week. When I asked about it, they responded, 'Of course, we didn't. It's because we're ridiculously busy.' It was helpful that I tried, failed, and learned that early on."

In 2011 LearnZillion launched its first Dream Team. Each year Learn-Zillion selects two hundred accomplished teachers to gather for TeachFest, three days of intense, collaborative lesson planning. The idea is to provide outstanding educators a chance to work with grade-level and content-area peers from across the nation, putting their best work together. Westendorf says, "What's interesting is how many people came to us after the experience and said, 'Oh, my God, it totally changed the way I think about myself as a teacher. The frustration was getting to me, but now, for the first time, I can really think of myself as a leader.' These are people who are used to not getting recognized. One of our California teachers got tapped for the state commission on implementing the Common Core because she was on the Dream Team. One thing leads to another once you're proactive. It starts with baby steps, but then it's a bigger step and a bigger one."

Westendorf says one of LearnZillion's goals is to remind teachers that they're professionals and should expect to be treated accordingly. With TeachFest, "we want it to be full of delight. We have them fill out a survey before they arrive, and we study those. While they're in line at registration, we can approach them and say, 'You must be Henry. That story you filled out about when you were six years old—that was amazing.' It's hard work, but it's fun. We offered teachers the night off for a *Ferris Bueller's Day Off* experience in Atlanta, but sixty chose to stay down in the basement room we had reserved to work on their lessons. It's engaging, empowering work. When we wrap up, people are really jazzed. There are tears, even singing, and teachers saying, 'This changed my life.'" This is a model that allows great teachers to grow, connect, and have a national impact—all while remaining firmly planted in their classrooms.

Sure, Westendorf has left the classroom to tackle this problem. But a cage-buster would have a hard time suggesting that he's left schools, teachers, or students behind.

Enriched: Solving the Substitute Teacher Problem

Andre Feigler liked teaching in Louisiana's St. Bernard Parish. "My administration was generally pretty supportive, though I never really felt like they were interested in my ideas about systematic changes." One of these ideas was her belief that substitute teaching could be dramatically improved. She says, "The substitute issue is something every teacher dreads. You worry that your class will be a [mess] when you get back. I'd spend so much time planning lessons, writing letters to my kids on the board. And then I'd still wind up leaving a movie and a busywork packet. They don't get anybody until the last minute, so the subs weren't prepared and they wouldn't care."

Feigler muses, "I never really said, 'Let's go to the principal and propose another system.' Maybe I should have. But I never felt like she was looking for ideas or inviting discussion from teachers. I wish that part of our PD had been them asking, 'What are the worst parts of your job? Why aren't the kids learning? Bring two or three ideas next week about what we can do.' But that wasn't the approach my administration took."

She notes that she "didn't fully realize how the substitute system works. The secretary has this yellow pad, starts calling names, and gets someone to show up. It's a scramble every morning." She started just trying to learn more about how it worked in different systems. "I asked everyone I could find, 'How does it work in your school? What's the worst part about this for you?' I talked to finance managers, operations people, HR directors, instructional coaches . . . As long as I approached it like, 'I want to learn from you, because here's something that might make life better for everybody,' people were pretty willing to share." Along the way, Feigler learned that the problem was even more significant than she'd known—that schools in the United States spend $4 billion a year on subs.

She says, "I talked to a teacher at KIPP who told me that the hardest thing was having to cover someone else's class once a week. They rely on internal coverage at a lot of the charter schools. It was his number-one frustration. He'd told KIPP he was thinking of leaving if they didn't figure that out, that teachers were burning out. He invited me to meet with his administration. I probably said ten words at that meeting, because he was making the case for me."

She launched a venture called Enriched. The first step was figuring out what exactly her solution was. She says the key was getting concrete: "Who's the user here? Is it the teacher or the office manager? How much will they pay for this? It helped me turn it into a workable model." When meeting with schools, "I usually don't need to tell them a lot. Schools already know how much of a headache this is, so what's most effective is when I say, 'I have a hunch you have this problem,' and then they jump in to say, 'Yes, we really do,' and, 'Can you help?'"

Enriched provides carefully vetted, trained subs who can teach well or who offer a unique experience. Feigler says, "We have accomplished local poets, artists, and authors. Our pool is 75 percent African American. So we offer something special. The proof is really in the pudding for the schools, but what makes us distinct is recruitment. We target presence. We want subs who can walk in and own the room. That's the main thing. But we also seek teaching experience and people native to the community. Then we work on preparation and training, take feedback seriously, and try to take care of our network of educators." Feigler's tale is a nice case of looking with fresh eyes at an old problem that often gets taken for granted, and then devising a solution to suit.

The Intersection: Solving the Student Engagement Problem

Cage-busters can sometimes find the classroom constricting. Zeke Cohen, executive director of the Intersection, a Baltimore-based community program, says, "I was teaching in a West Baltimore neighborhood that had open-air drug activity, churches, liquor stores, and not much else. My first year, I had this one young man who would get into it like clockwork," and nothing seemed to help. Finally, he says, "I raised the funds to take five of my eighth graders to New Orleans to do rebuilding work. This young man took over the crew. He was knocking down walls, pulling out nails. I'd never seen the kid smile. And he was suddenly a junior foreman. It was one of those teacher moments where I had to step back and ask what led to this crazy transformation. This kid had been so used to people hating or pitying him that doing something for someone else was profound. I thought of how many kids get lost in middle and high school but have incredible leadership potential."

Cohen muses, "People think about inner-city kids as part of the problem, or as victims." His goal was to change the lens so that they'd be seen, and see themselves, "as part of the solution."

> I got together with a couple of other teachers. We started with a group of nine kids out of the rec center, with no money and without nonprofit status. We built a whole course—public speaking, grass roots organizing, how to tell your story. We had the students ask people about challenges facing their community. The kids found that the community was a food desert; there was no access to fresh food. They found a lack of civic participation. They found a sense that the police work against the community. We turned it

back to the students and said, "Okay, what can we do about all this?" There was this abandoned lot next to the rec center filled with needles and junk. The kids hollowed it out and started this community garden. They started taking pictures of asbestos, lead paint, dumping . . . and got them run in the *Baltimore Sun*. They registered 118 people to vote. That summer we held a mayoral forum. We got the candidates for mayor to come, and our kids drilled them. It all just sort of worked. From there, we got a board, raised money, and formed a nonprofit.

One big advantage in launching the Intersection, says Cohen, is that he'd lived in Baltimore for twelve years. "I'd gone to college here, then taught here. Baltimore is my home. But, I'm a white guy, and I'm not *from* here. So, I had to earn that respect. I had to listen, learn, investigate, and really build relationships. My first board member was the president of Goucher College. The second was the board chair of the Walters Art Museum. Having folks with that credibility, who can vouch for you, makes a huge difference. One mistake I've seen is people come into places with great ideas but don't build relationships." Cohen's legwork made the enterprise workable and sustainable.

To start, we did it incredibly cheap. That first summer we raised a couple hundred bucks from friends and parents to pay for food for the kids, a camera, and a speaker system for the mayoral forum. Now, we've leveraged a bunch of partnerships. Teach For America provides tutoring for our kids. Johns Hopkins University has a guidance counselor program, and it provides 140 free hours of guidance counseling per semester. There's a program called First Generation College Bound that provides scholarships and mentoring. They'd long operated in Prince George's County but not Baltimore. We told their director what we were doing and he took us on as a test case. You've got to reach out. You don't need to reinvent the wheel.

By 2014 the Intersection had worked with scores of students. Students had earned the We Are the Dream Award, the Baltimore City Student Service Award, and the Princeton Prize in Race Relations. They'd been featured on National Public Radio, FOX45, and ABC2 News, as well as in the *Baltimore Sun* and the *Baltimore Business Journal*. They'd been invited to speak by Teach For America, President Obama's My Brother's Keeper initiative, and the Baltimore City Schools Leadership Academy. All of the program's graduates had enrolled in college. Not a bad start.

BetterLesson: Solving the Lesson-Planning Problem

Alex Grodd's classroom experiences led him to found BetterLesson, a venture that collects and curates lesson plans, classroom materials, and instructional resources from master teachers. Grodd started teaching in Atlanta, where, he says, "I realized early on that kids were the quietest and best behaved when you had a great lesson. When lessons were tight, had engaging Do Now's, and lively discussion, class went like clockwork. When you don't have that, you're outnumbered and things quickly devolve into this power struggle."

He says of lesson planning, "When you get it right, it's like a symphony. When I sat down to write my lesson plans, sometimes I could compose a symphony and sometimes I couldn't. When I couldn't, I'd lose control of the kids. When I did, I wanted to share my art. I didn't want to wait another year to do it again. I tried to find a way to collaborate with other Teach For America teachers in the area. We'd meet and exchange flash drives, but that didn't really work."

Taking a new job at Boston's Roxbury Prep, Grodd knew he'd be teaching a different subject and grade. He recalls, "I realized that all my art was going to be lost. The idea of all that creative output just dying on my hard drive viscerally affected me. Meanwhile, I was the only sixth grade English teacher and was searching for lessons. I tried to find people to collaborate with. I phoned local middle schools.

"That spring, I said, 'I'm going to try to solve this problem.' I'd been talking about a lesson-sharing Web site for a while. For three years, I'd been doing the market research." He teamed up with co-founders Erin Osborn and Jonathan Hendler and used modest "friends-and-family" financing to pay expenses, hire a coder, and build the prototype. He recalls that "none of us had any idea what we were doing" but that they made it through the first year. After that, support from the NewSchools Venture Fund put them on solid financial footing.

Grodd notes that the "teachers were supportive. They were like, 'Someone should do this.' Everyone recognized this problem should be solved in a better way. There aren't many companies started by teachers coming out of the classroom, but it seems sensible that teachers don't need to write every single lesson from scratch. They should be able to find good stuff and curricula from master teachers and then modify it to fit their students. When you make a movie, the director, screenwriter, and actor all have different jobs. But teachers have been expected to serve as the writer, director, and actor."

Grodd says,

> There may not be a lot of great ways to access master teachers in your school. We make it possible for teachers to find their soul mates. We've tapped 130 master teachers. Teachers are desperately seeking great content and the master teachers are psyched to share their craft. We pay the master teachers $15,000 a year. They're building out their entire curriculum and making it available. They're sharing maybe ten units, twelve lessons per unit, and they're breaking out those lessons in ways no one ever has. Usually, when you share material, there are gaps and holes. Or you're doing just what you have to, because it's for compliance purposes. Our lessons are being written to be consumed. We're working on having office hours for coaches and increasing access to mentors.

To those thinking about taking the entrepreneurial route, Grodd says, "Don't do it! That's a joke . . . but it's not. It's a half-joke. Entrepreneurship is hard. It's not a way to get rich. You've got to really believe deeply in your idea. The one thing is to be sure to find good mentors. That's the best advice I can give. Find people who have done it before and listen to them."

THE PROMISE OF TEACHER-LED SCHOOLS

Perhaps the cleanest way for teachers to marry accountability and authority is by creating schools where they run the show—just like the professionals do in a law partnership or medical practice. How does it work? It's pretty simple. Practitioners make the decisions and divvy up leadership responsibilities as they see fit. Al Shanker put it pithily: "If you want to hold teachers accountable, then teachers have to be able to run the school."[6]

Law partners manage their firm and are accountable for the results. Typically, one partner serves as managing partner. Firms can operate as they see fit so long as they generate the requisite revenues. Ted Kolderie, senior associate at the Minnesota-based think tank Education Evolving, has made the case for adapting this model to teacher-led schools, encouraging reformers to stop giving orders and to treat "teachers as professionals; telling them what we want and leaving it to them . . . to figure out how the job can best be done."[7] These teacher-led schools would be left alone so long as they deliver acceptable student outcomes.

There are dozens of teacher-led schools across the land today. The most prominent network of these schools is the EdVisions Cooperative, launched in Minnesota in 1994. EdVisions supports more than sixty teacher-governed schools across the nation, in states including Minnesota, Wisconsin, California, Nevada, Pennsylvania, and New Jersey. EdVisions provides schools with human resource and administrative support, but the teacher-owners are in charge of budget and staffing, hiring and evaluating faculty, curriculum, salaries, and academic outcomes. Teachers at the schools contract with outside vendors for things like transportation or food services.[8]

There's broad interest in teacher-led schools among both teachers and the public. In 2014, 49 percent of teachers thought that giving teachers a bigger voice in decision making would be the one change with "the biggest payoff for student learning." While 51 percent of teachers said they already have "a great deal" or "some" authority in schools (a classic cage-dwelling response, given how often teachers grumble that they have no say), 91 percent said they ought to have that authority. More than 80 percent of the public agrees that "teachers have the know-how to make schools run better" and endorses the idea of teacher-run schools. In fact, polling suggests the public is even more supportive of the idea than teachers are![9]

Earlier we met Lori Nazareno, who led a group of teachers in launching a teacher-led school with union support. When Denver Public Schools invited applications for new schools, Nazareno says, "we got a group of board-certified teachers, started with a blank sheet of paper, and designed the school we felt would best serve high-need students." She says, "While not every district is going to issue a request for proposals for new schools, almost everybody has schools in turnaround status or accepts applications for charter schools. What happens, though, is that teachers see those as opportunities for somebody else. They assume it's only for charter people. They don't realize that it's for them, too, that it's the exact same door that they can walk through with a teacher-led or a distributed leadership school."

Nazareno says the union's collective bargaining agreement wasn't a problem because the union partnered in creating the school. She notes, "We did have a problem with the state, because only principals can run schools, evaluate teachers, and suspend students—and our school wasn't going to have an administrator." They needed state waivers to go forward. Those took six months, but they came through. Nazareno says, "During the interview process, we had to tell people, 'You're not going to be evaluated by a principal but by your colleagues. And 100 percent of the time, people were like, 'Okay, where do I sign?'" More than five hundred teachers applied for a dozen teaching positions. The Math and Science Leadership Academy (MSLA) started in 2009 with 125 kids. By 2014 enrollment was over 300. Seventy percent of students were English language learners, and 95 percent qualified for the free and reduced lunch program. In 2013 student academic growth outpaced the state average in reading, writing, and math. After Kim Ursetta, the president of the Denver Classroom Teachers Association, stepped down from her union post, she went to teach at MSLA. Now, *that's* walking the walk.[10]

Although union leaders are often critical of charter schooling, NEA president Lily Eskelsen García sounds enthusiastic when discussing the ALBA charter school in Milwaukee, a bilingual teacher-led elementary school with a fine arts focus. She says, "These teachers had concerns and decided, 'We are not going to wait for someone to figure this out, or get on our hands and knees and plead with the principal.' They created an academy where they wrapped math, science, social studies, reading, everything really, around the fine arts, and they did it with the blessing of the Milwaukee Teachers' Education Association, which said this was what charters were always supposed to be about." She reflects, "When Shanker came up with the charter concept, he really wasn't thinking of companies and franchises. He was thinking of unleashing the passion of the educator." Three ALBA teachers were honored by *People* magazine as National Teachers of the Year in 2013, and the school was named a Wisconsin School of Distinction in 2014.

Now, there's nothing magical about law firms being run by lawyers. Law firms can be bureaucratic and stifling, with small-minded accountability systems that require even senior lawyers to obsess about billable hours. And keep in mind that the need for a managing partner can turn a partnership of equals into something else, especially with the passage of time. As schools or networks grow, cooperative arrangements can become more rigid and hierarchical, too. Recall George Orwell's *Animal Farm*, where the noble tenets of radical equality eventually gave way to a single dictum: "All animals are equal, but some animals are more equal than others."[11] Teacher-led schools are a great idea. But the cage-buster doesn't imagine that they're a cure-all. Cage-busting, in *any* school or system, is a mind-set, not a search for a quick fix.

MAKING ROOM FOR SQUARE PEGS

There is much that teachers can do right now, today. But there are also real limits to what teachers can do in roles, classrooms, and schools designed for the world of a century ago. These structures can limit the ability of teachers to make the best use of their talents or to reimagine stifling routines.

Teachers need to ask whether familiar job descriptions still make sense and, if they don't, how they should be changed. That means asking how specialization, the use of teams, new technologies, and unbundling might allow for better, more dynamic teaching and learning. If changes are called for, these are often difficult to pursue within an isolated classroom, or even within an existing school or system. That's why cage-busters push beyond those four walls and why cage-busting *can,* sometimes, lead teachers to follow nontraditional paths that take them into unusual roles or wholly new ventures. Following such a course should be neither a first choice nor a last resort. As always, it should be a question of a teacher pursuing the path that she thinks will allow her to make the highest, best use of her passion, time, and energy.

New tools and new school models make it possible for teachers to pursue great teaching and learning in all kinds of ways. Cage-busters choose the course *they* deem most promising, without guilt or apology. As Jeff Hinton says, "Teachers have very little influence over district reform. We're trapped in our little dungeons. We go in our classrooms and close our doors. But being Teacher of the Year gave me visibility, and now I'm running for state assembly. If I can't affect change from the classroom, I'll go to the legislature and try to do it there. I want to lead, but I don't want to become a dean of students to do it. That's not the path for me. If I have to, I'm going to make my own path."

In *The Bell Jar*, poet Sylvia Plath fretted, "I saw my life branching out before me like the green fig tree in the story. From the tip of every branch, like a fat purple fig, a wonderful future beckoned and winked . . . I saw myself sitting in the crotch of this fig tree, starving to death, just because I couldn't make up my mind which of the figs I would choose."[12] It's ironic: a notoriously depressed poet saw a world of possibility while even the most life-embracing of teachers can feel starved for options and opportunities. But that's a choice. Too often, teachers observe that green fig tree growing outside the school and they think, "That's not for me." But just as Lori Nazareno noted that charter schools are there for teachers to embrace *if only they choose to do so*, so, too, are all the futures represented by Cruz and Feigler and Cohen and Grodd. For this to happen, though, teachers need to see and embrace life beyond the cage . . . ideally to the point that they, too, are overwhelmed trying to choose among all the rich possibilities. Wouldn't *that* be a sweet problem for teachers to have?

8

You Are Braver Than You Believe

Man, it's the same bullshit they tried to pull in my day. If it ain't that piece of paper, there's some other choice they're gonna try and make for you . . . Let me tell you this, the older you do get the more rules they're gonna try to get you to follow.

—WOODERSON, IN *Dazed and Confused*

If ever there is tomorrow when we're not together . . . there is something you must always remember. You are braver than you believe, stronger than you seem, and smarter than you think.

—CHRISTOPHER ROBIN, from *Winnie-the-Pooh*

CAGE-BUSTERS DRAW ON the wisdom of both Wooderson and Christopher Robin—two fictional characters who constitute the most unlikely of duos. Wooderson, Matthew McConaughey's iconic stoner, knew that if you let others tell you to follow one rule after another, you'll wind up pacing in your cage. But he also knew that resistance isn't easy. For teachers stuck in bureaucratic schools and systems, it can be damn hard. Years of frustration can leave teachers feeling voiceless and powerless. Deference to familiar norms and a tendency to retreat to the classroom can leave teachers uncertain of their bravery, strength, and smarts—or that of their colleagues. But Christopher Robin was right: you *are* braver than you believe, stronger than you seem, and smarter than you think. It's those who remember that simple mantra who find ways to bust the cage.

It seems axiomatic that a respected profession needs to recruit and retain "effective teachers" and get rid of educators who aren't getting it done. But those policy debates are not the stuff that captivates the cage-buster. Cage-busting is not about finding more teachers who are good today, but about reshaping schools, systems, and the profession so that many more can be extraordinary tomorrow. That requires teachers to leverage all their authority. They must be prepared to address mediocrity, identify problems, pose solutions, and work with administrators and policy makers. (It's a funny thing, though. Done well, cage-busting inevitably addresses those questions of teacher retention and quality that so consume the policy discussion.) ▪

YOU HAD ME AT HELLO

Many successful cage-busters seem genuinely puzzled by the notion that "nobody cares what teachers think." They say they've found that people are eager to hear what they have to say. Jessica Waters, who teaches science at the Beacon Charter High School for the Arts in Woonsocket, Rhode Island, says, "Since early on, I always pushed myself to get out there. Not in a weird way, I just wanted them to know that I'm a professional, intelligent, and have experiences to share. Once I joined one state committee, one thing led to the next, and I started meeting the right people. I took myself out of the classroom at the end of the day and started networking. You really don't see much of that, you know. My husband is a CFO. That's his life. He networks. But you don't really hear about that kind of networking in the teaching profession."

Teachers can be uncertain about how to reach out. It can be easier than you'd expect, especially since principals, superintendents, and policy makers are starved for people to help solve problems. Louisiana state superintendent John White says, "I'm always looking for good ideas. Once a teacher connects, they become part of the club. Like everyone else, I have a network I'm always talking to. When we're stumped on an English language arts issue, I'll pull together eight teachers on the phone. I've got a group of counselors. These are people who reached out at some point in a way that was productive and positive." White explains, "If teachers e-mail me about how they personally were evaluated and how they disagree with their score, I'm not listening. But if they reach out with a suggestion on how we can improve student achievement or teaching across the state, I'm going to read the entire e-mail. A good leader wants to know about the things they don't know about, and teachers know what's happening in classrooms. That's the stuff state chiefs and superintendents don't know about. If a teacher says, 'I know something you can fix,' I'm interested."

Leaders may be jaded, but they're not fools. Building relationships isn't much different with state officials than with your local PTA. And modest up-front efforts can yield big, long-term benefits. Rhode Island's David Upegui connected with the state's commissioner of education when she visited his class. He says, "I didn't know she was coming. She saw us practicing for the science competition, and I explained to her what we were doing and why we'd win. The following year there was a conference. Her office called and asked if they could throw me in the mix. Now we have some back-and-forth. When I was in her office once, I saw she had student work displayed on her walls. So I sent her a book that some of my biology students had made for a child with leukemia, describing the science behind it and the treatments—all in a kid-friendly way. She's been very accessible. When I e-mail her, she gets right back."

Brad Clark, a fourth and fifth grade teacher in Woodford County, Kentucky, created the education arm of IdeaFestival Lexington, a student-led innovation conference where more than two hundred students observed student-created TED-style talks. Afterward, both the Center for Teaching Quality and the Hope Street Group's Kentucky teacher fellowship reached out to him to be a virtual community organizer.

But you needn't do grand things to open new doors. James Dunseith, a math teacher in Worcester, Massachusetts, and a BetterLesson master teacher, says opportunities are everywhere. He says, "It's on me to say, 'Hey, I'm going to go check that out.'" How did Dunseith become a BetterLesson master teacher? "I clicked on a link from a tweet from a guy I'd never met." It's important not just to be open to possibilities but to jump on through when that cage door swings open.

THIS IS GOING TO TICK OFF MY PRINCIPAL!

The fear that cage-busting will alienate your principal (or superintendent) is a rational one. That's why it matters so much *how* cage-busters go about things. Cage-busters take care to reach out productively. Just follow the advice your peers have offered in the course of these pages and you'll find that doing this isn't as difficult or as scary as it may seem.

Ann Bonitatibus, COO of Frederick County, Maryland, schools, says, "I feel like it's a Central Office obligation to listen to our teachers and to help when we can. We're happy to help there, because trust and autonomy are cheap—they don't cost anything. The union often claims that there are concerns of retribution when teachers try new things or challenge convention, but we don't see that happen. We say, 'Point to a time when retribution occurred,' and they can't."

Cage-busting isn't about rule breaking; it's about stretching the bounds of the permissible. Ken Halla, a social studies teacher and tech guru in Fairfax, Virginia, and author of *Deeper Learning Through Technology*, says his advice for other teachers is, "Just ask."[1] When he started his *World History Teachers Blog,* which registers 65,000 hits a month, he "went to the coordinator for K–12 social studies before I started and asked, 'Is there any problem with me doing this?' He told me, 'Just do it outside the school system.'" That sidestepped problems with privacy, restricted use sites, and district policy. An early blog prompted a parent to fire off a heated note to Halla's principal. In response, "my principal told me, 'I love what you're doing.' So the attempt to get me in trouble backfired. I tell teachers that you have cachet in your school. I knew that principal quite well. He knew what I was doing. I'd explained it. As long as I wasn't breaking rules, I was okay." Halla reflects, "Occasionally, I meet people who say, 'I thought you'd be this rule breaker.' But I'm not. I'm trying to innovate within the system." Halla rejects the "ask forgiveness, not permission" approach, noting, "I'm persistent. I'll come back three or four times to ask, 'How can we do this?' But I will ask."

Remember, there are cage-busting assistant principals, principals, district leaders, and superintendents searching for problem-solving teachers *they* can work with. Show them you're that teacher. As one big-district superintendent once told me, "Teachers complain that administrators are always saying no. The funny thing is that I talk to my good principals and area superintendents, and they say they *wish* that were the case! The fact is, teachers are generally so hesitant to bring ideas forward that it hardly ever happens." Are there times when you can push it too far or when you're wise to hold off? Of course. That's doubly true if you haven't yet done the requisite work to identify clear problems, build credibility, and find allies. Sometimes wisdom counsels prudence, and patience. But the cage-buster makes that decision deliberately and with calculation, not out of fear.

PASSION HAS A PRICE

Education is full of passionate people. Michelle Shearer observes, "That passion can be good and bad. Teachers often feel that they have no voice, so when they do speak up, all of that emotion comes to the surface. And it can come across as complaining or whining." Passionate people tend to be sure of their convictions and in a hurry to act on them. That can be good and admirable. But passion can also have real costs. It can leave us impatient, make us strident, and lead us to dismiss the views of others. It can make us better at talking than at listening. Passionate people aren't always great at understanding why others might disagree, which can make it hard to win people over.

Passion can lead people to say things that erode their credibility, making it harder to address their concerns. In early 2014, Michael Mulgrew, president of New York City's United Federation of Teachers, told 3,400 union delegates, "We are at war with the reformers." He said, "Their ideas will absolutely destroy—forget about public education, they will destroy education in our country."[2] Karen Lewis, former president of the Chicago Teachers Union, has said of "reform" advocates, "The key is they think nothing of killing us. They think nothing of putting our people in harm's way. They think nothing of lethal working conditions."[3] She called Chicago mayor

Rahm Emanuel the "murder mayor." She accused Teach For America of backing policies that "kill and disenfranchise children."[4] Lewis raised valid points on questions like teacher evaluation and school closings, but her invective ensured that these would get lost.

Angry chants and vitriolic signage are not how physicians, lawyers, bankers, or Marines have claimed influence or made their voices heard. These tactics are more the stuff of aggrieved college students and striking factory workers. If teachers want to be treated like professionals, they need to act the part. Jessica Waters recalls, "When Arne Duncan came to Rhode Island, there were people protesting outside. I was sort of embarrassed by them in comparison to other professions. I can't even begin to imagine people from other professions picketing outside with a T-shirt and a bandanna on. I just thought to myself, 'Is this how you convince them to treat you like a professional?'" Similarly, one state legislator said to me after chairing an education committee meeting, "I don't know what these folks are thinking. They're here to convince us that they've got the answers for our kids. But they're up against national experts, and they've got a crowd in T-shirts screaming at us like it's a Friday-night football game. This isn't abortion or guns. This is an area where people are ready to compromise and are open to being persuaded. Those teachers should take a look in the mirror and ask themselves if they'd expect to be convinced by a crowd like that."

It can be all too easy for teachers to let their frustration get the better of them. Teachers grumble, "Everybody thinks they're an educational expert because everybody went to school." Well, no. For one thing, most people *don't* think they're educational experts. For another, lawmakers have a job to do—which is write laws about how to spend money and provide services. They have to do this for lots of areas where they may not be expert, including national defense, bridge construction, space exploration, and public health. But, more to the point, many advocates and policy makers *do* have some expertise when it comes to schooling. They've spent years talking to educators, studying schools and school systems, crafting education laws, and wrestling with implementation challenges. They frequently know a lot more about the policy side of the equation than do classroom teachers. If practitioners want outsiders to acknowledge their passion and expertise, they'd do well to model that same respect. Make your passion work *for* you, not against you.

In the 2014 book *Teachers versus the Public: What Americans Think About Schools and How to Fix Them*, researchers Paul E. Peterson, Michael Henderson, and Martin West examine a slew of national surveys and find strong, persistent divides between teachers and the public on how to promote quality teaching. Two-thirds of the public supports merit pay, while just 16 percent of teachers do. Three-quarters of the public favors merit-based tenure, while the figure is just 29 percent among teachers.[5] These gaps remain after adjusting for differences in age, race, politics, and such. These results *don't* mean that the public doesn't like teachers; we've already seen that the public does. And they *don't* suggest that the public is "right." They *do* suggest that the public seems to favor some changes that educators don't. Given that, teachers have a choice. They can denounce talk of merit pay and merit-based tenure, or they can try to understand where the public is coming from, respond in measured tones, and propose alternatives that address the public's concerns while reflecting what teachers deem to be good for students and schools. Cage-busters know which course they favor.

HOW CAN THEY POSSIBLY DISAGREE?

Educators mostly operate in milieus where they're surrounded by people who see things like they do. This can make it all too easy to imagine that anyone who disagrees must have a nefarious agenda. That's a mistake. But it's one that's all too common in schooling today.

Now, I'm neither naïve nor soft-hearted. There are bad people in the world. There are people who blow up innocents and who attack children. But they generally don't wind up becoming educators, education researchers, or philanthropists. There are many better places to go if you're eager to do evil. I've been in education for a quarter-century now, and I've yet to meet an educator or advocate who hated kids or was seeking to ravage communities or undermine democracy.

You do yourself no favors by imagining that those who disagree with you must be ignorant or malicious. First, it's almost assuredly not true.

Second, focusing on bogeymen makes it easy to ignore more concrete points of agreement and disagreement.

A cage-buster finds it useful to ask, "Why might someone disagree with me?" Doing so can help us push ourselves to think through what we believe and recognize where others might see things differently. This can be especially useful for educators ensconced in schools among like-minded colleagues. For instance, when I talk to educators, they often ask:

- Why do reformers love testing?
- Why do reformers want to judge schools or teachers on reading and math scores?
- Why do reformers think charter schools are a miracle cure?

Here's the dirty secret. No one loves testing. No one thinks a good education is just about reading and math. And I don't know anyone who thinks charters are a miracle cure. These claims are caricatures. If you think that reformers are making these arguments, you're not spending enough time really listening to their views or challenging your own assumptions.

Like teachers, "reformers" are motivated by passion—in their case, by a fear that too many children are being ill-served or left behind. Now, that zeal causes *them* to have blind spots, too. Plenty of them put too much faith in tests or mechanistic systems, get overly impressed with themselves, or grow so frustrated with teacher pushback that they tune teachers out. (And I call them on this *a lot*. But this book isn't for them.) However frustrated you get, keep in mind that they feel what they're doing is right and necessary. Remember that it's a product of too many educators for too long shrugging off dismal results with little more than, "We're doing the best we can."

The truth is that there's much agreement on the broad strokes of what we want in schooling. I've never met a "reformer" who wants schooling to be only about test scores, or an antireformer who doesn't think troubled schools need to improve. I know no reformer who believes that teacher evaluation systems will fix education, or any teacher who rejects useful, teacher-driven evaluation and support. All the important disagreements are really about *how* to do these things and who ought to do them.

The debate about whether teacher evaluation should be tied to test scores, for instance, is less a battle of good and evil than a disagreement between people who see the question from different vantage points. "Reformers" are convinced that traditional systems do a poor job of recognizing excellence or addressing mediocrity and thus tend to see those scores as a better way to ensure hard decisions are being made. Teachers are more intimately familiar with the practical problems of using value-added scores to measure teaching performance and therefore tend to focus on the destructive side effects of doing this poorly. Both sides have reasonable points. More important, the two views are not mutually exclusive; it's easy to find points of possible agreement. But this requires partisans to actually understand the other side.

What can you do about this? One, presume that even your opponents have good intentions. Two, frame your ideas and solutions in ways that take your opponents' concerns seriously. Don't just preach to the choir. Three, realize that today's world of social media is polarized and exaggerated. Try to meet and talk to people who feel differently. It's a lot easier to reason and find points of agreement with a person than with a Twitter caricature (see *"Getting to Yes"*).

PLAY LIKE A PRO

So, how *do* you make your passion work for you? The same way you usually approach any endeavor that you're passionate about—whether it's bicycling, playing the piano, or mentoring a kid. Cyclists don't ride wildly on rocky terrain until they get hurt; they choose courses and regimens to help make the most of their talent. Pianists don't bang wildly at keys until their hands are sore; they worry about things like hand position, touch, and technique. Put simply, in any field, the truly passionate make it a point to *play like a pro.*

Actually, the seminal tip on what it means to play like a pro was captured in perhaps the best baseball movie ever made, the 1986 film *Bull Durham.* The tale revolves around the relationship between a knuckleheaded phenom, "Nuke" LaLoosh, and the savvy career minor leaguer,

Getting to Yes

Teachers spend a lot of time with students but usually spend much less time hashing things out with colleagues and supervisors. That can be a handicap. "Like it or not, you are a negotiator," explain Roger Fisher and William Ury, co-founders of Harvard University's Negotiation Project and authors of the best-selling negotiation manual *Getting to Yes*.[6] First published in 1981, the book is one of the longest-running best sellers on management. Fisher and Ury argue that workplace "pyramids of power" have increasingly given way to a world in which "to get what we want, we are compelled to negotiate."

Fisher and Ury warn that the most common negotiation strategies tend to misfire. One is the "hard strategy," in which we're so aggressive that we alienate our negotiating partner. The other is the "soft strategy," in which we give away the store in order to avoid conflict. They advise that the best approach is "principled negotiation," which has four key components.

- *Separate the people from the problem.* They advise that the human aspect of negotiation "can be either helpful or disastrous." People get "angry, depressed, fearful, hostile, and frustrated" when they feel attacked. Work to disentangle the person from the issues you're addressing.
- *Focus on interests, not positions.* Try to reconcile "interests rather than positions." For one thing, "for every interest there usually exist several possible positions that could satisfy it." For another, "reconciling interests rather than compromising between positions also works because behind opposed positions lie many more [common] interests than conflicting ones." Seek common ground by examining disagreements and asking yourself *why* the other guy feels as he does.
- *Invent options for mutual gain.* They explain that negotiators often get tunnel vision because, "in a dispute, people usually believe that they know the right answer." The problem is that fixating on the "single best answer" can "short-circuit a wise decision-making process" in which many possibilities are considered. Start by brainstorming possible solutions that might not otherwise emerge.
- *Insist on using objective criteria.* It can be hard to find agreement if the parties disagree on what they're trying to accomplish. If you

> can settle on a common aim—something that may be easier for a teacher and a principal than for two businessmen!—then you're on the way to finding grounds for agreement.
>
> It can be tough to negotiate with someone who has more power than you, like a principal or a policy maker. In that case, Fisher and Ury advise "negotiation jujitsu"—"If they push you hard, you will be tempted to push back." Instead, when offered a proposal, "neither reject nor accept it. Treat it as one possible option. Look for the interests behind it, seek out the principles that it reflects, and think about ways to improve it. [Ask] how they think [their solution] addresses the problem." Don't ask them to "accept or reject" your idea; instead, "ask them what's wrong with it."

Crash Davis, who's brought in to mentor him. Late in the film, Nuke learns he's been called up to the majors. In a drunken confrontation, a jealous Crash finally provokes his gifted protégé into punching him. From the ground, Crash groggily asks the pro's question:

CRASH: Did you hit me with your right hand, or did you hit me with your left? Huh? Did you hit me with your right hand, or did you hit me with your left?

NUKE: My left.

CRASH: Good! That's good. When you get in a fight with a drunk, you don't hit him with your pitching hand.

That's the thing. Pros control their passion. They don't throw wild punches in drunken brawls. They focus on what matters. For teachers, this means tapping their expertise and harnessing their moral authority.

HOW DO YOU PLAY LIKE A PRO?

Playing like a pro isn't really all that hard. In a lot of ways, it's just a question of seeing through fresh eyes, asking questions, offering solutions, managing up, and adding a big serving of common sense.

It's More Important to Act Like a Cage-Buster Than to Be One. When I talk about cage-busting, people frequently ask if I think person X or Y is a cage-buster. I usually shrug and say that what matters is not that teachers *be* cage-busters but that they *be willing and able to bust the cage when necessary.* Consider the veteran teacher who quietly observed that, over the years, he'd had his share of colleagues who weren't pulling their weight. "I don't know that I'd confront them or pull them aside," he explains. "Our principal and I have been together a long time. We have a solid relationship. What I'll do instead is sit down with her and give her a head's up on things she might not notice. Then she can say something on her next walk-through or do what's needed." Does cooperating with your principal to address problems and support good instruction make one a cage-buster? Who cares? It's best to spend zero time worrying about that. What matters is not whether someone *is* a cage-buster but whether their actions help bust the cage.

Help Them Say Yes. It's the cage-buster's job to make it easy for school or system leaders to say yes. How do you do this? Four steps are paramount. First, give leaders something they *can* say yes to. You need to give them a concrete, precise problem and solution. Second, give them something they'll *want* to say yes to. You need to explain why your idea is going to help solve a problem that *they* care about. Third, help them understand how they'll *justify* their yes to parents, school board members, or supervisors. Let them know what they can say to those who might be skeptical of the decision. Fourth, reassure them that they *won't regret* saying yes. How can they be sure that your request won't become a headache for them? It's the job of school and system leaders to help you solve problems, but it's your job to make it easy for them to do so.

Don't Accidentally Trigger Red Flags. You can get in your own way without ever realizing it. School and system leaders are operating with pressures and constraints that might not be obvious. Alice Reilly, who coordinates social studies for Fairfax County, Virginia, recalls that she wanted to help Ken Halla pursue an iPad adoption proposal but that it got harder after he innocuously mentioned to the district's IT team that he wanted to "pilot" the effort. She explains, "Ken had come across people he knew in our IT Department and innocently sent an e-mail saying, 'I'm going to be doing this pilot for this publisher.' But the word *pilot* was a huge barrier. You couldn't pilot a program without permission; it has to be evaluated first. Teachers don't always understand this big picture, and that's one place where problem solving comes in. If Ken had just known to avoid the word *pilot,* the whole thing would have been a whole lot easier." It can be tough to learn all the red flags. That's where it helps to have an ally in the principal's office or in Central, someone who can eyeball your proposal and offer some big-picture feedback.

Make Sure the Amateurs Aren't Speaking for You.   Because policy is written for everyone, your professional fate is linked to what people think of all teachers in your school or system. It's up to teachers to see that the face of the profession is the responsible majority and not the embittered few. Peter Greene, plain-spoken teacher and blogger, offers a crucial reminder: "There is a tremendous tendency to bundle all the people on the Other Side into one large homogeneous group. That is exacerbated by the tendency of people not to be critical of their allies. When I was the president of a striking teacher union, the school board president and I got together for breakfast regularly. One of the reasons we did it was, basically, to reassure each other that our wackiest constituents did not speak for everybody. 'You can't really pick your friends,' one of us said. 'Yes,' replied the other. 'Or get them to shut up, either.'"[7] It's easy for onlookers to assume that the loudest teachers speak for you. If they don't, you need to say so, clearly and forcefully. Even better, don't let it get that far. Cultivate relationships, build trust, and earn a seat at the table so that you can be sure the face of the profession is the one you want it to wear.

Tame the Green-Eyed Monster.   Winning awards can boost a teacher's clout, but can also pose challenges of its own. Maddie Fennell notes, "You have to walk a political tightrope. That's because of the whole 'green-eyed monster' [of jealousy] thing when you get recognized. If you're not careful, it can become an albatross." Celebrated teachers offer four tips for keeping things under control. First, let your colleagues know that you recognize your success is partly a reflection of their own efforts. After all, teaching is a team sport. Second, take care to acknowledge that your success may sometimes inconvenience colleagues. If you get a coveted temporary assignment, it can create disruptions and require adjustments from fellow teachers. Do what you can to minimize the fallout and to show your appreciation. Third, know that the personal touch can make a difference. Alex Kajitani says of his time as California Teacher of the Year, "If I was off-campus doing an event and saw something that reminded me of one of my colleagues, I'd try to bring something back. It was a little way to signal that my being named was good for all of us and not just me." Fourth, use your newfound clout to cage-bust on behalf of shared concerns and needs. That benefits your colleagues and makes your honor an asset *for them*.

Use the Sacred Cow Hunt. Cage-busting can be intimidating. If you're not sure how to get started, or fear that your principal is going to reject even your most constructive efforts to flag problems and suggest solutions, there's a gimmick that might help kick-start the cage-busting process: the sacred cow hunt. Houston Independent School District superintendent Terry Grier explains, "Back when I was superintendent in Williamson County, Tennessee, I was on an airplane with a guy and we got to talking. He asked me, 'Have you read the book, *Sacred Cows Make the Best Burgers*?' They required all their executives to read it. The idea was to give employees a chance to make recommendations that would make the firm more effective, and they'd give away prizes for the best ideas. I thought, 'If he can do that, so can I.' We had a hunt, and it was a hell of a way to give our people the license and freedom to question policies and processes and to make suggestions." Rather than offering specific recommendations, you're cracking the door by suggesting that the school or system would benefit from giving everyone a chance to weigh in. That's a pretty innocuous proposal, but it provides cover for the suggestions you'd like to make. It's tough for even the most close-minded principal or district official to flatly reject the idea that they should give employees the chance to be heard.

Power Map Your School. Cage-busters pay close attention to the sources of formal and informal power in their school. Jacob Pactor observes, "When I went into a big school, my first priority was to know who the players are. Usually that's going to be your department chair, the special ed chair, and the guidance counselor. If you build good relationships with them, when you go to your principal it's a whole new game. Rather than it being just me coming up with an idea, I can now tell my principal, 'I've been talking this over with A, B, and C, and we are all thinking . . .' and it's like you have the full force of the faculty behind you because you've secured the key players." Cage-busting is a team sport, and that requires knowing your teammates, their individual strengths, and how to put those strengths to work.

Plug in to the Policy Makers. Washington State's elected superintendent Randy Dorn offers practical advice on how to build relationships with elected officials. The thing, he explains, is that you've got to be willing to do what it takes.

> If you want to be someone that a state representative or senator actually listens to, pick one that's going to win, give them twenty-five bucks, and ask for a yard sign. You don't even have to put the sign up. Remember, a lot of the money in politics is from lobbyists or PAC money. When an individual gives you money, you notice it. I know how crazy that sounds. We're realistic; we know who makes money. The candidate will ask what you do. You say that you're a teacher. They'll ask what school you teach at. There are people at my fund-raisers whose job—if I'm talking to anyone for five minutes—is to come pull me over to the next person. Everyone who shows up will get two or three minutes with me. If they come to a second fund-raiser, by some crazy chance, and give another twenty-five, I'll know them, guaranteed. If you do that, I guarantee you the legislator will know you by your first name. Now, I'm talking about state reps and senators, not Congress. Once a legislator gets to know you and knows that you're a supporter, they'll believe they can call and ask you questions about education. Give them a straight answer. Teachers may think their unions are going to do this for them. But teachers are in the top three among trusted professions, while the two least trusted are union executives and politicians—and I say that as a politician and a former union official!

Readers may be saying, "Wait a minute! I want lawmakers to give my school more money, I'm not looking to give *them* money." Fair enough. But Dorn is talking about how real policy makers think and act. It's fine to opt for another approach. Just be sure that your efforts to plug into policy makers are informed by more than wishful thinking.

A FEW MORE TIPS FOR THINKING LIKE A PRO

Got all that? Good. But there are also a few more general pieces of advice worth keeping in mind. These are all things that I've touched on earlier—usually plenty of times—but they're also worth reiterating. These are less actionable, but they're terrifically useful tips for maintaining a cage-busting mind-set.

Patience Is a Virtue. Big changes take longer than small ones. And changing large public organizations, like schools or school systems, is never just a week's work. This means that cage-busters don't get fired up, raise a fuss, and then call it a day. Teachers know that changing a single classroom takes grit, so it's always funny when talented teachers throw up their hands at changing what their district does because it's going to be slow, complicated, and frustrating. As Alice Reilly says, "Change does not happen instantly. The wheels of change churn slowly."

If You Don't Want to Be Isolated, Don't Isolate Yourself. Heidi Welch, the New Hampshire music teacher we met in chapter 3, says it's vital to cultivate ties with your colleagues. "In a lot of schools, arts are lowest on the totem pole," she says. "Administrators and other teachers have no idea what's going on in art classes. Arts teachers can feel like they're on an island. Every student teacher I have, I tell them not to eat lunch in their room. They need to step out and become part of the lunchroom conversation. Sometimes, as a leader, that conversation can be hard to hear because there's so much venting. But it gives you a chance to talk to your fellow teachers. It's how I make sure my work is ingrained in the fabric of the school."

It Rarely Helps to Tell People You Think They're Useless. It's rarely much use to tell people you think they're awful. Yet, it's an easy mistake to make. As one teacher says, "Leading isn't something you can just do right the first time. It really will take trial and error." He laughs, "For example, I learned that it's not the smartest approach to just tell your union representative that the teachers unions aren't the real voice of teachers. They don't take it that well. Now, I understand how to approach that differently."

Trust Is a Two-Way Street, but . . . Teachers who want a major role in shaping education policy need to earn the trust of lawmakers. In response, teachers will say, "Fine, I hear you. But we're the ones in the classrooms with the kids every day. Don't they need to earn *our* trust?" The short answer: Yep, they do. The longer answer, though, is that educators are in an *asymmetrical* relationship with the lawmakers who control budgets, write policy, and legislate accountability systems. Think of a teacher dealing with students. Both teacher and student ought to try to earn the other's trust. But the teacher gets to set the rules, which means that students stand to gain more by winning the teacher's trust than vice versa. Such is life.

Skepticism Is Sensible, but It's Also Self-Perpetuating. Teachers have good reason to be leery of new initiatives, innovations, and attention-grabbing reforms. The truth is that most of these things are a horrendous, tedious waste of time. But some of them deliver the goods. Some reflect a real attempt to crack open the cage. And the frustration of principals, superintendents, and state leaders is that, when they *have* done these sincerely and well, they often feel like they've often encountered teacher apathy or disinterest. The challenge is one that can only be solved in tandem by teachers *and* administrators. So don't be a sucker; but don't be so jaded that you let opportunities go to waste.

Make Sure There Are No Weak Links. School and system leaders want teachers to succeed, and plenty are eager to empower teachers accordingly. A problem, though, is that these same leaders say they fear that too many teachers aren't yet equal to the challenge. As a result, school and system leaders can feel obliged to keep a firm hand on the tiller. The more teachers can convince their leaders that there's nothing to fear, the more autonomy they'll get. In fact, leaders can find it rewarding and energizing to loosen their grip. When everyone on staff is competent, working hard, and using good judgment, practitioners will find the cage doors swinging wide open. Inept or angry colleagues are not just a nuisance; they're the thing standing between responsible educators and professional freedom.

You Don't Need to Be the Star, but You Can't Stink Either. Teachers frequently ask, "How good a teacher do I need to be before I start cagebusting?" It's a great question. The cage-buster's authority flows from expertise and moral authority. You need enough of each that people will take you seriously. This means that you don't need to be an All-American Teacher to be a credible cage-buster—but you can't be a lousy one. You need to have earned some respect before you can effectively speak up or start assembling allies. Think of a football player. You don't need to be the *best* player on the team to be a leader, but it's hard to be a team leader if you're not good enough to be on the field.

DON'T LET OTHERS MAKE YOU FEEL CAGED

From time to time, we can all find ourselves in a workplace where we feel unappreciated, isolated, and stymied. In most professions, when people feel that way, it's natural to look elsewhere—for a place where they *can* do their best work. As Harvard research professor Susan Moore Johnson observes, "Usually, the great stories of teacher success are from a school or a district where there's real respect for the teachers. And choosing to just close the classroom door to dysfunction is less and less possible for teachers—because of things like benchmark testing and more aggressive observation." But teachers can feel so emotionally invested, or the hassles so routine, that they wind up feeling stuck.

A cage-buster resists being caged by others' expectations or norms. He is not guilted into staying, nor is he provoked into leaving. He chooses based on his values and beliefs. Now that can be difficult. It can be tough to walk away or to contemplate new possibilities. Angel Cintron, a middle school entrepreneurship and digital literacy teacher in Washington, DC, says, "It took leaving my school to see there's a whole different world out there. You can get lost in tunnel vision and the daily grind. Now, I ask myself, 'If I'm fighting a school or a system that's not going to change, is that right for me?'" Take Zak Champagne's situation in Duval County, Florida, shortly after he won the Presidential Award for Excellence in Mathematics and Science Teaching. After nine highly successful years at a school in Jacksonville, he got a new principal who "ripped" his performance and imposed a slew of mandates. Champagne says, "I never felt so defeated in my life. We had developed these 'problems of the day,' my colleague and I. We'd used them with great results. But the principal brought her own and mandated we use those." Champagne thought the problems were awful and spent hours scrutinizing them to flag errors. Ultimately, having had his fill of wasted time, passion, and energy, he decided to change schools— and found plenty of eager suitors.

Laura Strait, who hustled to get support at a massive Massachusetts middle school, found a powerful mentor in Principal Emily Murphy. When Murphy moved to Oakland to become principal of a charter school, Strait followed, and in short order she was named one of the four 2014 winners of TNTP's Fishman Prize. Strait says, "Emily gave me the help that really made a difference. I knew I had to follow Emily to become a better teacher. So when she moved out to California, I followed her a year later." It's not that cage-busters *should* emulate Strait but that they should feel unapologetic about choosing a path that lets them do their best work. In deciding what's right for you, keep four questions in mind.

1. Might doing your best work for kids in another school be a better use of your time, passion, and energy?
2. Is frustration compromising the caliber of your work?
3. Are you in a place where you have a chance to grow professionally and keep it going?
4. Does your staying in place serve to enable inept leaders who aren't doing what it takes to support, cultivate, and encourage terrific teachers?

Good teachers should know that they're going to have good options. Seth Andrew, founder of Democracy Prep, offers a rousing bit of wisdom that's worth hearing, even if it's not for you. He says of his early teaching experience, "It was this big, bad, 2,500-student school, and I just decided, 'So what if the principal is grumpy? I don't care about that. I'm going to do what I think is right.'" He advises, "If you're in the profession, you should always remember that the demand for good teachers is much bigger than the supply." (See "Ten Tips for Cage-Busters" for a handy cage-busting cheat sheet.)

"THEN, GOD, JED, I DON'T EVEN WANT TO KNOW YOU"

I've met terrific teachers who tell me they really don't want to get into the kinds of things we've discussed in this book. They say, "Look, I got into education because I just wanted to teach." They don't think "this cage-busting stuff" is relevant or that it ought to be their problem. I hear them. I get it. I'm sympathetic—right up until they launch into complaints about the dumb accountability system that's distorting their class, the petulant principal who's killing their program, or that god-awful professional development they had to suffer through last week. When I hear all that, I find myself thinking of a young Mrs. Landingham sighing, "Then, God, Jed, I don't even want to know you."

You don't know what I'm talking about? Okay, I'll back up. At the end of the second season of the iconic TV show *The West Wing*, President Jed Bartlett finds himself in dire straits. Mrs. Landingham, his indispensable secretary, has died suddenly in a car crash, the public has learned he suffers from a potentially debilitating genetic condition, and he faces crushing pressure to abandon his reelection bid. Amid his angst, Bartlett recalls a conversation with Mrs. Landingham from the time when she worked as a secretary to his father, the headmaster of a fancy private school. She was asking young Jed to urge his father to do something about the fact that the school paid the female teachers much less than the men. In her dry, flat cadence, Mrs. Landingham gives young Jed a talking-to worth remembering:

Ten Tips for Cage-Busters

Think of the following list of ten key concepts as your cage-busting cheat sheet. Just remember:

1. *The lucky get luckier.* In writing this book, I frequently chatted with educators who'd say, "Yeah, but these teachers you're talking about are the 'lucky' ones" because of their school, principal, or what-have-you. What these folks forgot was the wisdom in Thomas Jefferson's wry adage: "I am a great believer in luck. And I find the harder I work, the more I have of it."

2. *Knowledge is power.* Cage-busters figure out what's actually going on and what they're actually allowed to do. A ridiculous amount of what frustrates and impedes educators is the product of imprecision, confusion, and misinformation. If you know the true story, you have a shot at fixing it. If you don't look hard enough to clarify what you do and don't really know, you're likely to remain stuck.

3. *Focus on solving problems, not promoting grand agendas.* Cage-busting teachers are less interested in promoting someone else's grand agenda than in doing what it takes to solve important problems in their school and system. Cage-busters are less focused on causes than on addressing those things that drain their time, passion, and energy. This makes for successes that are concrete and ensures that activism isn't just about attending one more meeting or one more rally.

4. *Action changes culture.* Schooling is rife with talk of cultural change. But what sometimes gets lost in translation is that culture is changed by action—not by good intentions or impassioned words. It can be easy to put too much faith in urgent talk, stakeholder buy-in, or the catalytic power of some new policy. It's too easy for any of this to drift into the "think locally, act globally" trap. Cage-busters focus on discrete, concrete actions. They know that doing so eventually changes culture.

5. *Ask the six questions.* Cage-busting comes down to identifying precise problems, suggesting concrete solutions, and understanding what it'll take to make a solution work. There are six key questions that can help with this: Is X *important*? If so, how well *should* we be doing when it comes to X? How well *are* we doing with X? If we're

continued

not doing as well as we should, how can we *improve* X? What's *stopping* us from improving X? And finally, how do we *remove, blast through, or tunnel under the bars* stopping us from improving X?

6. *There's strength in numbers.* Because teachers lack positional authority there's only so much they can accomplish alone. To really tap into their moral authority and put their expertise to use, teachers need to join with like-minded colleagues. This can be a matter of a few teachers at a school, but it can also be a case where cage-busters can put the weight of the union to work. It's often wise to start with small, concrete steps that address practical problems and then to build your coalition of the willing from there.

7. *Ask, "How can we do this?"* If you charge into your principal's office and ask, "*Can* I do this crazy thing I have in mind?" it's a pretty safe bet she'll say, "No." Things are likely to go differently, though, if you identify a student-centered problem that matters to you both, offer a possible solution, and then ask, "*How* can we do this?" You may just find that your principal turns into a valuable partner.

8. *Make your principal a great principal.* I routinely hear that problem solvers were lucky to have great principals. It's easy to say, "I wish I had a great principal too." What's easy to miss, though, is that cage-busters *make their principals into "great" ones* by flagging problems, offering solutions, being responsive, and making it easy for the principal to get on board. Try that first, *before* concluding you need a better principal.

9. *Presume good intentions.* When you're frustrated, it's easy to assume opponents are malevolent. That's generally not the case. There are terrible people in the world, but few work in or around K–12 schooling. The truth is, people have very different notions about how to improve schooling. Rather than denouncing those who disagree, try to understand where they're coming from. That can help identify points of agreement and opportunities to influence their thinking.

10. *Cage-busting is half the equation.* You don't cage-bust *instead* of tending to your classroom practice. Cage-busters need to have their own house in order if they're going to muster moral authority or leverage their expertise. But if your house is in order, cage-busting enables you to amplify your best work and work to create a school and system where great teaching can thrive.

MRS. LANDINGHAM: The women . . . are afraid for their jobs. If they bring it up, they're afraid for their jobs. What is it you're afraid of?

JED BARTLETT: Why do you talk to me like this?

MRS. LANDINGHAM: Because you never had a big sister and you need one . . . You must know this by now, you must have sensed it. Look, if you think we're wrong, if you think Mr. Hopkins should honestly get paid more than Mrs. Chadwick, then I respect that. But if you think we're right and you won't speak up 'cause you can't be bothered, then, God, Jed, I don't even want to know you.[8]

That's a mantra that cage-busters can embrace. The truth is, there's only so much that a given teacher can do. There are only so many things anyone can do in a given year. But a cage-buster seeks possibilities. How might those dollars be better spent? How might that time be better used? How might that professional development or that PLC be made more useful?

There's nothing wrong with keeping quiet because you agree with what's going on. If you think it's reasonable to have the PLC operate this way or for teachers to spend hours filling out that paperwork, that's cool. And if you don't feel you have the standing to speak up, or if you think this is the wrong fight at the wrong time, that's fair. But if you think there are problems and that things need to change and you won't speak up "'cause you can't be bothered," a cage-buster thinks, "Then, God, Jed, I don't even want to know you."

Teachers who have promising ideas can get discouraged when they hear "no." But recall Jeff Charbonneau arguing that "no's" aren't final and that they create an opportunity to educate. Alice Reilly sighs, "When teachers see a policy, they take it as an absolute and don't realize that those can be changed. Those procedures were developed at one point; they can be undeveloped and changed." As Montgomery County superintendent Josh Starr says, "If teachers are bringing forward something useful to others and want to scale it, I'll listen. But, honestly, I don't get much of that."

A FINAL WORD

A few chapters back we heard from Rafe Esquith, author of *Teach Like Your Hair's on Fire*. He offers some pointed words that seem appropriate here: "First-rate educators have areas of expertise and a passion to share them. They have spent decades honing their craft to make lessons exciting. Good teachers get energized fighting the very System that seeks to suck the life out of learning, but imagine if the energy spent steeling their resolve was used to inspire their kids?"[9] Just imagine. Imagine if more schools and systems weren't impediments that sap teacher resolve but vibrant communities that turbocharged teachers' time, passion, and energy.

Remember, cage-busting is a complement to great classroom teaching, not a substitute for it. Teachers cage-bust so that they can focus on the things that matter most. They cage-bust so that they can spend less time in dull meetings and more time learning from colleagues. They cage-bust so that they spend fewer minutes watching students listen to announcements and more infusing students with their passion. They cage-bust so that they spend less energy fuming at pointless paperwork and more energy helping their principal become a great principal. They cage-bust so that they can better mentor, instruct, and inspire.

None of this is easy. It requires teachers to leave the comfort of their classroom and do things they usually aren't asked to do. It calls for taking risks and learning new skills. It means listening to those with whom you disagree, empathizing with administrators, and offering solutions instead of complaints. It's a tough deal, but a good one.

Cage-busters believe it's a deal worth taking.

APPENDIX A

Cage-Busting for Beginners

CHAPTER 1: THE CLASSROOM CAGE

What Is the "Cage"?

The cage is the routines, rules, and habits that exhaust teachers' time and energy, leading educators to close their classroom door and just try to teach their hearts out.

The Bars of the Cage

An "Overflowing Bucket" of Well-Intentioned Directives

Lawmakers and leaders feel obliged to try to make things better, producing a hail of rules, regulations, laws, and directives raining down on teachers.

Teachers Have Their Time Casually Wasted

It's natural for administrators to encourage teachers to spend more time filing comprehensive lesson plans, displaying student work, and posting "big goals" in their classroom. But the result can easily turn into busy-work, endless punch lists, and inane demands.

No Upside for Excellence

Too often in schools the reward for good work is more work. Now, it would be one thing if these requests came with recognition, compensation, or opportunities. But they usually come with nothing more than personal pleas, intimations of guilt, and assertions that it's the right thing to do.

Blindsided by Accountability

Cage-busters recognize that the push for accountability is well intentioned but can still feel bludgeoned by pointless tests, simple-minded accountability systems, and ludicrous expectations.

Who's to Blame?

Who is to blame for this? Everyone and no one. There are rules, regulations, and routines that have stacked up over the decades. The cage is the product of staffing norms, accounting practices, and collective bargaining agreements that have created a world where administrators won't think twice about having a talented educator waste an hour watching children board buses or eat lunch.

What *Is* Cage-Busting?

Cage-busting is concrete, precise, and practical. It asks what the problem is, seeks out workable solutions, and figures out how to put those into practice. Cage-busting teachers are less interested in what policy makers or district leaders *ought to do* than in how teachers can *make those things happen.*

What Cage-Busters Believe

Cage-busters believe that actions change culture and that talk does not. Cage-busters believe that teachers can have enormous influence but that they need to learn how to use their voice. Cage-busters believe that a focus on problem solving, precision, and responsibility can enable teachers to create the schools and systems where they can do their best work.

Teachers Possess Two Kinds of Authority

Teachers are often unsure of how they might bust the cage. After all, teachers don't have a lot of formal authority in schools. However, while they lack positional authority, teachers have two powerful sources of authority at their disposal: the authority of expertise and a potentially powerful moral authority.

Cage-Busting Mostly Gets Ignored

There's a lot of smart guidance out there for teachers seeking advice on instruction, pedagogy, curriculum, and culture. Indeed, because most of this advice emphasizes instruction and collegiality, it can have blind spots regarding policy, the policing of the profession, or the nitty-gritty of teacher leadership.

How Did We Get Here?

Teachers feeling isolated, frustrated, undervalued, and under attack is nothing new. In fact, that's kind of how our K–12 system was designed. Common School and Progressive reformers built schools in which docile educators were to be managed by powerful patriarchs. Teacher advocates won new protections for educators but strengthened the cage in the process.

Nobody Is Altogether on My Side

Teachers can feel pressured to be in either the "reformer" or "anti-privatizer" camp. They would do well to keep in mind the admonition of Treebeard, the wizened Ent from J. R. R. Tolkien's *Lord of the Rings,* who says, "Side? I am not altogether on anybody's side, because nobody is altogether on my side."

Cages Aren't Busted by Cheap Talk and Lip Service

Teachers get lots of lip service and misty-eyed declarations of admiration. These cloying tributes are ritually offered to more than three million teachers without qualifiers or challenges. This isn't how we talk to professionals. These platitudes are the fluff of political speeches and celebrity profiles. You don't lard buckets of mushy sentiment on people you really respect.

Cage-Busting Offers a Way Forward

Today we are in this destructive cycle where reforms garner more pushback, prompting calls for more aggressive and intrusive policy and yielding even more pushback. Is there a way out of this vicious cycle? Yep. It starts with cage-busting teachers. It starts with teachers earning, employing, and leveraging the authority that will make them masters of their fate.

CHAPTER 2: CHOOSE TO BE A PROBLEM SOLVER

Much of cage-busting comes down to a simple choice: whether or not to accept the cage. For many teachers, choosing to seek a way out can seem nerve-racking or unrealistic. Doing so requires teachers to start by unlearning the habits and fears that keep them trapped.

Seeing with Fresh Eyes

The bars of the cage are frequently farther apart and weaker than they appear, though this can be surprisingly hard to see. Problems and obstacles turn into immutable examples of "how things are done." The cage-buster chooses a different path. It starts with cultivating what Zen Buddhists term *shoshin*, or "beginner's mind."

What Problem Are You Solving?

The cage-buster's simple, clarifying mantra is, "What problem are you solving?" Ultimately, a problem-solving mind-set helps cage-busters focus on six key questions that can light their path:

- Is X *important*?
- If so, how well *should* we be doing when it comes to X?
- How well *are* we doing with X?
- If we're not doing as well as we should, how can we *improve* X?
- What's *stopping* us from improving X?
- Finally, how do we *remove, blast through, or tunnel under the bars* stopping us from improving X?

The Five Why's

If you're having trouble getting a good grip on how to ask or answer these questions, just look around and ask why things are the way that they are. A terrific tool for flagging easy-to-overlook dysfunction is the Five Why's approach. The key is asking "why?" enough times that we push ourselves to look at the matter with fresh eyes.

The Value of Precision

Ask yourself, "What is *my* vision of a terrific school?" Don't just ask how to run a good class. Rather, ask, "What kind of school would enable me and my students to thrive?" Talking unabashedly about "problems," and doing so with precise measurements, is useful. It helps pierce the fog of routine in order to see problems clearly and surface solutions.

Actions Change Culture

Schooling is rife with talk of cultural change. What sometimes gets lost in translation is that culture isn't changed by good intentions, impassioned words, or policy directives. It's changed by action.

Embracing Your Moral Authority

When you sit down with a principal or a lawmaker, you're going to be viewed not just as an individual but also as a member of a profession. This means that your fate is tied to the fate of the profession—it's in the hands of the other teachers in your school, system, state, and nation. The more teachers are trusted, the more weight their moral authority carries and the readier leaders and lawmakers will be to stand back and let you swing free.

The Teaching Profession Suffers for Its Reputation

No matter how impassioned or hardworking, teachers suffer from the profession's jaded stature. This isn't about blame, and it isn't personal. But the profession is paying for a lack of quality control.

It's Not about Picking Fights

Teachers don't win moral authority by picking fights, insulting colleagues, or proclaiming that lots of teachers are awful. It involves something much more practical and precise. Most of all, it requires finding a way to address the small percentage of teachers who are holding everyone back.

Giving Excellence Its Due

Would-be reformers talk a lot about getting bad teachers out of the classroom. Cage-busters think that kind of policing is essential. But cage-busters are even more interested in building schools and systems that nurture and reward excellence and that give good teachers the chance to shine.

Policing the Profession

It's one thing to talk about policing the profession and another thing to do it. Given their lack of positional authority, teachers don't have much formal ability to police their profession. So what can they really do? Think of that public safety poster—"See something, say something." Actions change culture.

Clarify the Norms

The first step is to be sure that norms are established and clear at your school.

Find Strength in Numbers

Don't try to be a lone ranger. Instead, focus on establishing those norms and then working to make sure that most colleagues embrace them and maintain them.

Make Your Principal a Partner

Teachers can quietly keep the principal up to speed on potential problems. They can help brainstorm solutions. They can go to the principal in numbers and let her know that the teachers have her back but also that they expect her to act.

Put Peer Pressure to Work

Be sure that the tone is set by colleagues who are focused on the right things.

Talk to Them Like Adults

If you can talk firmly and respectfully to a colleague about shared norms, sometimes that makes all the difference.

Choosing to Break Free of the Cage

State and system leaders already think they're listening to teachers. They say that they're trying to address the very concerns teachers raise and that teachers often don't realize it or don't respond to *their* efforts! Teachers who want to make change need to be clear about what should change and how to make that happen.

CHAPTER 3: MANAGING UP

Teacher mythology is littered with go-it-alone heroes. Cage-busting asks for more than martyrdom. In return, it offers more. Cage-busting helps teachers start to *dismantle* the cage and to morph that naysaying principal into a supportive one.

Pay No Attention to That Man Behind the Curtain

There are real bars in teachers' way, but they are fewer and weaker than is often imagined. Teachers have gotten used to hearing "you can't do this" or "you have to do that." When they ask why, they're told it's a rule, policy, or what have you—which is often nothing more than an order not to peer behind that curtain.

Influencing Up

Make it easier for your boss to work with you by finding constructive ways to tackle the things that are frustrating you. And keep in mind that disagreements can offer a chance to air questions and speak honestly. If you speak up respectfully and with an eye on solving a problem, disagreements can prompt creative thinking and build stronger, deeper relationships.

Think Like a Leader

When a teacher sits down with his principal, it's natural to focus on what that teacher thinks he needs for his students. But it's easy to forget that the principal thinks these are *her students too* and that things can look quite different from the other side of the table. Before sitting down, make it a point to put yourself in your principal's shoes.

"But My Boss Is a Jerk"

Before concluding that things are hopeless because your boss is a jerk, ask yourself if you've done all you can to make things work.

Treat Your Principal Like a Student

It's simple. Just treat your boss with the same understanding you show your students.

Solve One Problem at a Time

Giant problems are overwhelming. But you can make overwhelming challenges into manageable ones by breaking them down and tackling them one piece at a time.

Ask "How Can We Do This?"

Cage-busters prefer an approach that can win support, expand the realm of the possible, and create new possibilities for *everyone*. The biggest step in doing this is to stop asking *"Can I do this?"* and to start asking *"How can we do this?"* This shift is simple but profoundly important.

Let Leaders Know How to Help

Teachers will say that no one wants to hear from them, even as plenty of principals and superintendents insist that they're eager for input. Leaders are generally willing to help, but, in turn, you need to make it easy for them; you need to let them know what you need and to show that you're doing your part.

Make It Easy for Leaders to Say Yes

There are four steps to getting a "yes" from your school or system leaders. First, you need to give them something they *can* say yes to. Second, you need to give them something they'll *want* to say yes to. Third, you need to help them understand how they'll *justify* their "yes" to parents, school board members, or their supervisors. Fourth, reassure them that they *won't regret* saying yes.

What Will You Do If They Say Yes?

What happens if you talk to your principal or a district official and they say yes? Amazingly, a lot of teachers get stuck here! They get stuck because they're asking for things that leaders can't provide or control or because they've gotten so used to the idea they'll hear "no" that they don't have a solution to propose.

Knowledge Is a Powerful Lever

The way out of the cage starts with seeing clearly. That requires knowing what the facts are and what the rules actually say—not what people *think* they say.

Wasted Opportunities Have a Cost

Failing to take advantage of opportunities hurts in two ways. One, it adds to the pile of unnecessary and avoidable frustrations that teachers encounter. Two, it fuels distrust among those who feel like they've gone to bat to create opportunities for teachers only to see teachers reject the opportunity.

Make Your Principal a Great Principal

It's easy to *say* "I wish I had a great principal." What's easy to miss, though, is that cage-busters help to *make their principals into great ones*. They do this by flagging problems, offering solutions, being responsive, and making it easy for the principal to get on board.

CHAPTER 4: MILLIONS OF REGISTERED VOTERS— AND THEIR KIDS

Teachers are experts on teaching and learning and can be quick to observe that most policy makers are not. They're right. But it's rare that teachers then acknowledge that they're not experts in policy making, that there might be complexities and issues that *they* don't know much about. So it's useful to survey the world through the eyes of policy makers and understand their concerns.

Why Can't Politicians Get out of Schooling?

Talented educators regularly gripe about dumb accountability systems and teacher evaluation schemes. But public schools spend public dollars and hire public employees to serve the public's children. For better or worse, they're going to be governed by public officials.

Policy Is a Crude Tool

Policy makers can make people do things, but they can't make them do them well. Policy is a blunt tool: it tells people what they must do, or what they must not do, and that's about it. Most of what we care about when it comes to teaching and learning is about *how* you do things rather than *whether* you do them.

Laws Get Written for the Lowest Common Denominator

Rules are purposely written heavy-handedly, with an eye to stopping obvious stupidity, and are targeted at the irresponsible on purpose. Policy makers can't just make rules that only apply to bad actors.

Cage-Busters Make Their Peace with Policy

Cage-busters understand that policy makers have it pretty rough. Governors, legislators, school board members, and federal officeholders are all interested in making things better for kids and in responding to voter concerns. Yet, they have only the most rudimentary tools with which to do any of this. Cage-busters don't take policy personally.

The Accountability Thing

Absent professional trust, there are just three kinds of accountability. Lawmakers can hold public services accountable via input regulation, outcome accountability, and consumer choice. As much as they wish there were other methods, there aren't.

Big P versus little p Policy

When talking about policy, it's important to distinguish between *Big P* and *little p* policies. Big P policies are formal statutes and contractual provisions that present stubborn and hard-to-change barriers. Little p policies are local policies, accepted practices, or district conventions that can be more readily altered. Determining what kind of policy it is determines what you need to do to address it.

People Want to Hear What Teachers Have to Say

Believe it or not, teachers have a sympathetic audience. People are interested in what teachers think. After all, the public knows that teachers are closer to the classroom than anyone else. The question is what teachers choose to do with this influence.

What to Say to Policy Makers

When teachers talk to policy makers, they should emphasize shared concerns, offer solutions, and avoid asking for more money.

Don't Get Discouraged If They Happen to Disagree

People can listen carefully and still disagree with you. People value different things, have competing concerns, and see the world in different ways.

Check Your Stereotypes at the Door

Treat policy makers and advocates with the same courtesy that you'd like from them. Give them a chance before you make assumptions.

The Problem with Demanding "More Money"

Every single day, someone is asking policy makers for more. Cops, firemen, park officials, librarians, youth services directors, transit directors, public housing officials, college presidents, and public health providers are all saying, "What about us?" And they all want to know how anybody can oppose more funds for *their* valuable service. But if you convince policy makers that you're spending money wisely and well, they'll *show* you the money.

Policy Favors Those Who Are Prepared

Every so often, forces conspire to create "policy windows" during which it's possible to win the votes to pass new laws. Being informed, at the table and with a plan in hand, can make all the difference when those windows open.

Don't Stay in Your Corner of the Forest

Remember, policy is a crude lever. It's not nimble or easily targeted. And its impact depends on how it's implemented. This is why cage-busters tend to start small, tackling those problems in their school or system that drain time, passion, and energy, and *then* work their way up. That way, when they wind up talking to lawmakers, they're talking to them about solving specific problems that they themselves can't solve in their school or system.

CHAPTER 5: TACKLING EVERYDAY PROBLEMS

Teacher leadership is a good thing. In practice, though, it's historically added up to little more than pleasant words, having done little to tackle those things that sap teachers' time, passion, and energy

Why Teacher Leadership Is Often a Cruddy Deal

Teacher leadership can feel like a cruddy deal. Teachers sigh that it often means more work with not much say-so or satisfaction in return. The best case can involve spending time and energy on stuff that doesn't help you. The worst case is that that you're distracted from your kids and classroom.

Getting "Collaboration" Right

In K–12, we talk a lot about collaboration. And we should. Collaboration is a good thing. However, it's a term that's used so casually that it can become shorthand for "be nice." Cage-busters eschew vague talk of "collaboration" for a more precise and practical notion—that of the "coalition of the willing."

So, What Exactly Do You *Do* with Data?

Most teachers have some idea of how to use data to diagnose student needs, gauge progress, and adjust instruction. But most discussion of data tends to stop there. Unfortunately, however useful, this doesn't help do anything about the problems of the cage.

Don't Allow Data or Research to Substitute for Good Judgment

When presented with promising programs or reforms, ask the simple question: What are the expected benefits?

Be Sure That You're Collecting Data with an Eye Toward Solving Problems
Student achievement data is vital, but it doesn't tell you how well time is being used or how well the school is communicating with parents. To figure out what's going on behind the test scores, you need to ask the right questions and figure out how to measure what matters.

Metrics Need to Measure What Matters
Always be sure that you're not working for your metrics but that you've got them working for you.

Solutions That Work in One Place May Not Work Somewhere Else
This is especially true if challenges or conditions vary.

Think of Time and Dollars as Data, Too
Knowing where time and dollars go can be a powerful tool for finding solutions.

Flipping the Switch with Families

Cage-busters know they can't change rules and schools by their lonesome. They need allies. And parents can be powerful force multipliers, though their power often goes untapped.

Putting an End to Awful Meetings

Plenty of teachers grumble that they sit through lots of meetings that are a poor use of time. But teachers can turn this around. The simple way to start is by demanding that meetings be solution oriented and then holding everyone to that standard.

Rethinking the Deal with Professional Development

Teachers voice a lot of frustration with professional development. Asked about PD's unimpressive track record, teachers tend to voice a sense of helpless resignation—that this is just the way it goes. Cage-busters reject that hopelessness wholly and completely. They don't do this through vague calls for "professionalism." They do it by seeing the problem, putting forward sensible solutions, and working to make those real.

Viewing Technology as a Tool

Technology is too often hailed as a miracle restorative. Here's the thing: it's not the technology that matters but *how we use it.*

Putting the Media to Good Use

When teachers speak up about problems, solutions, and professional responsibility, they can use media to amplify their message. Engaging the media or writing for public outlets isn't as difficult as you might think. Truth is, the media is hungry for teacher voices.

Providing Leadership That Matters

Teacher leadership is not necessarily cage-busting. And it can be terrific even when it isn't. But a cage-busting mind-set equips teacher leaders to do more than help their colleagues be slightly better denizens of the cage.

CHAPTER 6: THE UNION QUESTION

Teacher unions are a lightning rod of controversy. Happily, the cage-buster need not wade into this broader debate.

Unions Aren't Monolithic

Unions can vary dramatically from one place to the next. They can play a constructive role at some times and in some places.

Aren't Union Leaders Enemies of Cage-Busting?

Precision is important. Cage-busters reject both vague assurances that union leaders are always eager to do what's best for students and claims that they never care about the kids. Cage-busters find it far more useful to think of union leaders the same way they think about school leaders or policy makers—as people who face a lot of demands but may well prove reasonable if given a chance.

Why Mess with the Union at All?

Unions are the primary vehicle for voicing teacher concerns and influencing policy. Trying to discuss educational practice or teacher empowerment without talking about the union is like discussing the beach without mentioning the ocean.

Contracts Can Be More Flexible Than You Think

Contracts, like policy, are generally the product of distrust, and it's hard to change the contracts before building that trust. Cage-busters don't allow themselves to be stopped by rumors or assumptions. If someone claims that the contract prohibits something, ask them to point out the relevant language. If they can't, the contract does *not* prohibit it.

Pushing the Union from the Inside

Union leaders are elected, and influence in union elections often comes down to credibility, preparation, and effort. Union bona fides can empower a cage-buster to push hard from the inside *if they choose to do so* and if they have the savvy and muscle to retain their support.

Don't Be Afraid to Challenge the Union

I frequently hear from teachers who feel that the union doesn't reflect their concerns. My question for them is the same one I ask any teacher frustrated by their principal—*What are you doing about it?*

Sometimes You Need to Start Your Own Team

Well-intentioned efforts may not be enough. After all, unions are big, stodgy organizations. It can be tough to really change things. One strategy for doing so is to join other dissatisfied teachers and together try to push the union more aggressively. Teach Plus and Educators 4 Excellence are two groups that cage-busters should look into in this regard.

There Are Times to Seek Another Way

Just as schools or districts may prove recalcitrant no matter how diligently you try to bust that cage, the same can be true of unions. At such times, cage-busters may opt out and choose to seek another way. The American Association of Educators (AAE) and the California Teachers Empowerment Network are two examples of what this looks like.

Remember Treebeard's Admonition

Cage-busters aren't pro-union or anti-union. They're for building schools where their time, passion, and energy are valued and amplified. The question is never whether a cage-buster is for the union; it's always whether the *union is for the cage-buster.*

CHAPTER 7: SQUARE PEGS AND ROUND HOLES

Cage-busters don't just want better schools or teaching. They want schools where educators and students can do their *best* work. That can require big changes, because the job description for the twenty-first-century teacher leaves something to be desired. Cage-busters wonder whether being a teacher should necessarily mean spending six hours a day in a classroom with twenty or thirty kids. They ask hard questions about what teachers *do* and how schools and systems can help them do it better.

Not "Just a Teacher"

For more than a century it's been largely assumed that teachers will do pretty much the same job, in the same room, for the same number of children on the first day of their first year and on the final day of their career. This has deprived teachers of the chance for professional growth.

Unbundling the Teaching Job

Teachers are asked to do a little bit of everything. The unstated assumption is that teachers are, more or less, similarly good at all of this. As a result, plenty of perfectly competent educators struggle just because it's hard to be good at everything.

Taking Specialization Seriously

You rarely see a thoracic surgeon or anesthesiologist unloading an ambulance, working the copier, or delivering food to patients. Instead, medical practice has been reconfigured so that they can do more of what they do best.

Taking Hybrid Roles Seriously

Hybrid roles allow teachers to remain in the classroom while also specializing and taking on new responsibilities. These roles include providing online instruction, supervising instructional teams, and more. The result allows for jobs that lets teachers make fuller use of their talents and increase their impact.

Taking Teams Seriously

Professional teams are typically built around the strengths of the most talented members, with recognition and pay reflecting those different contributions.

Cage-Busting Beyond the Classroom

Many teachers confess to feeling guilty about changing schools or changing roles. They shouldn't. Cage-busters see the classroom as a place of possibility, not a prison. Cage-busters celebrate those who choose to seek new possibilities, whether inside or outside of the classroom. Consider the paths of the founders of organizations such as EMERGE, LearnZillion, Enriched, the Intersection, and BetterLesson.

The Promise of Teacher-Led Schools

Perhaps the neatest way for teachers to marry accountability and authority is by creating schools where they run the show—just like the professionals do in a law partnership or medical practice. Practitioners make the decisions and divvy up leadership responsibilities as they see fit. There are dozens of teacher-led schools across the country today, and there's broad interest in teacher-led schools among both teachers and the public.

Making Room for Square Pegs

There is much that teachers can do right now, today. But there are also real limits to what teachers can do in roles, classrooms, and schools designed for the world of a century ago. These structures can limit the ability of teachers to make the best use of their talents or to re-imagine stifling routines. It's vital to ask whether the familiar teaching job still makes sense.

CHAPTER 8: YOU ARE BRAVER THAN YOU BELIEVE

Cage-busting is not about finding more teachers who are good today but about reshaping schools, systems, and the profession so that many more may be extraordinary tomorrow. That requires teachers to leverage all their authority. They must be prepared to address mediocrity, identify problems, pose solutions, and work with administrators and policy makers.

You Had Me at Hello

Many successful teacher leaders seem genuinely puzzled by the notion that "nobody cares what teachers think." They say they've found that people are eager to hear what they have to say. Principals, superintendents, and policy makers are starved for people to help solve problems.

This Is Going to Tick Off My Principal!

The fear that cage-busting will alienate your principal (or superintendent) is a rational one. That's why it matters so much *how* cage-busters go about things. A key part of cage-busting is to reach out productively. Remember, you can make your principal more receptive by approaching her the right way.

Passion Has a Price

Education is full of passionate people. But passion can come at real costs. It can leave us impatient, make us strident, and lead us to dismiss the views of others.

How Can They Possibly Disagree?

Educators (and advocates) tend to believe that what they're doing is good and important. And they mostly operate in milieus where they're surrounded by people who see things like they do. This can make it all too easy to imagine that anyone who disagrees must have a nefarious agenda. That's a mistake.

Play Like a Pro

So, how *do* you make your passion work for you? Think about how you approach any endeavor about which you're passionate—whether it's bicycling, playing the piano, or mentoring a kid. You harness your passion with discipline and focus.

How Do You Play Like a Pro?

Playing like a pro isn't really all that hard. In a lot of ways, it's just a question of seeing through fresh eyes, asking questions, offering solutions, managing up, and adding a big serving of common sense.

It's More Important to Act Like a Cage-Buster Than to Be One

When I talk about cage-busting, people frequently ask if I think person X or Y is a cage-buster. I usually shrug and say that what matters is not that teachers *be cage-busters* but that they *be willing and able to bust the cage when necessary.*

Don't Accidentally Trigger Red Flags

You can get in your own way without ever realizing it. School and system leaders are operating under pressures and constraints that might not be obvious.

Make Sure the Amateurs Aren't Speaking for You

Because policy is written for everyone, your professional fate is linked to what people think of all teachers in your school or system. If the face of the profession is to be the responsible majority and not the embittered few, teachers need to make that happen.

Tame the Green-Eyed Monster

Winning awards can raise a teacher's profile outside of school, but it can also present problems among his fellow teachers. Celebrated teachers take this in stride and keep things under control.

Use the Sacred Cow Hunt

The sacred cow hunt can give you and your colleagues a chance to weigh in on problems in your school.

Power Map Your School

Before going to your principal with a suggestion or proposal, figure out who the key players are in the school and how to get them on your side.

A Few More Tips for Thinking Like a Pro

Patience Is a Virtue

Big changes take longer than small ones. And changing large public organizations, like schools or school systems, is never one weekend's work. This means that cage-busters don't get fired up, raise a fuss, and then call it a day.

If You Don't Want to Be Isolated, Don't Isolate Yourself

You'll never be able to change things when you are sitting alone in your room.

It Rarely Helps to Tell People You Think They're Useless

It's seldom useful to tell people you think they're evil and awful.

Trust Is a Two-Way Street, but . . .

Teachers who want a major role in shaping education policy need to earn the trust of lawmakers. Teachers are in asymmetrical relationships with policy makers and administrators, and they should operate accordingly.

Skepticism Is Sensible, but It's Also Self-Perpetuating

Teachers have good reason to be leery of new invitations, innovations, and attention-grabbing reforms. But recognize that not all of these things are doomed. Some may reflect a real attempt to crack open the cage.

Make Sure There Are No Weak Links

The more that teachers can convince their leaders there's nothing to fear, the more autonomy they'll get. In fact, leaders can find it rewarding and energizing to loosen their grip.

You Don't Need to Be the Star, but You Can't Stink, Either

You don't need to be an All-American Teacher to be a credible cage-buster—but you can't be a lousy one.

Don't Let Others Make You Feel Caged

From time to time, we all find ourselves in a workplace where we feel unappreciated, isolated, and stymied. A cage-buster resists being caged by others' expectations or norms. He is not guilted into staying, nor is he provoked into leaving. He chooses based on his values and beliefs.

"Then, God, Jed, I Don't Even Want to Know You"

Some terrific teachers say they really don't want to get into the stuff of cage-busting. I hear them. I get it. And there's nothing wrong with keeping quiet when you agree with what's going on. But a cage-buster has no patience for someone who thinks things need to change but "can't be bothered" to speak up.

A Final Word

Cage-busting is a complement to great classroom teaching, not a substitute for it. Teachers cage-bust so that they can focus on the things that matter most. They cage-bust so that they spend fewer minutes watching students listen to announcements and more infusing students with their passion. They cage-bust so that they spend less energy fuming at pointless paperwork and more energy helping their principal become a great principal. They cage-bust so that they can better mentor, instruct, and inspire. None of this is easy. It requires teachers to leave the comfort of their classroom and do things they usually aren't asked to do.

APPENDIX B

Glossary of Terms

American Federation of Teachers (AFT)   The American Federation of Teachers is a labor union primarily representing educators. Founded in 1916, the AFT currently represents roughly 1.5 million members from more than three thousand local affiliates. The union is overseen by elected officials and convention delegates. Randi Weingarten is the current president.

Elementary and Secondary Education Act (ESEA)   The act, originally passed in 1965 as part of Lyndon B. Johnson's War on Poverty, emphasizes equal access to education and accountability and attempts to close the achievement gap by providing quality education and equal opportunities to all students. Since 1965, ESEA has been reauthorized every five years with various changes. The most recent reauthorization of ESEA was in 2001 with No Child Left Behind (see **NCLB**).

ESEA Waivers   In 2012, the U.S. Department of Education invited states to apply for waivers that offer flexibility to certain requirements of ESEA in exchange for states developing rigorous and comprehensive plans to improve student learning. States with waivers must prove that they are raising standards, improving accountability, and attempting to better assess teacher effectiveness.

Last in first out(LIFO)   Last in first out is a method of laying off teachers whereby the last teacher to be hired is the first teacher to be terminated. This practice is based entirely on seniority and is a prime concern for those who think staffing should take into account teacher or student performance.

Local education agency (LEA)   A local education agency is a public board of education or other authority that oversees elementary and secondary schools within a district, city, or other subdivision of a state. They are most often school districts but, in some states, charter schools can be their own LEAs.

Local superintendent   A local superintendent runs the local education agency or school district. The superintendent has executive and administrative oversight of schools, students, and educational services. The superintendent is appointed by the school board to recommend and implement educational policy for the district. Superintendent responsibilities include budgeting, facilities, personnel decisions, curriculum, professional development, contracts, and strategic planning.

Merit pay   This term encompasses a variety of strategies for linking teacher pay to job performance. There is controversy over the concept as well as over what criteria should be used to evaluate teachers.

National Board for Professional Teaching Standards (NBPTS)   Also known as the National Board, this nonprofit was founded in 1987 in order to develop and promote professional standards for teaching. The National Board developed a system to certify teachers based on those standards, manages the certification process, and seeks to involve Board-certified teachers in school improvement efforts. As of 2014, more than 100,000 teachers had been certified by the National Board.

National Education Association (NEA)   The National Education Association is the largest professional employee organization and labor union in the United States. It numbers 3.2 million members, with affiliate organizations in every state. NEA policy is set by its nine-thousand-member Representative Assembly, which also elects the national leadership. Lily Eskelsen García, first elected in 2014, is the current president.

No Child Left Behind (NCLB) The most recent reauthorization of ESEA, emphasizing standards-based accountability, No Child Left Behind requires states to develop state standards and administer annual standardized assessments to all public schools in order to receive federal funding. In 2012 the U.S. Department of Education started offering waivers (see **ESEA Waivers**) from provisions of NCLB.

Race to the Top (RTTT) Race to the Top is a grant competition first created by the U.S. Department of Education in 2009 in which states or school districts compete for federal funds. The initial and most famous version was the $4.35 billion RTTT program launched in 2009 as part of the federal stimulus bill. The 2009 competition emphasized standards, assessments, recruiting and retaining teachers and leaders, data systems, and turning around low-achieving schools.

State education agency (SEA) Also known as the state department of education, the SEA is the government agency in each state that's responsible for providing resources and guidance on education matters to school districts and citizens. The SEA oversees the local education agencies within each state.

State superintendent The state superintendent is either an elected or appointed officer (depending on the state) who serves as the chief executive official for a state education agency. This position is known in some states as the commissioner or secretary of education. The state superintendent oversees state activity, works with local school districts, implements education standards and policies, and manages administrative and operational duties of the state public education system.

Teach For America (TFA) Teach For America is a nonprofit organization that recruits, trains, and places "high-achieving recent college graduates" in schools in low-income areas. TFA corps members commit to teach for at least two years. In 2014 there were more than 11,000 active TFA corps members across the United States teaching more than 750,000 students.

Title I   Title I is a provision of the ESEA that provides federal funding to schools and school districts with a high proportion of students from low-income families. Funds can be allocated for "schoolwide programs" or for "targeted assistance programs."

U.S. Department of Education   Also known as ED, this is the cabinet-level department for education in the United States government. The department is primarily responsible for federal education policy, administering and coordinating federal assistance for education, collecting data on U.S. schools, and enforcing federal educational laws. ED is overseen by the U.S. Secretary of Education, who is currently Arne Duncan.

APPENDIX C

Teacher Voice Organizations

CENTER FOR TEACHING QUALITY (CTQ) COLLABORATORY

Locations: A virtual community that spans the country, with locations specific to Colorado, Florida, Illinois, Kentucky, North Carolina, and Washington

Membership: Any interested teacher or individual can join

Overview: CTQ seeks to connect and mobilize teachers who strive to improve the classroom experience for students. Through its Collaboratory, teachers can participate in teacher-targeted content labs and connect with other educators to discuss tasks, projects, and policy.

http://www.teachingquality.org

EDUCATORS 4 EXCELLENCE (E4E)

Locations: Chapters in New York City, Los Angeles, Minnesota, and Connecticut, and Chicago

Membership: All teachers who opt to sign E4E's "Declaration of Teachers' Principles and Beliefs"

Overview: E4E provides opportunities for teachers to learn about education policy, network with colleagues and policy makers, and advocate for policy changes. Its Teacher Leadership Program provides leadership development in areas like policy, advocacy, and organizing. E4E's advocacy work has led to changes affecting issues such as teacher evaluation, career ladders and differentiated compensation, restorative justice, school climate, and early childhood education.

http://www.educators4excellence.org

ELEVATING AND CELEBRATING EFFECTIVE TEACHING AND TEACHERS (ECET²)

Locations: National events across the country and regional events in Florida, Kentucky, Maryland, and Pennsylvania

Membership: Teachers selected after a peer nomination process

Overview: Sponsored by the Bill & Melinda Gates Foundation, ECET² holds conferences each year designed around recognizing great teachers and sharing their stories. Participants evaluate their work through lectures, workshops, informal dialogues, and networking. Hundreds of America's top teachers gather to exchange ideas for improving practice, engaging students, and policing the profession.

http://www.impatientoptimists.org/Posts/2014/02/Teachers-Voices-Matter-The-ECET2-Conference

HOPE STREET GROUP

Locations: National and state affiliates in Kentucky, Hawaii, New York, and Tennessee.

Membership: Teachers selected after competitive application process

Overview: Hope Street Group is a national nonprofit working to expand economic opportunity by addressing jobs, health, and education. The education team runs the National Teacher Fellows Program and several State Teacher Fellowship programs. It seeks to recruit outstanding teachers and equips them to advocate for local and national policy changes. Hope Street Group holds policy conventions, advises states on implementation of the Common Core standards, and creates online tools to connect reform-minded teachers.

http://www.hopestreetgroup.org

LEADING EDUCATORS

Locations: Greater Houston, Kansas City, New Orleans, Baton Rouge, Memphis, and Washington, DC
Membership: Determined by application process
Overview: Leading Educators partners with schools and districts to advance teachers' leadership skills and opportunities to provide frontline support and professional development to colleagues. Leading Educators offers a two-year fellowship program as well as a series of strategic support initiatives to schools and districts.

http://www.leadingeducators.org

NATIONAL BOARD FOR PROFESSIONAL TEACHING STANDARDS (NBPTS)

Location: Headquartered in Arlington, VA, with teachers certified across the United States
Membership: Educators may join by passing the National Board Certification exam
Overview: Founded in 1987, the NBPTS is an independent nonprofit organization with the interest of advancing the quality of teaching and learning by developing professional standards for accomplished teaching and offering a national, voluntary assessment, the National Board Certification. Currently more than 100,000 educators across the United States have been National Board certified.

http://www.nbpts.org

NATIONAL NETWORK OF STATE TEACHERS OF THE YEAR (NNSTOY)

Locations: National headquarters in Washington, DC
Membership: A teacher must have been a State Teacher of the Year and participated in the Council of Chief State School Officers' National Teacher of the Year program

Overview: NNSTOY is a hub for State Teachers of the Year to network around advocating for effective teaching practices and policies. It has partnered with the Council of Chief State School Officers to provide each State Teacher of the Year with training and opportunities in media outreach, policy, and advocacy.

http://www.nnstoy.org

TEACH FOR AMERICA LEADERSHIP FOR EDUCATIONAL EQUITY (LEE)

Locations: Membership and job opportunities available across the United States
Membership: Full LEE membership is open to Teach For America corps members, alumni, and staff
Overview: Sponsored by Teach For America (TFA), LEE is an organization dedicated to empowering Teach For America corps members and alumni to develop as leaders in their communities and to build the movement for educational equity. LEE offers training sessions, workshops, and fellowship programs for members to develop leadership skills in a variety of different areas within the education field. The LEE community provides a variety of resources, including career guidance and webinar sessions.

http://educationalequity.org

TEACH PLUS

Locations: Sites in Chicago, Indianapolis, Los Angeles, Massachusetts, Tennessee, and Washington, DC
Membership: Open to all educators
Overview: The Teach Plus Network is a network of educators eager to influence local, district, and national policy decisions. Members participate in interactive discussion series featuring expert speakers, teacher-driven discussions with policy makers, live polling, and professional networking receptions to discuss ways to improve the teaching profession.

http://www.teachplus.org

TNTP (FORMERLY KNOWN AS THE NEW TEACHER PROJECT)

Locations: In 25 cities across 21 states and the District of Columbia
Membership: Selected Teaching Fellows and TNTP Academy Program Participants
Overview: TNTP is a nonprofit organization committed to ending educational inequality. It offers a Teaching Fellows program as well as the TNTP Academy program, which both prepare professionals without a traditional education background to become effective teachers in high-need schools. TNTP also produces and publishes influential research on the state of the profession.

http://tntp.org

VIVA (VOICE, IDEAS, VISION, ACTION) TEACHERS

Locations: Chapters in Arizona, Colorado, Iowa, Massachusetts, Minnesota, New Jersey New York, and Pennsylvania
Membership: Open to all educators
Overview: Through the Idea Exchange Process, VIVA, sponsored by New Voice Strategies, allows teachers to get involved virtually through an open-invitation platform for teachers to share views on a policy issue. A small group of active participants in the exchange is invited to collaborate and craft recommendations which are then shared with public officials.

http://vivateachers.org

APPENDIX D

Fellowships and Leadership Opportunities

ALBERT EINSTEIN DISTINGUISHED EDUCATOR FELLOWSHIP PROGRAM

Sponsoring organization: U.S. Department of Energy, Office of Science
Duration: 11 months, full time
Stipend: $6,000 monthly, with $1,000 per month housing allowance; $4,500 travel stipend
Overview: Created by an act of Congress in 1994, this fellowship allows educators with a focus in STEM-related fields to work in the legislative or executive branch. Einstein Fellows spend a year in Washington, DC, working in congressional offices or at federal agencies. Accomplished educators who have been teaching at least five years full time, with most of that in a STEM-related field, are eligible.
http://science.energy.gov/wdts/einstein

AMERICA ACHIEVES FELLOWSHIP FOR TEACHERS AND PRINCIPALS (AAFTP)

Sponsoring organization: America Achieves
Duration: Ongoing, with semi-annual conferences and other programs throughout the year

Stipend: $500–$3,000

Overview: America Achieves offers several fellowships that join teachers and principals together to share ideas, learn from thought leaders, develop skills, and advise policy makers on local, state, and national education policies. America Achieves offers State and National fellowships, as well as America Achieves Lead Fellowships, which last two years and are awarded to approximately 20 teachers a year. The leaders in these programs help identify promising models and what is needed to help scale those models.

http://apply.americaachieves.org

CITYBRIDGE—NEWSCHOOLS EDUCATION INNOVATION FELLOWSHIP

Sponsoring organization: CityBridge Foundation and NewSchools Venture Fund
Duration: 1 year
Stipend: $5,000
Overview: The Education Innovation Fellowship focuses on providing teachers and educators with innovative strategies to implement blended learning models in their classrooms.

http://www.citybridgefoundation.org/Collaboration/Fellowship

FISHMAN PRIZE FOR SUPERLATIVE CLASSROOM PRACTICE

Sponsoring organization: TNTP (formerly known as The New Teacher Project)
Duration: 4-week summer residency
Stipend: $25,000
Overview: The Fishman Prize is awarded annually to exceptional teachers in high-poverty public schools. Educators who win the award are invited to participate in an intensive summer residency so that they can share their expertise, learn new practices, and explore larger educational issues.

http://tntp.org/fishman-prize

FULBRIGHT-HAYS SEMINARS ABROAD

Sponsoring organization: U.S. Department of Education
Duration: 4–6 weeks
Stipend: Covers a roundtrip flight, room and board, and program-related travel costs
Overview: The Fulbright program offers educators in the social sciences and the humanities the chance to travel abroad to countries outside of Western Europe in order to strengthen their understanding and knowledge of other nations and cultures. The program is geared toward educators who demonstrate the need to deepen their expertise through travel abroad.

http://www2.ed.gov/programs/iegpssap/index.html

FUTURE OF THE PROFESSION FELLOWSHIP

Sponsoring organization: NEA and Teach Plus
Duration: 1 year, part time
Stipend: $1,000 plus travel
Overview: Selected teachers are exposed to policy issues, interact with policy makers, and deepen their knowledge of advocacy. They have the opportunity to work with NEA staff and advise the union on ideas for engaging a new generation and enhancing the future of the profession. This cohort meets several times annually in Washington, DC, and engages monthly in virtual training.

http://www.teachplus.org/page/teach-plusnea-future-of-the-profession-fellowship-239.html

NATIONAL TEACHER FELLOWSHIP

Sponsoring organization: Hope Street Group
Duration: 18 months
Stipend: $5,000
Overview: The program enables educators with an interest in education policy to learn new skills and equips them to advocate for local and national

policy changes. Participants have the chance to influence policy through meetings with U.S. senators, representatives, and national policy leaders, as well as through attendance at national educator conventions and outreach to media.

http://hopestreetgroup.org/our-work/education/teacher-fellowship

RODEL TEACHER COUNCIL

Sponsoring organization: Rodel Foundation of Delaware
Duration: 18 months
Stipend: $1,500
Overview: The Rodel Teacher Council provides a venue for teachers to be heard on issues that affect educators and on the course of education reform throughout the state of Delaware. Members meet with education stakeholders, visit schools, and work to bring innovative practices to schools and districts. Each year, based on applications and interviews, 16 members are selected from across the state.

http://www.rodelfoundationde.org/who-we-are/teachercouncil

T3 (TURNAROUND TEACHER TEAMS) INITIATIVE

Sponsoring organization: Teach Plus
Duration: One mandatory three-day training session, along with ongoing training and professional development
Stipend: $4,000–$6,000 (commensurate with district policy)
Overview: The T3 Initiative recruits and develops experienced teachers to transform classrooms in underperforming schools. Participants receive professional development and weekly one-on-one coaching. The program seeks teacher leaders looking to lead their peers in efforts to improve instruction and boost student academic outcomes.

http://www.teachplus.org/page/t3-initiative-8.html

TEACHERS FOR GLOBAL CLASSROOMS GRANT PROGRAM

Sponsoring organization: U.S. Department of State and the International Research and Exchanges Board
Duration: 1 year
Stipend: Small stipend for international travel costs
Overview: The Teachers for Global Classrooms Grant Program for middle and high school teachers is an opportunity for educators striving to infuse a global perspective into their classrooms and curriculums. The program includes an online course to develop fellows' skills as ambassadors of globalized pedagogy and a Global Education Symposium in Washington, DC.

http://www.irex.org/project/teachers-global-classrooms-program-tgc

TEACHERS FOR TRANSFORMATION ACADEMY

Sponsoring organization: StudentsFirst
Duration: 1 year, part time
Stipend: Compensation varies by state
Overview: This fellowship is intended to engage teachers in education reform and help them acquire the resources and tools to organize local networks of educators. Fellows meet monthly for training sessions and twice for intensive weekend workshops in Sacramento, CA. Fellows attend events, meet legislators, and engage via various outreach initiatives.

http://www.studentsfirst.org/teacher-fellows

TEACHING AMBASSADOR FELLOWSHIP

Sponsoring organization: U.S. Department of Education
Duration: 1 year, full or part time
Stipend: Program compensation operates under the Intergovernmental Personnel Act
Overview: The Teaching Ambassador Fellowship program seeks to create a community of educators who can share their expertise and work with

policy makers to tackle national, state, and local education issues. There are two types of fellows: Washington Fellows take a year off from teaching and work as full-time employees in the U.S. Department of Education to share their knowledge and develop their understanding of the policy-making process. Classroom Fellows serve as part-time, paid federal employees facilitating conversation among local educators and collaborating with other fellows and federal officials.

http://www2.ed.gov/programs/teacherfellowship/index.html

TEACHING POLICY FELLOWSHIP

Sponsoring organization: Teach Plus
Duration: 1.5 academic years
Stipend: $2,400
Overview: The Teaching Policy Fellowship involves monthly meetings where the fellows interact with key education leaders, learn best practices for education reform, and advocate for policy to enhance their students' and fellow teachers' experiences. The fellowship emphasizes opportunity advocacy for policies that will better serve students and retain excellent teachers. Fellows typically have 2–10 years of classroom experience.

http://www.teachplus.org/page/teaching-policy-fellows-65.html

APPENDIX E

Resources for Rethinking the Profession

CARPE DIEM LEARNING SYSTEMS

Overview: Carpe Diem Learning Systems is a charter school management organization that focuses on a blended learning model in charter schools for students grades 6–12. After achieving remarkable results in its own redesigned schools, Carpe Diem has started to offer consulting to schools and teachers who want to apply the personalized blended learning model in their classrooms.

http://carpediemschools.com

CLAYTON CHRISTENSEN INSTITUTE FOR DISRUPTIVE INNOVATION

Overview: The Christensen Institute is a Boston-based think tank committed to exploring and explaining the key concepts of disruptive innovation. Founded to build on the work of Harvard Business School professor Clayton Christensen, author of *Disrupting Class*, it is a go-to resource on blended learning, the use of technology in schools, and devising promising models for digital learning.

http://www.christenseninstitute.org

EDUCATION ELEMENTS

Overview: Education Elements works directly with teachers, schools, districts, and states to develop and implement personalized learning strategies and methods. The company started by working with a single charter school and is now partnering with more than 100 public school districts across the country.

http://www.edelements.com

EDUCATION EVOLVING

Overview: Education Evolving deems itself a "design shop," working to redesign schooling to better suit student and teacher needs, new technologies, and the demands of the twenty-first century. The organization champions the notion of teacher-led charter schools. Education Evolving's Web site provides a comprehensive list of schools that have arrangements for teacher autonomy, with descriptions of what each arrangement entails.

http://www.educationevolving.org

EDUCATION RESOURCE STRATEGIES

Overview: Education Resource Strategies (ERS) seeks to boost student outcomes in urban schools by helping systems better use and organize resources, focusing on seven strategic areas: standards, teaching, school design, leadership, school support, funding, and partnerships. ERS consults with district and state leaders, maintains an extensive database of research and tools, and partners with communities to share research and support innovation.

http://www.educationresourcestrategies.org

EDUNOMICS LAB

Overview: Edunomics Lab, a research center based at Georgetown University, explores and models complex finance decisions within the education sphere. It studies best fiscal practices for districts and states, helps train principals in school-level budgets, and also brings relevant analyses to policy makers and school leaders.

http://edunomicslab.org

4.0 SCHOOLS

Overview: 4.0 Schools is an incubator for education start-ups based in New York and New Orleans. By bringing together entrepreneurs, educators, technologists, designers, and other creative thinkers, 4.0 Schools hope to find and fix problems in education. As investors in education ventures, they host workshops to explore hunches about the future of education, help define acute problems, and then quickly and cheaply tests solutions in order to launch new schools, programs, and companies.

http://4pt0.org

GETTING SMART

Overview: Getting Smart supports innovation and the shift toward personalized digital learning by providing consulting services, publications, and workshops. Getting Smart also has a blog that covers a wide range of topics, including developments in research, technology, entrepreneurship, and innovative strategies involving education today.

http://gettingsmart.com

LEARNZILLION DREAM TEAM

Overview: The Dream Team, sponsored by LearnZillion, is a group of 200 teachers from across the country who collaborate to create high-quality instructional materials. Members gather annually at TeachFest, a three-day event focused on devising outstanding Common Core–aligned lessons. Dream Team members receive a $2,000 stipend for their contributions.

http://learnzillion.com/dreamteam

NEW CLASSROOMS

Overview: New Classrooms seeks to create school models that help personalize learning. It helps design personalized models for classrooms and, using technology, works to reconfigure instruction into a series of learning stations that include such "modalities" as teacher-led instruction, computer-assisted instruction, virtual tutoring, and group work.

http://www.newclassrooms.org

OPPORTUNITY CULTURE

Overview: Opportunity Culture is an initiative intended to help redesign schools so as to create a culture of opportunity in which "all teachers have career opportunities dependent upon their excellence, leadership, and student impact." It offers a series of revamped staffing models intended to help extend the reach of terrific teachers, and it provides materials that address such topics as teacher compensation, career advancement within the classroom, teacher collaboration, and school redesign.

http://opportunityculture.org

ROCKETSHIP EDUCATION

Overview: Rocketship Education, a charter management organization that operates elementary schools, is a pioneer in blended learning. Using computer-assisted instruction to complement traditional instruction, Rocketship views technology as a tool to support teachers, help individualize learning for each child, and engage parents. Rocketship operates schools in California and Milwaukee.

http://www.rsed.org

AFT and NEA Initiatives

Fellowships

FUTURE OF THE PROFESSION FELLOWSHIP

Sponsoring organizations: NEA and Teach Plus
Membership: Selected NEA teachers
Duration: 1 year
Overview: Selected teachers are exposed to policy issues, interact with policy makers, and deepen their knowledge of advocacy. They have the opportunity to work with NEA staff and advise the union on ideas for engaging a new generation and enhancing the future of the profession. This cohort meets three times during the year in Washington, DC, and engages monthly in virtual training.

http://www.teachplus.org/page/teach-plusnea-future-of-the-profession-fellowship-239.html

TEACHER LEADERSHIP INITIATIVE

Sponsoring organizations: NEA, the Center for Teaching Quality, and the National Board
Membership: Selected NEA teachers
Duration: 1 year

Overview: The Teacher Leadership initiative exposes a select number of teachers to the latest thinking on three forms of teacher leadership: instructional leadership, policy leadership, and association leadership. The participants work through curricula on these subjects through the Center for Teaching Quality's online Collaboratory platform. The experience culminates in a formative, field-based capstone project solving a problem in their school or union or addressing a policy issue.

Resources

AFT INNOVATION FUND

Sponsoring organization: AFT
Overview: The AFT Innovation Fund was created in 2009 to provide resources for state and local AFT affiliates to support their ideas for improving education. It has supported initiatives including new designs in teacher evaluation; the creation of lessons, units, and professional development on the Common Core State Standards; various types of charter schooling; expanded learning time (with an emphasis on teacher collaboration); and early childhood initiatives.
https://www.aft.org/about/innovate/

THE NEA FOUNDATION

Sponsoring organization: NEA
Overview: The NEA Foundation awards grants to innovative educators and to teacher-led pilot projects. It has also targeted several districts in its Closing the Achievement Gap initiative to implement and evaluate approaches to reform. The Foundation offers online courses in everything from The Brain to Teachers Unions and Education Reform.
https://www.neafoundation.org/

SHARE MY LESSON

Sponsoring organization: AFT

Overview: Share My Lesson is an online resource for teachers that contains more than 300,000 free lessons. Users can sort through the Web site and search based on grade level, subject area, and content concentrations or subtopics. Each lesson can be rated and reviewed to note how helpful it was.

www.sharemylesson.com

WORKS4ME

Sponsoring organization: NEA

Overview: Works4Me is a Web site where teachers can share tips on classroom management, pedagogy, peer and student relationships, etc. Users can rate the tips on a scale of 1–5 stars and leave comments. There is also a discussion board where teachers can connect virtually and discuss mutual concerns or solutions to problems.

http://www.nea.org/tools/Works4Me.html

APPENDIX G

Questions for Further Thought and Exploration

This appendix is intended to serve as a jumping-off point for further discussion and reflection. My hope is that readers will use these questions as an opportunity to think through and apply what they've read and as a way to connect the stories and suggestions to their own experience. After all, this book is really successful only to the extent that readers put it down with an eye to identifying and acting on cage-busting opportunities in their own schools and systems.

CHAPTER 1: THE CLASSROOM CAGE

- The chapter opens with some examples of what the cage looks like. Do any other stories come to mind from your experience that make you think, "That's the cage!"? When you think back on those stories, what sticks out in your mind?
- Consider Sarah DuPre's account of how little control she had over her instructional day. Do you ever feel that way? Map out how you spend the minutes in your day. How much time a day do you spend on teaching and learning? How much on other stuff? What changes would help you spend more time on teaching and learning? What would those changes require? Who would be able to help you make those changes happen?

- Chapter 1 discusses four key bars of the cage. What are they? Can you recall a time when you experienced any of these? Can you think of other bars that aren't mentioned here? What would you call them?
- Recall an occasion when you invested a lot of time, passion, and energy in a project or program. Thinking back, are you confident that your energy was well spent? If not, try to think of some of the ways in which your effort was wasted. What impediments were responsible for this, and what could you do about them?
- Jacob Pactor tells of a success that required the school secretary helping him with his plan to access student data more quickly. Do you have ideas to help teachers get data, resources, or support more readily? Who could help make your idea a reality?
- Casie Jones "flipped the table" by taking her colleagues' complaints and transforming them into concrete recommendations. Have you ever been in a meeting where this happened? How did you, or your colleague, manage to flip the table? Then think back to a meeting where this didn't happen. What steps could you have taken to flip that table in an unproductive, negative meeting?
- Jeffrey Charbonneau tells a story of how he got his students college credit for his science courses. What were some of the key steps that he took? Can you think of a similarly ambitious project you'd be inclined to take on? What can be learned from Charbonneau's example?
- Platitudes like "all teachers are heroes" can drown out real professional respect. What kind of praise would you like to hear from public officials? From parents? From your peers? What can you do to attract the kind of acknowledgment that would feel significant and serious?

CHAPTER 2: CHOOSE TO BE A PROBLEM SOLVER

- In Peter Skillman's spaghetti story, the kindergarteners succeeded because they didn't assume constraints. Because they didn't know any better, they were unafraid to ask a simple question. Sit down with a colleague and try to think about some constraints in your school that may not make any sense. What questions might a kindergartener think to ask that you've skipped right past?

- Get together with a colleague and identify a place where you think your school could be doing much better. Use the six questions offered in the chapter to help identify an opportunity that you think is important. What should happen, and what's standing in the way?
- With that same colleague, think of what you just identified as standing in your way. Why is it there, and how might you deal with it? Try asking "why?" five times as you tackle this and see where that takes you!
- Paul Ramirez found himself wasting dozens of hours each year grading quizzes before he looked around for an alternative that saved him a tremendous amount of time. Ramirez found the solution to his "spaghetti problem" by looking with fresh eyes. Can you think of a situation at your school where you feel similarly frustrated? If so, try to imagine a better solution and identify some of the assumptions that have kept you from pursuing it.
- Roxanna Elden offers some sound advice on how a teacher should approach her principal. With a colleague, select a problem and think through how you would offer to do most of the work when taking the solution to the principal.
- Is there someone in your school who everyone knows isn't doing their job? If so, has anyone taken any actions to address this? How did those turn out? What else might be tried? How would you go about respectfully doing so?
- Joseph Manko's school is an example of how a uniformly strong faculty makes it possible for principals to vest a lot of trust and authority in their teachers. Are there any weak links on your faculty? If so, how might you go about addressing them? Do you believe your principal would give teachers more authority if you strengthened or eliminated those weak links?
- Building moral authority requires policing the profession. Role-play with a partner. One of you is an accomplished veteran; the other is a colleague who is struggling and has developed a negative, destructive

attitude. What might the veteran say, and how should she say it? How might she draw on colleagues without having to involve the principal?

CHAPTER 3: MANAGING UP

- When confronted with a recalcitrant principal, Evan Stone found strength in numbers. Can you think of a time when you tried to go it alone but might have fared better by trying to work with allies? Why did you decide to do it alone? How did that turn out? In retrospect, how might you have done it differently?
- Michael Dunlea was frustrated by a policy that wasted his time without helping his students. When he brought the issue up, they changed the policy as he suggested. Are there policies in your school that don't make sense for your students? What kind of change would help? How would you make the case to your principal?
- Louisiana state superintendent John White tells of changing a policy after meeting with a teacher. Imagine reaching out to your state superintendent. What one problem would you flag for him? What makes it a state-level issue? What would you recommend as a solution? Presume you only have two minutes to make your case—that's about 250–300 words. Work with a colleague to prepare what you would say.
- Recall John Solet's patient effort to change things for his students. He didn't think in terms of one grand solution but instead focused on solving one practical problem at a time. Think of one big challenge facing your school. How might you break that problem down into discrete parts and then tackle each of those?
- Every teacher has at least one good suggestion she's been hesitant to share. Working with a colleague, take Michelle Shearer's advice and write your ideas down and then share them with one another. What's good and useful about each idea? How could it be sharpened or made more actionable? How can it be made more appealing to the school administrators?
- Think of a time you saw a colleague handle a situation with her peers or principal that made you think, "She knows what she's doing. She's

a savvy operator!" Ask her for the story. Don't focus on the result; ask her how she went about it, step by step.

- Try to remember an interaction with your principal when you didn't get the answer you wanted. Think back on how you made your case. Did you make it in a way that reflected the principal's concerns? Did you try to understand the principal's point of view and offer appealing solutions? What might you do differently next time?

CHAPTER 4: MILLIONS OF REGISTERED VOTERS— AND THEIR KIDS

- Rebecca Mieliwocki's frustrations with distrust-based policy are pretty common. Of course, teachers frequently adopt distrust-based policies in their own classrooms. Rules like "no talking during tests," "students need a note if they're late to class," or "no late homework accepted" are not written for the students who teachers trust; they're written to the lowest common denominator. The idea is to put a floor under student behavior. How many lowest common denominator policies can you list from your classroom? What could students do that would convince you to relax those policies? How might you make use of those tactics in dealing with your school administration?
- Tammie Schrader asserts that policy makers are smart people trying to do right by kids with the tools that they have but that they can't always anticipate how policy can get garbled during implementation. Can you think of one policy you've seen in your school or system where you've thought, "That makes no sense at all! What were they thinking?" Do you know what the policy makers intended? Work with a colleague to research what the policy makers thought they were doing. See if the idea makes any more sense, and, if it does, see if you can figure out where it's gone awry and how you might help policy makers fix it.
- Reflect on the lesson of No Child Left Behind. Why did the law become so much more ham-handed than what President Clinton had proposed several years earlier? Can you identify a similar dynamic

playing out on other education issues today? If so, what could help alter that dynamic?

- Reflect on the "Seven Tips for Dealing with Lawmakers" sidebar. What's one piece of advice offered there that you hadn't thought of before? What about it struck or surprised you? How might you make use of it next time you talk to a public official?

- Reflect on a policy that's gotten in the way of your own efforts. Do you know where that policy comes from? Is it a Big P or a little p policy? Do you know whether it's based on federal law, state statute, or local interpretation? Is it actually written down anywhere? Once you've found out just what and where it is, think about how you might go about changing it.

- Gerry Spence encourages people to frame their argument as a story. Reflect on something you'd like to convince your school administration to do. How can you craft your points into something that will be compelling? What would you say? Presume you have two minutes to make your case—that's about 250–300 words. Sketch out your argument.

- Get together with a colleague and think of a challenge you face where a change in policy might help. Precisely what kind of change in policy would you like to see? Each of you should write a pitch for a policy maker that concisely makes your case but also signals that you understand the policy maker's concerns, constraints, and possible reservations. Be sure to explain why your idea will help kids not just in your classroom but also in your district or your state. (Your whole pitch should run no more than two or three minutes—so keep it short and sweet!)

- Randy Dorn says that asking a policy maker for something is like asking a stranger for $10. He argues that it's tough to get money from a stranger but much easier to get a loan from someone who knows you. Do you think this is true? If so, what are some ways you might reach out to a district leader or a policy maker and help him start to feel like he knows you?

CHAPTER 5: TACKLING EVERYDAY PROBLEMS

- Courtney Fox and her colleagues forged a coalition that built and maintained a program for more than 15 years. What were some of the key steps they took to make that happen? If you were to launch a similar effort, which colleagues would you start with? What would your first steps be?

- While schools have lots of information on reading and math scores, the more interesting data that teachers might find useful often goes uncollected. Can you think of any examples from your experience? What's one thing at your school that you wish you had more information about? If you had that data, what would you do with it? How might you go about collecting the data you need?

- Consider "Ms. Bullen's Data-Rich Year." Do you ever feel like the point of data is more about helping others keep an eye on you than on helping you do your job? If so, what are some suggestions on how data might be made more useful to you? What would be collected? How would you and your colleagues put it to use? Who in the administration would you need to talk to in order to make these changes?

- Play "School Budget Hold 'em" with a partner. Each of you should play with a goal of reducing the budget by 1 percent. After you've done so, show each other your "hands" and see which approach you prefer.

- Karen Mapp says families can be untapped resources for change. What's one change you'd like to see that would benefit from parental support? What would you need from the parents? How much time? What kinds of actions? What would it take to make that happen? Try to devise a plan that offers a path from here to there.

- Have you ever been in a school meeting where it felt like a waste of your time? How did you feel? What made it so wasteful? Did you try to let anyone know how you felt, or try to ensure that next time it would be different? If so, how did you go about it? If not, why not? Looking ahead, how might you use the *Meeting Wise* template to figure out what specifically could be changed?

- Can you remember having been through an unhelpful professional development experience? What made it unhelpful? What would need to change for it to have been worth your time? Did you let anyone know how you felt? If so, how did you go about doing so? If not, why not? Who would be responsible for making the changes you'd like to see?
- Curtis Chandler argues that educators are often more able to create or customize professional development than they realize. Work with a colleague to dream up a PD module, session, or day that you'd love to participate in, that you think you and your peers could really use. Then ask yourself, "How could I make this happen? What would the steps be? Who could I call in from the outside? Who would I need to talk to? Who has the authority to provide resources, support, and approval for professional purposes?"

CHAPTER 6: THE UNION QUESTION

- Unions aren't monolithic. The union local that Dan Montgomery revered was very different from the one that David Upegui reviled. Where does your union fall on this continuum? If you're not sure, inquire as to what the union is focused on and why it's focusing on those things. Do those strike you as the right things?
- When Larry Campbell talked to the teachers in his charter school as they unionized, he found out that while they wanted basic job protections, they were more interested in how the union could help them professionally. Talk to a few of your peers. If they could start their union from scratch, what would they want it to focus on? What would you want it to focus on? If that's not what your union is focused on, how do you start to move it from here to there?
- Bill Raabe argues that teachers can do much more than they think their collective bargaining agreement allows. Is your school covered by such an agreement? If so, have you ever read it? How long was it?

If not, where can you find it? Peruse it. What strikes you about the language or surprises you about what it does (or doesn't) say?

- Think about Montgomery County's Peer Assistance and Review process. What do you like about it? What do you dislike? How would you feel about being referred to that process? How would you feel about participating as a "consulting teacher" who provides the assistance and review? If you could wave a magic wand and implement the process in your school or district, would you?

- Contracts can be hard to interpret if you're not a lawyer, especially if you're not sure what you're looking for. Get together with a couple of colleagues and talk about things you'd like to see happen that you've been told are difficult to enact because of the contract. Can you find provisions in the contract that speak to the problem? What exactly do they say? Is the language as ironclad as you'd heard? Who might you go to for help in deciphering exactly what the contract means?

- Have you talked to your local union steward to share your views on the union and what it should be doing? If yes, how did she react? Did she listen to you and seem interested in what you had to say? Did you get a sense of how you can be more involved if you wanted to be? If not, who is your steward? Try reaching out and hearing what she has to say.

- Do you know your union's position on key local, state, and federal policy questions? If yes, which ones do you support and which do you disagree with? If not, how would you go about finding out? Can you find them online or is there a particular individual you need to talk to? What, if anything, surprised you about the union's positions? In either case, what might you do to be sure your voice is being heard?

- New teacher organizations are pushing the unions to change in certain ways. Educators 4 Excellence is one such entity. Its members all sign a statement of principles. Some of those principles are mentioned in the chapter, but go online and read the full statement. Which principles do you agree with? Which do you disagree with? Do you think an organization like E4E is constructive? Why or why not?

CHAPTER 7: SQUARE PEGS AND ROUND HOLES

- Teacherpreneurs are educators who stay in the classroom while taking on new roles. Does that model appeal to you? Does it seem like it would stretch you too thin? Can you think of other roles you'd like to play while retaining a full-time teaching schedule?
- Reflect on the concept of unbundling. Not all teachers have identical strengths. What are some areas in which you're especially strong? What are some in which you think you're weaker than your peers? Can you imagine how the school might be better able to take advantage of your talents and cover for your weaknesses?
- If you could write your own job description, what would it say? What would you want it to include? What would the specific responsibilities and duties be? What else would need to change to make it work smoothly as part of the school?
- Think about the five new models of the teaching job sketches by Public Impact. Which of these models most appeals to you, and why? Which strikes you as least appealing, and why?
- What were some of the key things that Rick Cruz did right in building his program and in agreeing to take a job in central administration? Are there things that you think he got wrong? Is there a similar venture that you'd like to tackle? What would be the first steps in getting started?
- Of the five cage-busting teachers who left their districts to launch new endeavors, which one did you find most interesting? Why? What were some of the lessons you took away?
- Teacher-led schools are an opportunity to align accountability and autonomy. What was your reaction to the discussion of teacher-led schools? What seems exciting about them? What makes you skeptical? If you were to start a teacher-led school, which colleagues would you want to do it with? Describe the school. How would you craft teacher roles? The school day? The academic program? (Remember that any teacher-led school has to operate with the same per-pupil funding as any other school—unless you raise extra money privately.)

CHAPTER 8: YOU ARE BRAVER THAN YOU BELIEVE

- Have you ever seen a colleague's passion get in the way of what he was trying to accomplish? Has this ever happened to you? Grab a colleague and practice presenting a frustration that drives you crazy without letting your passion get the better of you. What are some strategies you can take from the book that will help ensure that your passion is working for and not against you?

- Jessica Waters thinks teacher protestors should dress and act in ways that other professionals do. At the same time, she says there are things, such as networking, that teachers *don't* do that other professionals tend to do. Do you think she has a point? In either case, what are other things you can think of that teachers do that other professionals don't do? And what are some things that you see other professionals do that teachers don't do? What do you make of this?

- Teachers can be afraid to speak up for fear of alienating their principal. But Ann Bonitatibus says that she has never seen an example of retribution in her school district. Have you seen examples of retribution? If so, what were the details? If not, do you think the fear of principal retribution is ever overblown?

- Ken Halla accidentally made it harder to pursue a proposal because he used the word *pilot* in his proposal. Sit down with a colleague and think of the red flags in your school or district. When have you seen people get tripped up for silly reasons, like because they used this word or forgot to speak to that person first? What are some strategies you can use to avoid triggering concerns? Who can you count on to help steer you in the right direction?

- The sacred cow hunt is a clever way to kick off a conversation about changing comfortable routines. It asks participants to find routines that don't make sense or costs that can be cut. When Superintendent Terry Grier conducted his hunt, he found that the best ideas for tackling Department A would inevitably come from someone in Department B. What might explain that? What's one thing you would flag about your school or system if your district held a sacred cow hunt?

- Jacob Pactor suggests making a "power map" of your school so you know who you need to have on your side to promote an idea. Who are the power players at your school? What makes them important?
- Have you ever seen a problem and had a solution to propose but kept quiet anyway? Why? Do you think you did the right thing? If the same situation arose next week, would you react the same way? If yes, what would it take for you to react differently? If no, why not?

Notes

Chapter 1

1. Michelle Collay, "Teaching Is Leading," *Educational Leadership* 71, no. 2 (2013): 73.
2. Harry K. Wong and Rosemary T. Wong, *The First Days of School: How to Be an Effective Teacher* (Mountain View, CA: Harry K. Wong, 1998), 24.
3. National Network of State Teachers of the Year, "Unintended Consequences," *ED Blog*, n.d., http://www.nnstoy.org/unintended-consequences.
4. Author calculation, National Conference of State Legislatures, "Education Bill Tracking Database," http://www.ncsl.org/research/education/education-bill-tracking-database.aspx.
5. Ibid.
6. Geoffrey Phelps et al., "How Much English Language Arts and Mathematics Instruction Do Students Receive? Investigating Variation in Instructional Time," *Education Policy* 26, no. 5 (2012): 631–662; Jodie Roth et al., "What Happens During the School Day? Time Diaries from a National Sample of Elementary School Teachers," *Teachers College Record* 105, no. 3 (2003): 317–343; Helen Abadzi, "Instructional Time Loss and Local-Level Governance," *Prospects* 37, no. 1 (2007): 3–17.
7. American Speech-Language-Hearing Association, "General Talking Points for Increased Salaries," http://www.asha.org/slp/schools/salaries/talk-points.
8. "NCTQ Teacher Contract Database," *National Council on Teacher Quality*, http://www.nctq.org/districtPolicy/contractDatabaseLanding.do.
9. Ann Duffett et al., "Waiting to Be Won Over: Teachers Speak on the Profession, Unions, and Reform" (Washington, DC: Education Sector, 2008), 4, http://www.educationsector.org/usr_doc/WaitingToBeWonOver.pdf.
10. Frederick M. Hess and Chester E. Finn Jr., "Crash Course," *Education Next* 7, no. 4 (2007): 40.
11. "America's Teacher on Teaching in an Era of Change," in *Primary Sources Poll*, 3rd ed. (New York: Scholastic, 2013), http://www.scholastic.com/primarysources/PrimarySources3rdEditionWithAppendix.pdf.
12. Sarah Rosenberg and Elena Silva, *Trending Toward Reform: Teachers Speak on Unions and the Future of the Profession* (Washington, DC: Education Sector, 2012), 6, http://www.educationsector.org/publications/trending-toward-reform-teachers-speak-unions-and-future-profession; Brandon Busteed and Shane Lopez, "Teaching May Be the Secret to a Good Life," *The Gallup Blog*, March 27, 2013, http://thegallupblog.gallup.com/2013/03/teaching-may-be-secret-to-good-life.html; Shane J. Lopez and Preety Sidhu, "U.S. Teachers Love Their Lives, but Struggle in the Workplace," *Gallup Well-Being*, March 28, 2013, http://www.gallup.com/poll/161516/teachers-love-lives-struggle-workplace.aspx.

13. Dana Markow, Lara Macia, and Helen Lee, *The MetLife Survey of the American Teacher: Collaborating for Student Success* (New York: MetLife, 2013), 5, https://www.metlife.com/assets/cao/foundation/MetLife-Teacher-Survey-2012.pdf.

14. Ann Duffett et al., *Waiting to Be Won Over,* 4; Rosenberg and Silva, *Trending Toward Reform,* 11.

15. Lopez and Sidhu, "In U.S., Newer Teachers Most Likely to Be Engaged at Work."

16. Dana Markow and Andrea Pieters, *The MetLife Survey of the American Teacher: Collaborating for Student Success* (New York: MetLife, 2010), 49, https://www.metlife.com/assets/cao/contributions/foundation/american-teacher/MetLife_Teacher_Survey_2009.pdf.

17. Ellen Behrstock-Sherratt, Allison Rizzolo, Sabrina Laine, and Will Freidman, *Everyone at the Table: Engaging Teachers in the Evaluation Reform* (San Francisco: Jossey-Bass/Wiley, 2013), 5.

18. Lopez and Sidhu, "U.S. Teachers Love Their Lives, but Struggle in the Workplace."

19. Peter Dolton, Oscar Marcenaro-Gutierrez, Vikas Pota, Marc Boxser, and Ash Pajpani, *2013 Global Teacher Status Index* (London: Varkey Gems Foundation, 2013), 12, https://www.varkeygemsfoundation.org/sites/default/files/documents/2013GlobalTeacherStatusIndex.pdf.

20. Frederick M. Hess, *Spinning Wheels: The Politics of Urban School Reform* (Washington, DC: Brookings Institution Press, 1998).

21. Suzy Brooks, "Six Planes, Six Plans," *Purposeful Teacher Accidental Leader Blog,* February 23, 2014, http://edge.ascd.org/blogpost/six-planes-six-plans.

22. Larry Bossidy and Ram Charan, *Execution: The Discipline of Getting Things Done,* (New York: Crown Business, 2002), 89.

23. The Commission on Effective Teachers and Teaching issued a report well worth the cagebuster's while: *Transforming Teaching: Connecting Professional Responsibility with Student Learning* (Washington, DC: NEA, 2011).

24. Behrstock-Sherratt et al., *Everyone at the Table,* 118.

25. Julia G. Thompson, *The First-Year Teacher's Survival Guide: Ready-to-Use Strategies, Tools, and Activities for Meeting the Challenges of Each School Day* (San Francisco: Jossey-Bass/Wiley, 2013), 80.

26. Charlotte Danielson, *Teacher Leadership That Strengthens Professional Practice* (Alexandria, VA: Association for Supervision and Curriculum Development, 2006), 126.

27. Ibid., 55–56.

28. Each list ranked from most popular to least: Google list: *The First Days of School: How to Be an Effective Teacher,* Harry Wong (Harry K. Wong, 2009); *Educating Esmé: Diary of a Teacher's First Year,* Esmé Cordell (Algonquin Books, 1999); *The Courage to Teach: Exploring the Inner Landscape of a Teacher's Life,* Parker Palmer (Jossey-Bass, 2007); *Teaching Outside the Box,* LouAnne Johnson (Jossey-Bass, 2011); *The Reluctant Disciplinarian,* Gary Rubenstein (Prufrock Press, 2010); *Fred Jones's Tools for Teaching: Discipline, Instruction, Motivation,* Fred Jones (Fredric H. Jones, 2007); *The First Year Teacher's Survival Guide,* Julia Thompson (Jossey-Bass, 2013); *What Great Teachers Do Differently,* Todd Whitaker (Routledge, 2013); *Teaching with Love and Logic,* Jim Fay and David Funk (Love and Logic Press, 1995); *Teacher Man,* Frank McCourt (Simon & Schuster, 2005); *The Freedom Writers' Diary,* Erin Gruwell (Broadway Books, 2009); *The Shame of the Nation,* Jonathan Kozol (Three Rivers Press, 2005); *I Read It, but I Don't Get It,* Cris Tovani (Stenhouse, 2000); *Classroom Instruction That Works,* Robert Marzano et al. (ASCD, 2012); *Never Work Harder Than Your Students,* Robyn Jackson (ASCD, 2009); *Why Didn't I Learn This in College?* Paula Rutherford (Just Ask, 2009). Good Reads list: *The First Days of School: How to Be an Effective Teacher,* Harry Wong

(repeat); *The Book Whisperer: Awakening the Inner Reader in Every Child*, Donalyn Miller (Jossey-Bass, 2009); *Teach Like Your Hair's on Fire: The Methods and Madness Inside Room 56*, Rafe Esquith (Penguin, 2007); *Readicide: How Schools Are Killing Reading and What You Can Do About It*, Kelly Gallagher (Stenhouse, 2009); *Teach Like a Champion*, Doug Lemov (Jossey-Bass, 2010); *Educating Esmé: Diary of a Teacher's First Year*, Esmé Codell (repeat); *The Essential 55: An Award-Winning Educator's Rules for Discovering the Successful Student in Every Child*, Ron Clark (Hyperion Books, 2003); *Teaching with Love and Logic*, Jim Fay and David Funk (repeat); *Teacher Man*, Frank McCourt (repeat); *In the Middle: New Understandings about Writing, Reading, and Learning*, Nancie Atwell (Boynton/Cook, 1998); *The Courage to Teach: Exploring the Inner Landscape of a Teacher's Life*, Parker Palmer (repeat); *Lies My Teacher Told Me: Everything Your American History Textbook Got Wrong*, James Loewen (Touchstone, 2007); *I Read It, but I Don't Get It*, Cris Tovani (repeat); *Strategies That Work: Teaching Comprehension for Understanding and Engagement*, Stephanie Harvey and Anne Goudvis (Stenhouse, 2007); *Pedagogy of the Oppressed*, Paulo Freire (Bloomsbury, 2000); *The Freedom Writers Diary*, Erin Gruwell (repeat); *When Kids Can't Read: What Teachers Can Do: A Guide for Teachers 6–12*, Kylene Beers (Heinemann, 2003); *Other People's Children: Cultural Conflict in the Classroom*, Lisa Delpit (The New Press, 2006); *Savage Inequalities*, Jonathan Kozol (Crown, 1991); *Mosaic of Thought: Teaching Comprehension in a Reader's Workshop*, Ellin Keene and Susan Zimmerman (Heinemann, 2007).

29. Author's calculations based on Amazon searches of the twenty-nine texts.

30. Doug Lemov, *Teach Like a Champion: 49 Techniques That Put Students on the Path to College (K–12)* (San Francisco: Jossey-Bass/Wiley, 2010); Steven Farr, *Teaching as Leadership: The Highly Effective Teacher's Guide to Closing the Achievement Gap* (San Francisco: Jossey-Bass/Wiley, 2010).

31. Elizabeth Green, *Building a Better Teacher: How Teaching Works (and How to Teach It to Everyone)* (New York: W. W. Norton, 2014), 111–112.

32. Dan Lortie, *Schoolteacher: A Sociological Study* (Chicago: University of Chicago Press, 2002), 12.

33. Frederick M. Hess, *The Same Thing Over and Over* (Cambridge, MA: Harvard University Press, 2010).

34. Jal Mehta, *The Allure of Order: High Hopes, Dashed Expectation, and the Troubled Quest to Remake American Schooling* (New York: Oxford University Press, 2013), 38–42.

35. Dana Goldstein, *The Teacher Wars: A History of America's Most Embattled Profession* (New York: Doubleday Press, 2014), 4.

36. J. R. R. Tolkien, *The Two Towers: Being the Second Part of the Lord of the Rings* (New York: Mariner Books, 2012), 75.

37. Arne Duncan, "A Call to Teaching," speech delivered at The Rotunda at the University of Virginia, 2009, https://www2.ed.gov/news/speeches/2009/10/10092009.html.

38. Valerie Strauss, "Matt Damon: 'We Would Never Let Businessmen Design Warheads. Why Would You Cut Out Educators When You're Designing Education Policy?'" *The Answer Sheet Blog*, February 8, 2014, http://www.washingtonpost.com/blogs/answer-sheet/wp/2014/02/08/matt-damon-we-would-never-let-businessmen-design-warheads-why-would-you-cut-out-educators-when-youre-designing-education-policy.

39. Michelle Collay, *Everyday Teacher Leadership: Taking Action Where You Are* (San Francisco: Jossey-Bass/Wiley, 2011), 50.

40. Amy Wallace, "Wicked Smaht," *GQ*, January 2012, http://www.gq.com/entertainment/movies-and-tv/201201/matt-damon-gq-january-2012-cover-story-article.

41. Benjamin Summers, "Hero Worship of the Military Is Getting in the Way of Good Policy," *Washington Post*, June 22, 2014, A19, http://www.washingtonpost.com/opinions/hero-worship-of-the-military-presents-an-obstacle-to-good-policy/2014/06/20/053d932a-f0ed-11e3-bf76-447a5df6411f_story.html.

Chapter 2

1. Melissa Bailey, "Randi Weingarten, American Federation of Teachers Head, Declares Ed Reform Victory in New Haven," *New Haven Independent,* May 7, 2013.

2. Thomas J. Kane, "Capturing the Dimensions of Effective Teaching," *Education Next* 12, no. 4 (2012).

3. Dana Goldstein, *The Teacher Wars: A History of America's Most Embattled Profession* (New York: Doubleday Press, 2014), 221.

4. Shunryu Suzuki and Trudy Dixon, *Zen Mind, Beginner's Mind* (New York: Weatherhill, 1970), 1.

5. Michael Fullan, *Leading in a Culture of Change* (New York: Jossey-Bass/Wiley, 2001), 44.

6. For the whole story on Project RESTORE, see the five-part *Indianapolis Star* series by Matthew Tully: "When Every Minute Counts," February 13, 2011, http://www.indystar.com/article/20110213/NEWS08/102130364/1101/NEWS08/IPS-elementary-school-making-every-minute-count; "Students Rise to Challenge of Rigorous State Tests," February 16, 2011, http://www.indystar.com/article/20110216/NEWS08/102160324/; "School's Peacemakers Are Key to Its Turnaround," February 20, 2014, http://www.indystar.com/article/20110220/NEWS08/102200369; "High Expectations Inspire High Goals," February 24, 2011, http://archive.indystar.com/article/20110224/NEWS08/102240411/Tully-High-expectations-inspire-high-goals; "Arlington Woods' Formula for Success Is Simple: Just Do It," February 27, 2011, http://archive.indystar.com/article/20110227/NEWS08/102270379/Arlington-Woods-formula-success-simple-Just-do-it.

7. All material in the sidebar is adapted from Roxanna Elden, *See Me After Class: Advice for Teachers by Teachers* (New York: Kaplan, 2011), 4–141.

8. Peter Greene, "What Happened to the Trust," *Curmudgucation Blog*, June 21, 2014, http://curmudgucation.blogspot.com/2014/06/what-happened-to-trust.html.

9. Ila Towery et al., *Perspectives of Irreplaceable Teachers: What America's Best Teachers Think About Teaching* (Washington, DC: TNTP 2013), 19, http://tntp.org/assets/documents/TNTP_Perspectives_2013.pdf.

10. Nithya Joseph, Nancy Waymack, and Daniel Zielaski, *Roll Call: The Importance of Teacher Attendance (Washington, DC: National Council on Teacher Quality, 2014)*, 3.

11. Daniel Weisberg, Susan Sexton, Jennifer Mulhern, and David Keeling, *The Widget Effect: Our National Failure to Acknowledge and Act on Differences in Teacher Effectiveness* (Washington, DC: TNTP, 2009), 6.

12. Dana Markow, Lara Macia, and Helen Lee, *The MetLife Survey of the American Teacher: Collaborating for Student Success* (New York: MetLife, 2013), 5, https://www.metlife.com/assets/cao/foundation/MetLife-Teacher-Survey-2012.pdf.

13. Scott Reeder, "Diplomacy Undermines Teacher Evaluations," *The Hidden Costs of Tenure Report*, 2005, Small Newspaper Group, http://thehiddencostsoftenure.com/stories/?prcss=display&id=266561.

14. Education Next, *Program on Education Policy and Governance—Survey 2014,* http://educationnext.org/files/2014ednextpoll.pdf.

15. Frederick M. Hess, "Aftermath: My Note to the Gates Foundation," *Rick Hess Straight Up Blog,* April 24, 2014, http://blogs.edweek.org/edweek/rick_hess_straight_up/2014/04/aftermath_my_note_to_the_gates_foundation.html.16; Sarah Rosenberg and Elena Silva, *Trending Toward Reform: Teachers Speak on Unions and the Future of the Profession* (Washington, DC: Education Sector, 2012), 11.

16. Scholastic, "America's Teacher on Teaching in an Era of Change," *Primary Sources Poll,* 3rd ed., 2014.

18. Richard Ingersoll, *Who Controls Teachers' Work: Power and Accountability in America's Schools* (Cambridge, MA: Harvard Education Press, 2003), 244–45.

Chapter 3

1. *The Wizard of Oz,* directed by Victor Fleming (Los Angeles: Metro-Goldwyn-Mayer, 1939).

2. Allan R. Cohen and David L. Bradford, *Influencing Up* (Hoboken, NJ: John Wiley & Sons, 2012), 8.

3. David L. Bradford, "How Do You Manage Up in the Workplace?" October 8, 2013, Insights by Stanford Business, https://www.gsb.stanford.edu/news/headlines/david-l-bradford-how-do-you-manage-up-workplace.

4. Ibid.

5. Ibid.

6. Ibid.

7. All material in the sidebar is adapted from Dale Carnegie, *How to Win Friends and Influence People* (New York: Pocket Books, 1998), 109–192.

Chapter 4

1. Rafe Esquith, "Why Great Teachers Are Fleeing the Profession," *Wall Street Journal,* July 17, 2013, http://blogs.wsj.com/speakeasy/2013/07/17/why-great-teachers-are-fleeing-the-profession.

2. *Ghostbusters,* directed by Ivan Reitman (Los Angeles: Columbia Pictures, 1984).

3. *A Time for Results* (Washington, DC: National Governors Association, 1991).

4. William J. Bushaw and Shane J. Lopez, *Which Way Do We Go? The 45th Annual PDK/Gallup Poll of the Public's Attitudes Toward the Public Schools,* 12, http://pdkintl.org/noindex/2013_PDKGallup.pdf.

5. Patrick McGuinn and Andrew P. Kelly, *Parent Power: Grass-Roots Activism and K–12 Education Reform* (Washington, DC: American Enterprise Institute, 2012), 13.

6. All material in the sidebar is adapted from Gerry Spence, *How to Argue and Win Every Time* (New York: St. Martin's Press 1995), 47–204.

7. Geoff Decker, "Joel Klein Says Curriculum Is His Legacy's Lone Dark Spot," *Chalkbeat New York,* December 13, 2013, http://gothamschools.org/2013/12/13/joel-klein-says-curriculum-is-his-legacys-lone-dark-spot.

8. John W. Kingdon, *Agendas, Alternatives, and Public Policies* (New York: Pearson Longman Classics in Political Science, 2010).

9. A. A. Milne, *Pooh's Little Instruction Book* (New York: Dutton, 1995), 52.

Chapter 5

1. Iowa Department of Education, "Guidance on the Iowa Teacher Leadership and Compensation System," July 15, 2013, https://www.educateiowa.gov/sites/files/ed/documents/2013-07-15GuidanceOnTheTLCSystem.pdf.

2. Teacher Leader Exploratory Commission, *Teacher Leader Model Standards,* http://teacher-leaderstandards.org/downloads/TLS_Brochure.pdf.

3. Julia G. Thompson, *The First-Year's Teacher Survival Guide* (San Francisco: John Wiley & Sons, 2013), 56.

4. Anna Egalite et al., "Finding the Right Fit: Recruiting and Retaining Teachers in Milwaukee Choice Schools," *Journal of School Choice* 8, no. 1 (2014): 113–140.

5. John H. Tyler, "If You Build It Will They Come? Teachers' Online Use of Student Performance Data," *Education Finance and Policy* 8, no. 2 (2013): 168–207.

6. *Teacher Data Literacy: It's about Time* (Washington, DC: Data Quality Campaign, 2014), http://www.dataqualitycampaign.org/files/DQC-Data%20Literacy%20Brief.pdf.

7. Frederick M. Hess, *Cage-Busting Leadership* (Cambridge, MA: Harvard Education Press, 2013), 77.

8. John Merrow, "Assets or Liabilities," *Taking Note: Thoughts on Education from John Merrow,* July 18, 2014, http://takingnote.learningmatters.tv/?p=7075.

9. All material in the sidebar is adapted from Education Resource Strategies, "School Design: Leveraging Talent, Time, and Money," 2010, http://www.issuelab.org/resource/school_design_leveraging_talent_time_and_money.

10. Steve Shelden and Darcy Hutchins, *The D.C. Family Engagement Partnership: Findings from a Descriptive Evaluation* (Baltimore: Johns Hopkins University, 2014).

11. Steven G. Rogelberg, Desmond J. Leach, Peter B. Warr, and Jennifer L. Burnfield, "'Not Another Meeting!' Are Meeting Time Demands Related to Employee Well-Being?" *Journal of Applied Psychology* 91, no. 1 (2006): 88–96.

12. Kathryn Parker Boudett and Elizabeth A. City, *Meeting Wise: Making the Most of Collaborative Time* (Cambridge, MA: Harvard Education Press, 2014), 13–14.

13. Ibid., 15.

14. Steven Rogelberg, Linda Shanock, and Cliff Scott, "Wasted Time and Money in Meetings: Increasing Return on Investment," *Small Group Research* 43, no. 2 (2012): 236–245.

15. Ibid.

16. Gary Rubenstein, *The Reluctant Disciplinarian* (Fort Collins, CO: Cottonwood Press, 1999), 26–27.

17. Boston Consulting Group, "The Professional Development Marketplace" (webinar presentation, 2014).

18. Linda Darling-Hammond et al., *Professional Learning in the Learning Profession: A Status Report on Teacher Development in the United States and Abroad* (Palo Alto, CA: Stanford University, National Staff Development Council and the School Redesign Network, 2009), 2.

19. All material in the sidebar is adapted from Boudett and City, *Meeting Wise,* 13–137.

20. Dana Markow and Andrea Pieters, *The Metlife Survey of the American Teacher* (New York: Metlife, 2012), 6, http://files.eric.ed.gov/fulltext/ED530021.pdf.

21. Scholastic and the Bill & Melinda Gates Foundation, *Primary Sources: America's Teachers on Teaching in an Era of Change* (Seattle: Bill & Melinda Gates Foundation, 2014), http://www.scholastic.com/primarysources/PrimarySources3rdEdition.pdf.

22. For extensive discussion on this count, see Frederick M. Hess and Bror Saxberg, *Breakthrough Leadership in the Digital Age: Using Learning Science to Reboot Schooling* (Thousand Oaks, CA: Corwin, 2013).

23. Matt Pasternack, head of growth for Clever, Inc., personal communication, June 6, 2014.

24. Albert Shanker, "The Revolution That Is Overdue" (speech delivered at Herbert H. Lehman College, City University of New York, 1987), https://www.reuther.wayne.edu/files/64.28.pdf.

25. All material in the sidebar is excerpted from Alex Kajitani, *The Teacher of the Year Handbook: The Ultimate Guide to Making the Most of Your Teacher-Leader Role* (CreateSpace Independent Publishing Platform, 2013), 7–96.

Chapter 6

1. Commission on Effective Teachers and Teaching, *Transforming Teaching: Connecting Personal Responsibility with Student Learning* (Washington, DC: NEA, 2012), 9, http://www.nea.org/assets/docs/Transformingteaching2012.pdf.
2. *Rebalancing Teacher Tenure: A Post-Vergara Guide for Policymakers* (New York: TNTP, 2014), http://tntp.org/publications/view/rebalancing-teacher-tenure-a-post-vergara-guide-for-policymakers.
3. Joe Williams, "Where We Think DVR Is Right," *Democrats for Education Reform Blog*, June 16, 2014, http://www.dfer.org/blog/2014/06/where_we_think.php.
4. National Right to Work Foundation, "Frequently Asked Questions," http://www.nrtw.org/b/rtw_faq.htm.
5. Stephanie Simon, "Teachers Unions Face Moment of Truth," *Politico*, December 8, 2013, http://www.politico.com/story/2013/12/education-teachers-unions-moment-of-truth-national-education-association-american-federation-of-teachers-100813.html.
6. "Heavy Hitters: Top All-Time Donors, 1989–2014," OpenSecrets.org, https://www.opensecrets.org/orgs/list.php.
7. Jal Mehta, *The Allure of Order: High Hopes, Dashed Expectations, and the Troubled Quest to Remake American Schooling* (New York: Oxford University Press, 2013), 151.
8. Gene I. Maeroff, "Shanker Urging Shift in Strategy to Aid Teachers," *New York Times*, April 28, 1985, http://www.nytimes.com/1985/04/28/nyregion/shanker-urging-shift-in-strategy-to-aid-teachers.html.
9. Richard D. Kahlenberg, *Tough Liberal: Albert Shanker and the Battles Over Schools, Unions, Race, and Democracy* (New York: Columbia University Press, 2007), 297.
10. Sarah Rosenberg and Elena Silva, *Trending Toward Reform: Teachers Speak on Unions and the Future of the Profession* (Washington, DC: Education Sector, 2012), 3, http://www.educationsector.org/sites/default/files/publications/REPORT-TeacherSurvey3f.pdf.
11. Ibid.
12. For a critical but authoritative look at the teacher union influence, see Terry M. Moe, *Special Interest: Teachers Unions and America's Public Schools* (Washington, DC, Brookings Institution, 2011).
13. Jennifer Martin, "For Real Teacher Advocacy, Don't Forget Unions," *Education Week Teacher Blog*, June 19, 2013, http://blogs.edweek.org/teachers/teaching_ahead/2013/06/working_together_for_positive_change.html.
14. Richard D. Kahlenberg, *Tough Liberal: Albert Shanker and the Battles Over Schools, Unions, Race, and Democracy* (New York: Columbia University Press, 2007), 308–312.
15. Saul Avery Rubinstein and John E. McCarthy, *Reforming Public School Systems Through Sustained Union-Management Collaboration* (Washington, DC: Center for American Progress, 2011).
16. For an extensive account of Montgomery County's reform efforts, see Stacey M. Childress, Denis P. Doyle, David A. Thomas, *Leading for Equity: The Pursuit of Excellence in the Montgomery County Public Schools* (Cambridge, MA: Harvard Education Press, 2009).
17. Charles Taylor Kerchner, Julia E. Koppich, and Joseph G. Weeres, *United Mind Workers: Unions and Teaching in the Knowledge Society* (San Francisco: Jossey-Bass, 1997).

18. All material in the sidebar is adapted from Teach Plus, *Rock the Union: An Action Plan to Engage Early Career Teachers and Elevate the Profession,* (Washington, DC: Teach Plus and NEA, 2014), 3–17, http://www.teachplus.org/uploads/Documents/1401225385_rock_the_union_ultra_compressed.pdf.

19. Educators 4 Excellence, "A Declaration of Teachers' Principles and Beliefs," http://educators 4excellence.zissousecure.com/register.

Chapter 7

1. All material in the sidebar is adapted from Barnett Berry, Ann Byrd, and Alan Weider, *Teacherpreneurs: Innovative Teachers Who Lead But Don't Leave* (San Francisco: Jossey-Bass/Wiley, 2013), 8–92.

2. Frederick M. Hess, "Revitalizing Teacher Education by Revisiting Our Assumptions About Teaching," *Journal of Teacher Education* 60, no. 5 (2009): 450–457.

3. Robin Tepper Jacob, Thomas J. Smith, Jacklyn A. Willard, and Rachel E. Rifkin, *Reading Partners: The Implementation and Effectiveness of a One-on-One Tutoring Program Delivered by Community Volunteers* (MDRC Policy Brief, June 2014), http://readingpartners.org/wp-content/uploads/2014/06/Reading-Partners_final.pdf.

4. Dana Markow, Lara Macia, and Helen Lee, *The Metlife Survey of the American Teacher: Challenges for School Leadership* (New York: MetLife, 2013), https://www.metlife.com/assets/cao/foundation/MetLife-Teacher-Survey-2012.pdf.

5. Brooke Peters, "Building a School Around Teacher Leadership," *Teaching Ahead: A Round-table Blog,* March 19, 2013, http://blogs.edweek.org/teachers/teaching_ahead/2013/03/building_a_school_around_teacher_leadership.html.

6. Beth Hawkins, "Teacher Cooperatives: What Happens When Teachers Run the School?" *Education Next* 9, no. 2 (2009), http://educationnext.org/teacher-cooperatives.

7. Ibid.

8. Ibid.

9. Education Evolving, "Teacher Powered Schools: Generating Lasting Impact Through Common Sense Innovation," May 2014, http://www.teacherpowered.org/resources/tps-white-paper.pdf.

10. For a nice discussion of the school's creation, operation, and related issues, see Lori Nazareno, "Teachers Lead the Way in Denver," *Phi Delta Kappan,* March 28, 2014, http://www.edweek.org/ew/articles/2014/04/01/kappan_nazareno.html.

11. George Orwell, *Animal Farm* (New York: Harcourt Brace, 1945), 118.

12. Sylvia Plath, *The Bell Jar* (New York: HarperCollins, 1971), 67.

Chapter 8

1. Kenneth P. Halla, *Deeper Learning Through Technology: Using the Cloud to Individualize Instruction* (Thousand Oaks, CA: Corwin Press, 2015).

2. Patrick Wall and Geoff Decker, "Making His Case, Mulgrew Says New Contract Draws Battle Lines in 'War with the Reformers,'" *Chalkbeat New York,* May 8, 2014, http://ny.chalkbeat.org/2014/05/08/making-his-case-mulgrew-says-new-contract-draws-battle-lines-in-war-with-the-reformers.

3. Trevor Tenbrink, "Crowd Laughs as Chicago Teachers Union President Talks about Killing the Rich," *Education Action Group,* January 7, 2013, http://eagnews.org/crowd-laughs-as-chicago-teachers-union-president-talks-about-killing-the-rich.

4. Stephanie Simon, "Name-Calling Turns Nasty in Education World," *Politico,* November 8, 2013, http://www.politico.com/story/2013/11/education-debates-rhetoric-99556.html.

5. Paul Peterson, Michael Henderson, and Martin West, *Teachers versus the Public: What Americans Think about Schools and How to Fix Them* (Washington, DC: Brookings Institution Press, 2014), 17–19.

6. All material in the sidebar is adapted from Roger Fisher, William Ury, and Bruce Patton, *Getting to Yes: Negotiating Agreement Without Giving In* (New York: Penguin Books, 2011), 1–125.

7. Peter Greene, "What Happened to the Trust?" *Curmudgucation Blog,* June 11, 2014, http://curmudgucation.blogspot.com/2014/06/what-happened-to-trust.html.

8. "Two Cathedrals," *The West Wing* (NBC, aired May 16, 2001).

9. Rafe Esquith, "Why Great Teachers Are Fleeing the Profession," *Wall Street Journal,* July 17, 2013, http://blogs.wsj.com/speakeasy/2013/07/17/why-great-teachers-are-fleeing-the-profession.

Acknowledgments

I'm indebted to those who provided the counsel, insight, and support that made this volume possible. First and foremost, I'd like to offer my heartfelt thanks to the astonishingly talented duo of Max Eden and Sarah DuPre for their indispensable role in researching and crafting this book. Max and Sarah were more than research assistants; they were invaluable partners. They managed and helped conduct hundreds of interviews, coordinated focus groups, examined thousands of pages of transcripts, worked closely with dozens of organizations, plunged into polling, and offered incisive feedback and whip-smart editing. I also owe a vote of thanks to their current and former colleagues Daniel Lautzenheiser, Michael McShane, Elizabeth English, Jenn Hatfield, and Taryn Hochleitner, as well as to all-star interns Dennis Zeveloff, Emily Levine, and Brendan Bell.

This is a book informed and shaped by the wisdom of teachers. Max, Sarah, and I spoke with hundreds of teachers as well as union leaders, advocates, administrators, academics, and public officials. Those conversations form the backbone of this book. I owe a special thanks to all those who made time to talk to us or to help us along the way, including the raft of teacher organizations that I name in the preface. I also want to offer a special word of appreciation to the dozens of teachers who were gracious enough to peruse the manuscript at various stages of development, offering suggestions and feedback.

I owe the deepest appreciation to the American Enterprise Institute and its president, Arthur Brooks, for the support and backing that allowed me to pursue this work. I know of few places where I would have the autonomy and remarkable staff that make it possible to write a book like this. I also want to thank the terrific team at Harvard Education Press. I've had the privilege of working with HEP for more than a decade, and that relationship continues to be a joy and a privilege. I want to offer particular thanks to HEP publisher Douglas Clayton for his faith in this project and for his unwavering friendship and support. I'd also like to thank Josh Edelman and Irvin Scott for their friendship and support in bringing this project to fruition.

As always, I'm indebted to my wife, Joleen, for her love, understanding, and droll editorial support. These have helped carry me through this project just as they have through so many others. I owe big thanks to my loving parents for so much, including steadfast support and impeccable copyediting.

Finally, it goes without saying that any mistakes, flaws, or inanities are mine and mine alone, while all the good stuff was inevitably cribbed from some savvy practitioner. But, as Kurt Vonnegut Jr., might have put it, "So it goes."

About the Author

Frederick M. Hess is resident scholar and director of education policy studies at the American Enterprise Institute. An educator, political scientist, and author, Hess studies a range of K–12 and higher education issues. His books include *Cage-Busting Leadership, Breakthrough Leadership in the Digital Age, The Same Thing Over and Over, Education Unbound, Common Sense School Reform, Revolution at the Margins,* and *Spinning Wheels.* He is also the author of the popular *Education Week* blog *Rick Hess Straight Up.* Hess's work has appeared in scholarly and popular outlets such as *Teachers College Record, Harvard Educational Review, Social Science Quarterly, Urban Affairs Review, American Politics Quarterly, Chronicle of Higher Education, Phi Delta Kappan, Educational Leadership, U.S. News & World Report, National Affairs, The Atlantic, National Review, USA Today, Washington Post, New York Times,* and *Wall Street Journal.* He has edited widely cited volumes on the Common Core, education philanthropy, urban school reform, how to stretch the school dollar, education entrepreneurship, the federal role in education, and No Child Left Behind. Hess serves as executive editor of *Education Next,* as lead faculty member for the Rice Education Entrepreneurship Program, as senior fellow for the Leadership Institute of Nevada, and on the review boards for the Broad Prize in Urban Education and the Broad Prize for Public Charter Schools. He also serves on the boards of directors of the National Association of Charter School Authorizers and 4.0 Schools. A former high school social studies teacher, he teaches or has taught at Georgetown University, Rice University, the University of Pennsylvania, Harvard University, and the University of Virginia.

Index